PRAISE FOR

LIFE, INCORPORATED

"I read—and wrote all over—my copy of *Life, Incorporated* in two back-to-back sessions. The reason it was two sessions rather than one was that I had to stop, gather myself, and reflect on the lessons I'd already learned from the first two chapters alone. Halley Bock hasn't written just another self-help tome for a narcissistic generation; she's written a searingly honest, immediately practical road map for anyone who wants to find, rediscover, reposition, or just polish their North Star. Buy it, learn the lessons, work the exercises, and I guarantee you'll put down Life, Incorporated with a renewed sense of who you are and what you're here to do."

—LES MCKEOWN, best-selling author of *Predictable Success: Getting Your Organization on the Growth Track—and Keeping It There*

"Our work has always supported the fact that living with purpose and intention and staying connected to the process will drive results. In *Life, Incorporated*, Halley proves yet again that you can choose your life and daily action to drive your success."

—BEN NEWMAN, performance coach for five straight NCAA Division I Football Champions and author of Leave *YOUR Legacy: The Power to Unleash Your Greatness*

"Mindfulness may not be an easy skill to master, but Halley Bock's *Life, Incorporated* will help you get there. Through personal anecdotes and practical tips anyone can employ right now, she takes the reader on their own journey of self-discovery in the process."

—KRISTIN MCGEE, celebrity yoga instructor

"At last, we have an author who has taken the genre of self-help and completely transformed it into what it should be: a real, practical, and essential roadmap for life. Halley tells a story that will engage you and then backs it up with approachable, actionable, and most of all, doable steps you can take immediately to take control of your life and make it what you want it to be. Halley's tested and well-researched guidance, combined with an easy-to-read style make this book a must-have for anyone looking to make their lives better."

—ANN HERRMANN-NEHDI, CEO and coauthor of
The Whole Brain Business Book

Life,

incorporated

A PRACTICAL GUIDE

TO WHOLEHEARTED LIVING

Life,

incorporated

HALLEY BOCK

GREENLEAF
BOOK GROUP PRESS

Published by Greenleaf Book Group Press
Austin, Texas
www.gbgpress.com

Distributed by Greenleaf Book Group

For ordering information or special discounts for bulk purchases, please contact Greenleaf Book Group at PO Box 91869,
Austin, TX 78709, 512.891.6100.

Design and composition by Greenleaf Book Group
Cover design by Greenleaf Book Group

For permission to reprint copyrighted material, grateful acknowledgment is given to the following sources:

Many Rivers Press, Langley, WA: From "What to Remember When Waking" from *The House of Belonging* by David Whyte. Copyright © 1996 by Many Rivers Press.
Seth Godin: "Linchpin Manifesto" by Seth Godin.
Avery, an imprint of Penguin Publishing Group, a division of Penguin Random House, LLC: From *Play: How It Shapes the Brain, Opens the Imagination, and Invigorates the Soul* by Stuart Brown with Christopher Vaughan. Copyright © 2009 by Stuart Brown.
TED: From "Serious Play" by Stuart Brown, 2008.
Hal Leonard LLC: Excerpt from lyrics from "Any Road," words and music by George Harrison. Copyright © 2002 by Umlaut corporation. All rights reserved.

Cataloging-in-Publication data is available.

Print ISBN: 978-1-62634-355-9

eBook ISBN: 978-1-62634-356-6

Part of the Tree Neutral® program, which offsets the number of trees consumed in the production and printing of this book by taking proactive steps, such as planting trees in direct proportion to the number of trees used: www.treeneutral.com

TreeNeutral®

Printed in the United States of America on acid-free paper

16 17 18 19 20 21   10 9 8 7 6 5 4 3 2 1

First Edition

For Niko and Uma, whose infectious curiosity and exquisite courage make it absolutely impossible for me to play it safe.

CONTENTS

PREFACE xi

ACKNOWLEDGMENTS. xvii

INTRODUCTION. 1

PART 1: THE SOIL: FOUNDATION

CHAPTER 1: Inner Life 25

CHAPTER 2: Physical Well-being. 57

CHAPTER 3: Environment. 81

PART 2: ROOTS: INSPIRATION

CHAPTER 4: The Inspired Life 113

PART 3: BRANCHES: EXPRESSION

CHAPTER 5: Expression 1: Play 149

CHAPTER 6: Expressions 2 and 3: Avocation and Vocation 165

CHAPTER 7: Expression 4: Key Relationships. 191

CHAPTER 8: Crafting Your Living Tree 203

PART 4: LEAVES: IMPACT

CHAPTER 9: Intention. 239

CHAPTER 10: Attention 265

CHAPTER 11: Conclusion 279

JOURNAL 283

INDEX 305

ABOUT THE AUTHOR 315

PREFACE

In spring of 2014, I was asked if I would write a book on behalf of the training company I led at the time. It's typical in the training industry for resident thought leaders to churn out a book every few years as a means to market their companies and remain relevant. After a little hemming and hawing, I agreed, even though I struggled with what I would write about. I didn't want to write about being a female executive. Gag me. I didn't want to write about the nuts and bolts of business. Snooze. There was a brief moment when I thought I wanted to write about risk, but it turned out to be a fleeting affair.

For nearly a decade, I both taught and studied human dynamics, specifically relationships and their impact on personal and business success. My organization focused on developing the art of conversation as the vehicle for creating connection among teams, employees, leaders, and individuals. I repeatedly found that organizations that created deep and meaningful connections with their employees financially outperformed their peers year after year. The more time I spent in the field, the more it became clear that successful leaders put people first.

I, too, shared a penchant for prioritizing the well-being of my employees, and every quarter I challenged myself to create an even more supportive workplace. The goal was to foster a trusting, respectful environment that honored how incredibly wicked smart and dedicated we all were yet also tended to the very realness of life, how terribly unpredictable it could be.

If my employees could deliver excellence in their work, then they could certainly manage their needs when life inconveniently occurred at 3 p.m. on a Tuesday or 9 a.m. on a Thursday, laying waste to the well-intentioned plans of living a neat and tidy life. Flex schedules, unlimited paid time off, full medical benefits for employees and their children, and telecommuting options all became part of the fabric of my company. We were named a best place to work year after year while concurrently landing on *Inc.* magazine's annual list of fastest growing companies. You put people first, and the profits will come. You put profits first, and your people will leave—along with some profit.

Creating sustainability in the workplace was what I knew, and that's what I began writing about. I see organizations as ecosystems that thrive or become diseased based on the strength of the connection they build with their employees, their mission, and their customers. If weak links exist along this chain, problems arise, such as low employee engagement, high employee turnover, poor profits, and low customer retention. Any one of these can be fatal to an organization's ability to grow.

But as I spent more and more hours out on the road speaking with business leaders and employees on the topic of connection, I noticed something disturbing: I was working to create healthy ecosystems within organizations, yet many of the individuals who worked in those organizations were operating on shaky footing themselves. So many people were lost. Stressed. Unwell. Beleaguered. Spent. Raw. At sea. I realized this malady was not a flash-in-the-pan problem or one that afflicted only a few. It was an epidemic. We have become a nation lost to ourselves; our focus is more and more centered on who or what can "fix" us—give us a sense of worthiness—instead of fostering our own ecosystem of total well-being that generates its own self-worth.

Sitting side by side, shoulder to shoulder with the blue haze of our phones illuminating our faces, we have forgotten how to connect with others. We've also lost the most essential ability needed to thrive: the ability to connect deeply with ourselves. We've lost touch with our physical bodies, so we pour pharmaceuticals down our throats to feel "well" and make up for our own lack of caring. We've lost touch with our inner world, so we grasp for self-worth through social media "likes" in what's now become the gamification of life. We've lost touch with our own passion and purpose, instead feeding a ravenous, bottomless pit with empty gestures and crisp paychecks. And we've lost touch with our loved ones as we overreach, trying to be enough or have enough for everyone *but* ourselves.

The following list presents a few indicators of the prices we pay for this always-on, never-enough lifestyle:

- We are obese. Thirty percent of adults and seventeen percent of youth in America are grossly overweight.[1]

- We are in debt. US consumers have racked up over $3.5 trillion in outstanding debt.[2]

- We are addicted to the Internet. One in five Americans is "almost constantly" online, and thirty-six percent of eighteen- to twenty-nine-year-olds are always connected.[3]

- We are medicated. The United States has five percent of the world's population and consumes seventy-five percent of the world's prescription drugs.[4]

---

1 C.L. Ogden, M.D Carroll, B.K. Kit, K.M. Flegal. "Prevalence of childhood and adult obesity in the United States, 2011-2012," *Journal of the American Medical Association* 311 (2014): 806-814.

2 Board of Governors of the Federal Reserve System, "Federal Reserve statistical release: Consumer credit, January 2016" (Washington, DC: Federal Reserve, 2016), https://www.federalreserve.gov/releases/g19.

3 A. Perrin, "One-fifth of Americans report going online 'almost constantly,'" *Pew Research Center* (December 8, 2015), http://www.pewresearch.org/fact-tank/2015/12/08/one-fifth-of-americans-report-going-online-almost-constantly.

4 United Nations Office on Drugs and Crime (UNODC), *World Drug Report 2011* (2011), http://www.refworld.org/docid/4e809b422.html.

- We are depressed. Approximately 18.8 million American adults, almost ten percent of the US population age eighteen and older, have a depressive disorder.[5]

Clearly something's broken. The good news is that this "something" lies within us and is ours to repair, but it has to be done from the inside out. Through the work in this book, we will create deep, intentional, energizing connections with ourselves that enable us to live a wholehearted and rewarding life. I have learned that there can be no meaningful relationships and authentic connection with others if we haven't forged the same, first, with ourselves.

It was upon this discovery that I began applying everything I knew about relationships, human connectivity, and sustainability in health and wealth to repairing our relationship with ourselves. I also picked up new research along the way. That work culminated in the crafting of this book and the models and exercises found within.

About the time I decided to shift the subject of my book from organizational well-being to individual well-being, my entire world was dumped upside down, resulting in a complete "yard sale" of my life. This upheaval included a severe turn in my career, my finances, and the necessary, yet painful, loss of some long-held relationships. While writing, I had to dig deep and lean on the same key strategies and exercises I had developed for others to get me through my own difficult phase. Every component of this book was put through its paces and rigorously tested. If at first an exercise or a concept fell short, I worked with it until it held strong.

As you progress through the following pages, you will witness my journey of healing and rebuilding, and you'll hear about others who also had to forge a new way forward. The exercises and practices that follow grant you the opportunity to lift up every stone and address every corner of your life. While I needed a near total overhaul, you can also use the guidance to tune up specific aspects of your life, such as

---

5   W. E. Narrow, "One-year prevalence of depressive disorders among adults 18 and over in the U.S.: NIMH ECA prospective data" (unpublished, 1998).

stepping into a healthy lifestyle, healing old wounds, creating meaning in your work, or repairing a relationship. No matter where you are in your life, there is a place for you to dig deeper and cultivate more of what you desire. You'll learn how in the following pages.

BARNES&NO

cheryl van gelder
4626 Via del Rancho

Newbury Park
CA
91320-6742
UNITED STATES

	ISBN	TITLE
=	9781626343559	Life, Incorpor

If you are not satisfied with your order, you may return it within 30 c
items may be returned to the address on the packing slip or returne

LI - 9 5 5 5 1 7 7 *

BLE.com

Shop:	BNCDF
Buyer Name:	cheryl van gelder
Order Date:	05/06/2020
Order Number	BNCDF4096831813-25

	QTY
ted: A Practical Guide to Wholehearted Living	1

ACKNOWLEDGMENTS

For me, writing this book meant slamming into walls, picking myself up, and scaling those walls only to slam into another—an epic journey that tested and strengthened every facet of myself. It has been stressful and complicated, but most importantly, it's been a meaningful labor of love and certainly a task one doesn't accomplish alone. While a thank you seems hardly enough, I want to express my heartfelt gratitude to all of the special people who accompanied me on this journey.

First and foremost, to Deli and my children, Niko and Uma: The unwavering love, patience, understanding, and encouragement you consistently surround me with is the reason I possess the courage to pursue what matters. Pushing me to follow my dream is a gift I will always cherish. I love you all so very much.

To the hundreds of people who have shared their stories with me and allowed me to share mine. Your vulnerability sparked a revolution in my heart, and this book would not have found its way without you. Thank you for teaching me and trusting in me so I could bring this work forward.

To Debbie Potts: Your belief in me and this topic repeatedly amazed me. Your strength, encouragement, insights, and companionship were instrumental in the writing of this book and will never be forgotten.

To my editors, Jay Hodges and Meredith Bailey: a special thank you for your keen editorial assistance, your skill and clarity in shaping the content, and your enthusiasm for the book.

To Steven Pecoraro, my insanely gifted designer: Thank you for bringing your talents to this project and taking such care. Your creations are beautiful and take my breath away.

To all of the exceptional staff at Greenleaf Book Group: Thank you for your belief in the need for this book. Justin Branch for saying yes. Nathan True for overseeing this immense project. Emilie Lyons for guiding me from start to finish, and Neil Gonzalez for the beautiful cover design.

To my incredible community of friends: Thank you for supporting me with love, smiles, pats on the back, introductions, feedback, and an occasional cup of coffee: Ann Herrmann-Nehdi, Paul Horner, Julie Schell, Les McKeown, Neal Potts, Nancy Mendelson, and the rabble-rousers who stir my heart: Robin, John, Angela, Teri, and Deneen.

And finally, a special thank you to my dad, Charlie Bock, and his wife, Pat: Your unconditional support and profound love are deep oars in the water. And to Frank and Mitra Moussavi, who have become a second set of parents: I adore you. Thank you for embracing me wholeheartedly.

INTRODUCTION

Can you call me? I think my marriage is over.

These were the words I punched into my phone. My thumb trembled over the "Send" button as the terror of acknowledging this stark possibility washed over me. I feared that transmitting this message would somehow manifest the reality already confirmed by the latest exchange of verbal blows. I sat, head in my hands, defeated. Hopeless. How could this be happening to me . . . to *us*? How could my wife and I be so close to becoming yet another dismal statistic in the overloaded column of failed marriages? It didn't seem possible, yet here we were. Precariously hanging on to the last strand of hope in what had once been a relationship tightly bound by love, affection, respect, and an unfathomably deep connection.

It was the summer of 2014 and I had just completed my first Half Ironman triathlon—an event that tested the thresholds of my physical stamina and, in hindsight, the tolerance threshold of my marriage. The grueling pressure exerted on my marriage was not due to the sport itself but rather my extreme approach to the sport. It is a form of extremism that has become an epidemic in America, leaving so many individuals more cut off than ever. Let me explain.

Right now, there are more active mobile devices than people in the world, and the growth of mobile devices is outpacing the human population by a factor of five.[6] While this doesn't mean everyone

---

6   Zachary Davis Boren, "There are officially more mobile devices then people in the world," *Independent*, (Oct. 7 2014) http://www.independent.co.uk/life-style/gadgets-and-tech/news/there-are-officially-more-mobile-devices-than-people-in-the-world-9780518.html.

in the world owns a mobile device, it does mean that those who do carry more than one gadget, such as a smart phone and a tablet. Even in economically depressed countries, approximately 89.4 mobile subscriptions exist for every one hundred inhabitants.[7]

No matter how you slice these numbers, it's clear we have more capacity for connection than we've ever had, yet it is my opinion and my experience that we are the most disconnected we have ever been. We are disconnected from ourselves, our passions, our loved ones, our lives. How many of us park ourselves in front of our computer and attempt to experience life through a machine? Attempt to create deep, meaningful connection through a DSL cable? Choose to stare into pixels instead of eyes? Share status updates instead of intimacy? We choose to plug into the binary code of a computer over the DNA of another person. Don't get me wrong, I was a button-mashing Atari child of the '70s and later went on to have a career in high tech so I get the draw, but what was intended to entertain and inform has become a way of life. Simply put, we have lost the skill to connect deeply with another person because we've turned the task over to technology, a task too big even for the best and brightest in Silicon Valley.

In addition to allowing ourselves to be consumed by technology, we have become swept up in the self-imposed, achievement-based, drone-producing norms of society. There exists more and more pressure to keep up though the bar never seems to stop rising. This is because we have lost the ability to define "enough" for ourselves. Instead, we cast it out for others to decide and invariably fall short with each well-intended effort, because we've borrowed the masthead from someone else's ship and have set sail on a course that has no destination. We judge our worth by how many "friends" we have on social media, how many cars are parked in the garage, how many appointments fill up our Day-Timer, how many alerts are flashed upon our

---

7   Tim Fernholz, "More people around the world have cell phones then ever had landlines," *Quartz*, (Feb. 25, 2014) http://qz.com/179897/more-people-around-the-world-have-cell-phones-than-ever-had-land-lines/.

screen, how many flags we can capture in our reckless slalom through an impossible life. And when we find ourselves exhausted and unfulfilled—yet again—we point the finger at work-life balance, which is not only a bullshit move, it's a bullshit term.

Here's why. First, I don't believe balance is achievable when we're addressing a matter as complicated as life itself. Balance requires some predictability, and life is anything but predictable. The best we can do and expect of ourselves is to gain the ability to hold our own center—our own vision for ourselves—while maintaining the ability to adapt to reality on a moment-to-moment basis. This requires us to clearly define what's "enough" instead of running someone else's race. And it also requires us to let go of what we *think* success looks like.

Second, the term "work-life balance" not only pits the two against each other, meaning one must always be at risk of losing, but it also carves work out of life as if to say that our lives can be compartmentalized. This only reinforces the disconnection we experience in life. But this separation doesn't begin and end with work. We live our entire lives in a compartmentalized fashion like a series of buckets, each with a different label: "Work," "Family," "Marriage," "Health," "Me-Time," and "Friends/Community." You get the idea. And we tend to these buckets on an as-needed basis. We're busy stirring and filling the Work bucket only to turn around and find that our Marriage bucket has sprung a leak or, worse, the bottom has fallen out! So we run over and try to stretch our reach between the two, furiously (and often clumsily) repairing and refilling Marriage while continuing to tend to Work. And then, hang on, we look down and find that we can no longer spot our toes beyond our protruding belly. Or a doctor's appointment didn't go so well and, come to find out, all that extra stress, fast food, or lack of sleep has put our health at risk. So then we rush to locate, uncover, and dust off the Health bucket so we can furiously right that ship while desperately trying to keep up with the other areas. But, unfortunately, we often drop one bucket as our split focus can only keep eyes on one or two key areas at a time. Forget about ever making it over to Me-Time, or watch out when we do, as we're likely to overindulge, becoming drunk on our own company while our other relationships starve.

In this paradigm of compartmentalizing life, each disconnected link in the chain is not only weakened but also easily lost in the fray of all that consumes us. It is no wonder we find ourselves adrift in an epidemic of stress and burnout given the manner in which we approach and live out our lives. To try and harness life into equal measures is like trying to fence in the weather. While a noble and curious effort, it is doomed for failure, not to mention exhausting, and creates a propensity for overcorrection and extremes. This is what happened as I trained for my triathlon—I threw myself into a new interest after years of setting my needs aside to focus on raising a family and building a company. Unfortunately, I overdid it. I became too myopic in my renewed focus on myself, and I got dangerously close to losing one of my most important key relationships–my marriage.

Perhaps something similar happened to you. You landed your dream job, and the promise of reward coupled with the high sense of achievement you experienced daily swept you off your feet. You were wholeheartedly connected to your passion and, for a time, it was an avenue to create rich connection with your partner, not to mention a great source of personal pride. But as the workaholic months chained together into years, your relationship with your loved one became ever distant and fragile. Eventually, you found yourself emotionally burned out, yet you remained handcuffed to the corporate ladder that promised yet another set of stock options if you could just wait it out another six months. You negotiated with yourself, with your partner, and with your future as you put off living "now" for "someday."

Or maybe you have become painfully untethered from yourself, unsure of who you are or if you are even worthy of love. Perhaps you grew up in an environment that wasn't accepting, and you had to modify which version of yourself you presented in order to get approval, hoping more often than not you would land safely on the preferred flavor of the day. Or love was simply withheld and used to manipulate your self-confidence by dialing it up or down, depending on the whims of another. Whatever the case, your sense of self and belonging were never fostered, leaving you unable to anchor in your own self-worth. Instead, you people please and act as a chameleon, hoping someday donning the costume of another will deliver to you the "home" you never had.

These are just three examples of disconnection that I have found more common than not. At the very least, each example represents a seed that exists in many other stories. That seed may not have sprouted into the outcomes illustrated in my examples, but as long as the seed exists, the potential looms. And as long as we're on this planet, with proven theories that confirm our inclination for chaos and negative thought patterns, we should do our best to understand how it is we can begin in a place of such promise yet end up in a place that is foreign and isolated.

THE DRIFT

One of my favorite places to be is in the sea. Being a resident of the Pacific Northwest requires an annual escape to the Hawaiian Islands to stave off Seasonal Affective Disorder (SAD), a type of depression related to changes in season that tends to strike in the fall and winter. When you live under constant cloud cover for months on end, it can make you a bit . . . well . . . sad. So as most Seattleites do, my family searches out the sun at least once during the heavier, grayer months.

As soon as my family hits the beach, I eagerly dive into the ocean, reaching beyond the break where I can safely swim along the shoreline. This is something I could do for hours if my body would allow it, but after a time, I head back toward my family, find my perfect patch of water in front of where they are parked on the shore, stick my toes up, and float. My senses are alive as I feel my buoyed body undulating atop waves, tiny licks of saltwater lapping my ears. Again, I could stay atop nature's water bed for hours if left to my own devices, but eventually this meditative state lapses, and I feel inclined to check on my family. However, upon looking back, rarely are they in direct sight on the beach; more often than not, the gentle current working underneath me has swept me down shore, and I must search for them.

Just like in the ocean, there are currents at work in every facet of life, moving us along—whether we know it or not—as we try to maintain some level of connection with ourselves, our passion, our work, and our relationships. We initially charge forward with our sights laser focused on our intentions, wholeheartedly connected to the equation on the other side—a vocation that aligns with our personal mission, an endeavor that speaks to our passion, a person with whom we desire to plug into each day, a newfound hobby or practice that brings us home to ourselves. The initial outset is as invigorating as my annual inaugural swim in the ocean. We don a fresh pair of lenses to see the world and admire it from a perspective we hadn't yet discovered or had all but forgotten. It's exhilarating and, for a while, we actively nurture these endeavors, this sensation of connection at its fullest, and it nurtures us in turn.

But over time, we inadvertently ease off the oars as predictability and inertia creep in and lull us into our own form of sleep. We rest upon the cushion of familiarity, putting our endeavor on autopilot, assuming we are maintaining the status quo. Until one day, something compels us to wake up only to find that we have drifted dangerously down shore, completely disconnected and disoriented from where we began. Perhaps the wake-up call is realizing you and your loved one have drifted from soul mates to awkward companions, or your vocation has drifted from life work to corporate grind, or your emotional bank account of self-worth, once overflowing, has become bankrupt.

The reality is that there is no such thing as holding the status quo when it comes to our connections. Everything worthwhile takes effort. I have never seen someone deposited to greatness by default. Nor have I seen anyone in a rich relationship with themselves, others, or what they do without equal parts strength, vulnerability, and attention. If we want to live a life in which we are *fully* engaged on all fronts, we have to actively pursue, revisit, and practice connection.

WHAT DOES BEING CONNECTED MEAN?

So what does it mean to be connected? We've talked about what it isn't: copper wires, landlines, or radio towers. It doesn't consist of logging into a local hot spot and mindlessly numbing out via an endless drip of data. And it certainly doesn't entail staring into the blue haze of a phone, swiping this way and that to build relationships with "friends," an exercise I, frankly, find more anesthetizing than moving.

The kind of connection I'm referring to comes from a different source that isn't marked with a bar code or accessible via password. It's energetic. It's reciprocal. It's life affirming. When fully in play, it resembles a dance that leads as much as it follows, an infinite loop that nourishes us to the extent we nourish it.

Connection, for the purposes of this book and our lives, is the intentionality and effort in which we engage with something or someone, including ourselves. It isn't an intellectual exercise; rather, it's a heart-based calling that electrifies our very existence, instilling it with purpose. Connection has "teeth" that pulls us forward, ever closer to our particular North Star—who we are at our very core and how we express our individuality. It doesn't leave us chewed up. But it does leave us energized and, undoubtedly, bruised and nicked; bearing battle scars is a natural result of participating in something that requires the vulnerability and risk that connection requires.

In his book *Flow: The Psychology of Optimal Performance*, Mihaly Csikszentmihalyi speaks of experiencing this kind of connection at its apex, when we are completely absorbed in an activity and time stands still. Think of musicians getting lost in the music or artists becoming one with their creations. If you want to see this kind of poetry in motion, google Stevie Ray Vaughan, select any of his live concert footage, and watch the man become his guitar time and time again. This psychological state is one in which we experience suspended bliss, where we are so present with what we are engaged in that everything else falls to the wayside. We become *presence* itself.

While we may experience bursts of the kind of transformative connection that Csikszentmihalyi refers to, we usually experience connection in much more subtle—though just as important—ways. Connection could look like any of the following:

- A partner intuits the needs of a loved one by meeting an unforeseen, harrowing, late day at work with dinner on the table accompanied by two glasses of red wine.

- A program manager nearly misses the bus home due to being so wrapped up in an inaugural project.

- An ultramarathoner crosses the finish line caked in mud and soaked to the bone, with fingers nearly frostbitten, yet is grinning from ear to ear.

- A parent senses a child's tears the moment before they come pouring out and wraps the stiff-upper-lipped little one in a hug.

- A friend picks up the phone and asks, "How can I help?" immediately upon learning you've been laid off.

- A person in your life acts as a steady force of calm, compassion, and belonging in this manic, yo-yo world.

These are all examples of people connected to their loved ones, their career, their avocation, or themselves. Many of us achieve these connections in one area of life, perhaps two or three if we're lucky. But it's often sporadic—the result of either spinning the plate that is most obvious to us or the one in the most danger of shattering. Our goal is to create and foster an ongoing web of connection throughout all aspects of our life. And in order to do so, we must start with connecting to ourselves.

CONNECTION STARTS WITH YOU

We are all familiar with the phrase "Secure your own oxygen mask before assisting others." This used to bother me as a new mother. I couldn't imagine tending to myself before ensuring my son or daughter was safe from harm, but now I get it. If we don't help ourselves first, we flail and grasp in our efforts to help another, panic quickly depleting us of our own oxygen supply and ability to survive, not to mention our ongoing capacity to assist others.

This phenomenon plays out in the exact same way when we attempt to live our lives from the outside in. How many of us have had the experience of living our lives for others only to find we are as empty and exhausted as ever? We stay in a job because it feels like the right thing to do for our family. We put aside the hobbies we once enjoyed because we have other adult responsibilities that should take precedence. Or we spend all of our efforts helping others because it keeps us numb to the vortex of pain we cannot bear to touch in ourselves.

When we engage in life this way—attempting to gain self-worth and belonging through means outside ourselves—we are destined to fail. We cannot manifest self-worth, self-love, and long-term contentment by stuffing achievements, accolades, and good deeds into our well of being when we haven't yet defined that space for ourselves. Those efforts may momentarily satiate, but they just as soon fall away, rattling around like pellets in a hollow container that has become foreign to us. Until we define who we are and what we are, we will remain the proverbial bottomless pit or a shape shifter, borrowing someone else's identity in the hopes we will finally experience contentment. The reason these strategies fail is because they are not of our own creation; they don't serve our particular needs. They are plagiarized stories of which we are not the authors. They may look good on the surface, but the surface is all we have. We are attempting to live life from the outside in instead of from the inside out. See table I.1 for some examples of the differences between the two.

Outside In	Inside Out
You measure success as a comparison against others.	Success is determined by your own measure.
Money is a means to acquire things that excite you.	Money is a by-product of doing what you are passionate about.
Life is for display and "likes" on social media.	Life is intimate and for those you love.
You pursue happiness as a goal.	You experience happiness due to the way in which you live.
Life expands to fill all your time.	Time expands as you live a full life.
Self-worth is externally achieved.	Self-worth is self-generated.

Table I.1. Living from the Outside In vs. Inside Out

We can easily fall into the trap of living a life from the outside, in or how I might term it "Life, Inc." Life, Inc. is the life that has no unique song to sing, no courageous tale to tell. While it promises a more youthful appearance, greater popularity, lower interest rates, a better smelling car, a spiffier resume, a whiter smile, and so on, it is a life lived on the surface—an inch deep, rooted in nothing that could nourish a soul. It's a life we live on behalf of others because we cannot anchor ourselves to our own purpose.

An incorporated life, in short terms, is the antithesis of Life, Inc. It's a purposeful life—one deeply rooted in personal passion, and one lived with blatant disregard for what others down the block or through the halls are doing with theirs. It's not as if you're living in a vacuum, unaware and uncaring of others. Rather, it's that your life is specific to you and not available for comparison. Your joy comes from within, not from winning in comparison to others. It also brings together all the fragments of our lives that have gotten away from us: Our relationships, our well-being, our passions, and what we do for a living so that we can live a fuller, more robust and rewarding life.

To craft an incorporated life—one that can deliver us the full spectrum of wholehearted living—we need to forge an intimate connection to ourselves. As the saying goes, we need to come back home. Whether it's been a momentary lapse in which we've become ungrounded and lost our center or decades since we cracked open the door and stepped inside, we need to begin if we are to ever experience what it is to truly be "enough."

IS IT POSSIBLE TO RECONNECT?

Connection can be as intermittent as a ship-to-shore call hailing from the middle of the Arctic Ocean, so developing the ability to tune back in is essential. Life is impermanent by nature, so it's to be expected that we will lose a bowline from time to time. Thankfully, not only is it possible to reconnect with yourself but it's also possible to reconnect with any facet of your life that has gone unnoticed, ignored, or unattended. The good news is that as long as we're available to the choice, the choice is available to us.

In my own life, I have had many opportunities to reconnect as I, too, have employed all the failed strategies I spoke about in my endeavor to live Life with a capital *L*, the life that's sold to us but cannot be delivered.

As a twentysomething in the high-tech industry, I was present for my company's initial public offering (IPO), which turned out to be one of the many jaw-dropping, wealth-creating events in the dotcom bubble of the late '90s. If you want to see the embodiment of a heady experience, watch a group of young high-tech hipster nerds see a company through its IPO. It was intoxicating, surreal, and distracting beyond belief.

I remember vividly the steady stream of Porsche Boxsters flowing into the parking garage that had, until recently, only housed Ford Broncos and well-loved (read: beat-up) Saabs. In an instant, life was different. The conversations had once revolved around who owned whom in foosball and ping-pong; now everyone talked about their personal finance managers, their portfolios of diversified stocks, their new homes, their new wheels, and their new designer duds (or at least a new sweatshirt to replace the one with more holes in it than a Wiffle ball). Suddenly, we all had access to options once reserved for those who lived beyond our means, giving us a new and profound sense of power.

But as with so many things in life, there were two sides to the coin. Along with the spiffy list of shiny cool things came the dark trappings of wealth. New mortgages, new car payments, new headaches, new stressors, new expectations of ourselves and our potential, new distractions, new demands, and a new bar for what made life complete—the amount of money in one's checking account rather than the amount of meaning, love, and happiness in one's life. It's an easy mistake to make when the only delicacy you've known prior is piping hot ramen noodles delicately perched upon a saltine cracker.

Clearly, my partner and I weren't living any sort of high life before the IPO, but at the time it didn't matter; we couldn't have cared less. The company—a pioneer in streaming media technology—was involved in something incredibly meaningful to the world, and I was deeply passionate about the work. The fact that we were barely making ends meet was tolerable. High-tech salaries were almost laughable at the time; the real potential was in the stock options. But until the mid-to-late '90s, options had never paid off to any great extent. You could expect a little extra income for your sixteen-hour workdays but nothing like what occurred during the dotcom bubble.

When our stock soared, then split, then soared, then split again, it was an opportunity to get carried away. And there I went, choosing to stash my money away like some paranoid squirrel filled with apocalyptic visions. I wanted to secure a future for my wife and eventual family. I wanted to close the chapter, permanently, on Top Ramen. But before I knew it, I was caught up in the disorienting spin cycle of the high-tech bubble. I no longer sought downtime and closeness with my wife. Instead, I chose work, and I said yes to more and more projects and roles that were farther and farther away from the passion that had brought me to this career. I thought that if I could achieve such a high level of wealth, why shouldn't I achieve more?

The iron was hot, and it was time to strike. I happily threw myself at every launch, project, idea, and opportunity, and then between the hours of 2 a.m. and 8 a.m., I would curl up on my giant beanbag chair in the corner of my office to catch some Z's. I showered at work, ate dinners in the hallway, married my wife between trips, became a feared ping-pong contender, and cultivated my entire social network with the people who shared a wall with me.

While there were a lot of wonderful outcomes I can attribute to this time in my life—namely, marrying my wife and creating a close circle of friends—the rest was, well, somewhat unfortunate. The fast growth of the organization along with the surreal become-a-millionaire-over-night environment made it more and more difficult to stay tethered to my original reasons and passion for being there. Eventually, I became a cookie-cutter drone. I was overweight, overworked, and becoming more and more empty with each passing day. I was fueling *all* aspects of my life via a single outlet—work. I was making decisions based on money and counting down the months until I vested in another batch of stock options. I had replaced my internal engine for generating happiness with distracting material objects, and I had happily snapped on the golden handcuffs and allowed them to become my North Star. I had sold out, and it happened so quickly and so effortlessly that it took me nearly two years to notice. When I finally snapped out of my fog, I recognized that I was no longer living *my* life; I was trespassing on someone else's dreams.

A decade later, my marriage was about to collapse—a result of the same kind of tunnel vision, but this time it wasn't about work. It was about my connection to myself. After leaving my high-tech job but prior to settling down and starting a family, my wife, Deli, and I led eclectic lives. I ran a media and design agency, studied acting, spent hours tooling around on my motorcycle, and danced my booty off every Friday and Saturday night at our favorite club. Deli was building a new organization, studying sound healing, working on her memoir, and dancing with me on the weekends. It was great. It was its own era.

When our son, Niko, and then our daughter, Uma, were born, my life and heart were happily overtaken. Friends would beg me to come out and play, and I would say no. Offers to join a theater company or take part in a production would come in, and I would say no. The only thing I said yes to were my three amigos. They became my world, and I was happy. The rush of being responsible for myself as well as my growing family was intoxicating, and I bellied up to the bar. I sold my agency to pursue a more stable career, exchanged my motorcycle for a minivan, and deposited all of my efforts into building a loving and secure home for my family. Totally predictable? Yes. Totally normal? Yes. Totally honorable? I used to think so, but now I know otherwise. When we set ourselves aside for too long, we develop tunnel vision; either we become overly focused on others or, when we finally snap to, we become overly focused on ourselves, which was what I did. After five years of setting aside my own needs for the sake of raising a family, I became hyper focused on myself.

In both cases, I was able to find a way back: In my 30s, I reconnected to my passion for work by leaving my high-tech job and starting my own agency, and in my 40s, I reconnected to my wife by understanding where my frantic energy around triathlons was stemming from so I could relax and settle back into ease. While I had to discover my own path, cues, and practices for finding my way back, I'll share the model I developed that others, including myself, now use to forge and thread connection throughout all facets of life.

A PLAN TO RECONNECT

The visual model I've chosen for this work is a tree. One of the many pleasures of living in the Pacific Northwest is the evergreen trees that fill up the landscape year round: hemlock, cedar, pine, dogwood, madrona, Douglas fir, and the list goes on. From old-growth forests to new growth, the variety is astounding. While admiring a tree one particular day, it dawned on me: Here is a living organism that displays for all to see the health of each vital connection required for its overall well-being, not to mention how its ecosystem affects its capacity to survive and thrive.

The quality of the soil affects the tree's ability to extend upright and its level of access to the nutrients that nourish and sustain growth.

The integrity of the root system determines how well the tree is able to withstand the forces of nature and draw up precious nutrients from the soil.

There is a mindfulness in the outlay of branches that displays the tree's ability to grow thoughtfully and purposefully; branches are marked by symmetry and health or tangles of dead wood from overgrowth.

Finally, there's the canopy of foliage overhead, indicating whether or not the tree is successful in ultimately fulfilling its purpose. Does new life spring from each limb? Has the tree listed to one side by leaning too far into the sun, compromising the other facets of itself and spurring uneven foliage? Or are the limbs altogether barren?

While the ailing connections in our own lives may not be as visually noticeable as those of a tree, I have witnessed people struggle with the exact same issues time and time again. I have seen those who are deeply connected to their passion and have found a magnificent way in which to express that passion, yet their relationships are barren. I have seen those rich in relationships with much to show for all their doing, yet the way they regard themselves is black with disease. I have seen more than my fair share of individuals who are one bad day away from toppling over.

It's time we cease compartmentalizing our lives and learn how to create interconnectedness throughout all facets of our being. To do this, we will borrow the vital components of the tree to represent each of those areas in our life: The soil will be our foundation. The roots will be our inspiration. The branches will be our expression. The leaves will be our impact. See figure I.1. Each component will be discussed in its own section of the book.

In part 1, "Foundation," you will learn how to cultivate and

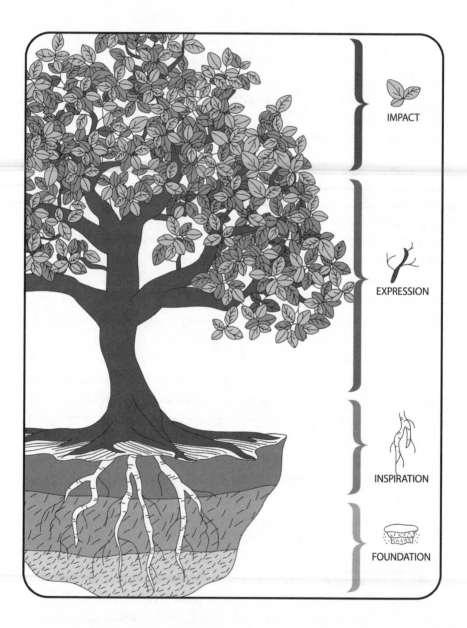

nourish wellness in the areas that ultimately determine your ability to thrive—your emotional, spiritual, and physical well-being and your environment.

In part 2, "Inspiration," you will identify what makes *you* tick along with the values that are essential for navigating toward your goals.

In part 3, "Expression," you will become aware of the forms of expression humans need in order to live life to the fullest. You will discover your original path as it pertains to your vocation, avocation, and expressions of play while also defining the key relationships in your life.

Finally, in part 4, "Impact," you will turn your attention to how your actions, thoughts, and beliefs are affecting you and your relationships with others. Here you will essentially learn how to become a good steward of your ecosystem.

Throughout the book, there are exercises to help you become attuned to each essential component of your life. Those of you who use e-readers or who prefer to keep your copy of the book pristine will find all of the exercises available as downloadable PDFs on the website www.lifeincorporated.co.

For the purposes of structure and what I find most important, the book begins with addressing your foundation, because I find this to be one of the *most* overlooked and undervalued yet most essential aspects of life. What we root ourselves in has everything to do with our ability to reach up and out in a meaningful way. That being said, it is okay to start with any part of the model that calls to you. You may feel solid in your foundation yet struggle with finding what inspires you. Or perhaps you have identified your passion but have difficulty managing your relationships. Because we are all so unique, please make this your own adventure and start wherever you feel drawn. Just one caveat—and this is coming from someone who loves to jump to outcome-based endeavors—if you start at the top of the tree, please find the time to come back down to the roots and soil. It's tempting to chase the fruit and place focus on output or outcome. But as with so many things, the most essential work is often in addressing the areas we cannot see or touch. For how we *feel* is how we will *live*.

Part 1

THE SOIL: FOUNDATION

"Vitally, the human race is dying. It is like a great uprooted tree, with its roots in the air. We must plant ourselves again in the universe."

—D. H. Lawrence, *Lady Chatterley's Lover*

Not long ago, a news story about a home that had tumbled into the ocean gave me pause. A lot of resources had been poured into building this beautiful house. But, apparently, an engineer hadn't assessed the stability of the land, or the builders had ignored the assessment: The *cliff* the house was built on crumbled and fell into the sea. I thought, "How many of us race ahead or ignore warning signs for the sake of projecting external magnificence?"

To build something that will exist over time, you must first lay a solid foundation and be mindful of that foundation on a consistent basis. This is true for a building of any size, it is true for a tree that wishes to thrive for decades, and it is true for each of us. If we do not consistently plant ourselves in a foundation that can nurture our growth and sustain our physical and spiritual well-being, we are constantly at risk of sliding into an outcome we'd rather not experience. We can place all the attention we want on the structure everyone can see, but if we place no attention on how we anchor ourselves, we limit the very nature of our potential. It's a slippery slope when our roots have nothing substantial to grab on to.

For me, I ran headlong into this phenomenon while leading an organization through growth curve after growth curve. I was deeply connected to my life purpose at the time, had found a brilliant way in which I could outwardly express that purpose, and was admittedly struggling with awareness of how my hectic schedule was negatively affecting the well-being of my family, but I was somehow threading the needle. What I had completely failed to manage was my own health—my foundation.

When I speak of health, it's easy to assume I'm referring to physical well-being. And in fact, that's exactly where I first turned my attention when I began to sense some discomfort in inhabiting my own body. One look at myself in a swimsuit was all the visual evidence I needed that I had drifted somewhere I didn't want to be. After many years of working in an office, eating hotel food, and sitting on airplanes, I had become doughy. I also wasn't managing stress well and often stayed up into the wee hours and then poured coffee down my throat the moment the alarm went off. Having been healthy and fit prior to this new version of myself and knowing how wonderful it felt to be physically strong, I regained my focus and set out to reclaim my vigor. I did, and I remain committed to this day.

Once I regained my physical well-being and reconnected with my body, I realized I was still at risk for collapse thanks to a sudden, unexpected departure from my job. This experience, made worse by its entanglement with a family member, exhausted all my coping mechanisms and revealed an inner life full of toxicity. Mired by a cluster of loss and feelings of unworthiness, I had to let go of a fantasy I had painstakingly crafted over several decades. When this veil was ripped off, I was stripped bare, left emotionally raw, painfully vulnerable, and alone. My only way out was to sit in the rubble with my emotions and rebuild from scratch. So I did just that. I now take time each day to nurture a healthy inner life.

Unlike the first two components of our foundation—physical well-being and inner life—the third component is external in nature but still capable of having a tremendous impact on us, and that is environment. Through the process of sorting out my life and what was and wasn't working, it became clear that the people I was surrounding myself with and where I was spending my time were having a profound effect on my spiritual and physical well-being. Those consequences were good or bad, depending on the particular alchemy between me and them. There are people I choose to spend time with and places I go *just* to be lifted up. On the other hand, there are people and places that rob me of joy, that are nothing but vacuums, vortexes, and black holes that leech my positivity.

Strangely, we often choose to remain in an environment or a relationship that is toxic to us even though it can bring unwanted drama and trauma. I think I sometimes choose to stay because I have hope. I feel I could make the person or situation better or that, perhaps, I am the problem, and if I fix myself then I can fix the relationship. I also possess a tendency to be the eternal optimist, and while I've been told to never lose that quality, it does make walking away or throwing in the proverbial towel harder. I also *loathe* being called a quitter, so that doesn't help either! However, in the end, we only harm ourselves when we engage in a futile endeavor such as wishing to change the dynamic of another or willing ourselves to be someone we aren't.

When it comes to the short, precious time we have, there are boundaries we must draw and choices we must make if we are to ensure our ability to live a peaceful, positive life brimming with love and possibility. I said good-bye to some very difficult places and people, a few of which societal mores dictate should be in my life but can't be if I am to live free of the incurable negativity that comes with those relationships. While the landscape may be new and foreign, and there remain a few empty chairs, I am free, peaceful, content, and happy without them.

These are the three elements necessary for laying a healthy and enduring foundation: inner life, physical well-being, and environment. Nested within each element are specific strategies and tools to assist in attaining, sustaining, or perhaps regaining these critical components.

Just as a gardener carefully prepares the soil before planting a sapling, ensuring it contains the vital nutrients required for the tree to thrive, we, too, must cultivate our own soil, the foundation in which we root our lives. We need to be mindful of what we add, keep, or remove from our foundation, the soil that will nourish us as we set down roots and begin to grow.

INNER LIFE

*"Until we find self-love, the roots of our tree cannot
grasp the rock or the soil."*

—Halley Bock

When I originally sketched out the structure of this book, I thought physical well-being should be the first foundational element, followed by environment, and finally, inner life. As with most Americans, I tend to gravitate toward what I can *show* as it speaks to my results-minded slant. Plus, it's quite gratifying to be able to present the physical evidence of working on oneself by flexing in front of the mirror after an intense workout session. But in the process of digging up and cultivating my own foundation, I quickly realized I had it backward. Looking solid on the outside bears no weight and has no connection (minus the brief endorphin high) with spiritual and emotional health. A tree can have a strong root system and an impressive outgrowth of branches, but if the foundation—the soil—in which it's rooted cannot support its continued growth, then the tree will eventually fail because the roots have nothing substantial to grasp.

I can also assure you that there is no magic pill we can ingest to fortify our centeredness, our spiritual grit. No inner life "sea monkeys," if you will, that can spring up to fill a void or make things happy and okay. There is also nothing exterior, no scaffolding to bolt on that can compensate for lack of emotional health and connection with self.

Focusing on the external as a means to heal our inner life is akin to erecting a facade in front of a derelict building. We merely mask the truth of what begs for our attention. We choose to look the other way, betraying the exquisiteness that lies beyond what our eyes can see—the crumbling walls and forgotten rooms—shaming and running from ourselves instead of embracing our own human nature.

The path to peace and inner fullness has no signpost, no neon lights, no catchy slogan. It is a tiny, meandering, lush footpath that can go easily undetected in our fast-paced, results-driven lives if we aren't careful.

SHI(F)T HAPPENS

I'll pause to share the life-changing event that uprooted me from the earth—thanks to a lifetime of leaving my internal world unattended to—and how, like millions of people, I employed all the techniques previously mentioned to try and fix myself. I exhausted each and every one of them until I landed on the powerful insights and new strategies that would heal the pain and allow me to build a healthy emotional ecosystem, once and for all.

When I began the initial undertaking of authoring a book, I was the CEO and shareholder of a training organization. I was passionate about the work, had a formidable tribe of dedicated employees, landed the company on several well-respected business lists, and was exalted as a leader in the industry for both my business acumen and my approach in creating a people-first culture. For nine years, I worked my knuckles to the bone to turn what was a boutique lifestyle company into a force to be reckoned with.

On April 2, 2015, my boss waltzed into my office as if walking on air, with a delicious grin curling up the sides of her mouth. She invited me into a conference room, where she sat me down and delivered these words: "After careful consideration, the company no longer requires your services and wishes to part ways. Your employment has been terminated, effective immediately." She slid a folder across the table, and that was it. My life changed forever.

Here's the plot twist: That boss was my mother. The reasoning and style of her delivery baffled many, including me, but her world—seemingly made of extremes—had always been peculiar to me. There was often no middle ground. From an early age through adulthood, I was either in fashion or outmoded, good or bad, adored or tolerated, right or wrong. Too often, I landed on the wrong side of the coin, as I did that day in the conference room.

As a child and daughter, I always struggled with the feelings of never being enough when it came to my relationship with my mother. Needless to say, I spent a great deal of my life trying to be enough of an asset or creator of assets to justify my existence, to find a sense of belonging. I was constantly reaching for approval and doing *anything* to grasp that trophy, which always seemed out of reach because it wasn't mine to take. It was hers to give, and she wasn't capable of extending it to me—at least not in a way that I could sense. I get it now, and I don't fault anyone for it. But in the absence of engaging in that struggle for unconditional love, I had to face the void that remained within me.

THE ART OF BUSY

The first two weeks following my dismissal were pretty much a shitstorm. No joke. My body rejected anything I tried to consume. Determined to prove that I was fine, I kept up with my already demanding workout routine and literally ran myself into the ground. After vomiting during a run up a particularly steep hill, I passed out on the downhill side and came to in front of the house of a very surprised, incredibly sweet retired woman. She begged to give me a ride home, but I turned her down and staggered back to my car. She must've thought I was out of my mind. She would've been right.

In another effort to prove to myself and the world that I could handle what had happened as if it were no big deal, I began to seek a way to provide for my family. Within these same two weeks, I hung up my shingle as an executive coach and growth consultant and had my first signed contract in hand. For this, I was elated. Overjoyed! This first gig gave me a much appreciated and well-timed boost of confidence. It is work that I remain passionate about to this day.

Two months later, my wife and I sold our home. We could no longer afford to live the life we had created, and there were a million adjustments we would have to make for ourselves, our children, and our future. In short, I was busy. As a born visionary and problem solver, I was making mincemeat out of these seemingly mountainous challenges while looking forward to the new adventures that would come with completely overhauling our lives. What I didn't take into account was the silent but devastating spiritual, psychological, and emotional damage that had taken place due to the teeth, the buzz saw, of incredible loss and pain.

Looking back, I see clearly what I was doing. My theory was that if I kept achieving goal after goal, I would build up enough self-worth and positive feelings that when I finally did sit still, I wouldn't implode from hurt. A steel structure of inner peace and fortitude would be my prize for all my *doing*.

I was wrong. Though I could keep myself incredibly busy mentally and physically, there were inevitable lulls when the emotional pain would creep in. And my steel structure? Well, it was more of a sand castle. There was no escaping the emotional tide and the fragility of my inner life when I sought to strengthen it through external validation instead of from within. It was simply an altered version of what I had been doing for forty-something years. Recognizing that this strategy of keeping busy wasn't going to be my ticket to "just-fineness," I began to see it for what it was. I realized I needed to find out why I defaulted to this mode. The reason, I discovered, was the seemingly unachievable need of feeling loved and worthy.

By the time I was an adult, this constant striving for love and acceptance had become an unconscious pattern. But when the veil of fantasy was forever ripped off, what I didn't know—the insecurity, the fragility, the still desperate five-year-old fighting for a parent's love—took center stage. As the Japanese poet Mizuta Masahide so eloquently put it, "Barn's burnt down. Now I can see the moon." For me, the "moon" was the recognition that I would never receive the kind of love and belonging I craved from my mother, that this wasn't what the universe had in store for me during this lifetime; I would have to provide that love and sense of belonging for myself. But before I gained that ability, I had to deal with the ashes—the sheer, guttural pain that comes from letting go of what could have been. After spending years guarding my emotions and allowing callouses to form around my heart, I was confronted with my own pain, my loss; it was almost too much to handle.

That's where I was in the weeks following my termination—busy on the outside cobbling together a new life while hate mounted on the inside. The scariest part was that there was little outward indication of the pressure that was building within me. There were momentary, sporadic outbursts of negative emotions, but those were nothing like the emotional outpouring and collapse that would soon follow.

WHAT LIES WITHIN

It's true that we discover who our real friends are when we fall on hard times. I was fortunate enough to have Deli alongside me, a handful of close friends who managed to keep me upright, and the collective support of a larger community. During this time I learned what family meant to me and discovered the true, raw power of love—the beauty and life force that comes in its presence and the brittle emptiness that remains in its absence. I learned that love, like balance, is an inside job. It's not freely available to give or receive until we can create and sustain it within ourselves.

Once I stopped filling my life with busyness, I ran face-first into my feelings about myself. It was like slamming into a mirror. The experience left me dazed, confused, and fragile, yet full of clarity. The insight I gained is that how we treat others—what we say about others, what we believe about others, and how we care or don't care for others—is often a direct reflection of what we believe and feel about ourselves. I would say this is generally true in day-to-day life when we aren't actively projecting ourselves onto others. However, during times of extreme stress or emotional trauma, it is one hundred percent dead on. In these moments, it's not uncommon for the true, honest feelings and beliefs we have about ourselves to emerge.

As I mentioned, Deli and a small circle of close friends stood with me during this time of chaos. Unfortunately, to both my wife and closest friends, I became a monster. I began acting in a way unfamiliar to myself. I assumed friends hung out with me out of obligation, not because they really wanted to. If there was *any* way to twist a text, action, gesture—anything—into a sign of rejection, I would make it so. Time after time, I would emotionally implode or verbally explode when I perceived that my wife or friends were not fully accepting or supporting me. I actually believed that, deep down, they didn't really like me, that they already had one foot out the door, and that it was just a matter of time before they fully absented themselves from my life.

Of course, none of this was true! But I projected my own feelings about myself onto them, feelings I had formed in childhood. The sad reality is that the sheer force of my will to hate myself was leaving them no choice but to opt out of having a relationship with me. The more they loved me, the harder I pushed them away.

It's really sad how hard, mean, impatient, and unkind we can be to ourselves. I know I was heartless. Ruthless. The pain I experienced as a child was nothing compared to the pain I inflicted upon myself. It was only when my wife and close friends began to pull away for reasons of self-protection that I realized what I was doing, and if I didn't stop and change, all the behaviors I exhibited would prove me right: that I was unlovable, that I didn't belong, and that total abandonment was not a question of *if* but *when*. When the impending isolation closed in after I succeeded in forcing one of my closest friends out of my life, I realized it was the *last* thing I wanted. I embarked on an immediate emotional and spiritual journey to save my life.

THE PATH FORWARD

Each morning, I remind myself that the real work is the inner work. I can set the tone for the day, or I can let external forces set it for me. This is the difference between living life from the inside out and the outside in. The most important aspect of my life will not be defined by accolades, positions, accomplishments, possessions, or the results I achieved. The most important aspect of my life will be how I *felt* during my gifted time here and, equally as important, how I made others feel. It's the experience brought on by the time and attention I afford my inner life, not what life can afford me.

In an effort to create the foundation upon which we can spring forth and live fully, let's set aside our desire for pursuing results. Don't get me wrong! Having goals is great *and* necessary. We'd be lost at sea in an oarless boat without them. But life is to be experienced and enjoyed on the *path* from here to there—not only when we attain something or arrive at a destination.

One cannot pursue happiness as a goal or expect it to be a by-product of achieving a goal. When we throw happiness outside ourselves or make it a task, then we lose the essence of it. When we try to regulate our emotions based on how or what we achieve, the feeling is short-lived, if not missed altogether. However, when the basis of those feelings and emotions is internal and we focus on experiencing them daily, what we find is long-lasting, attainable joy. Or peace. Or confidence. Or whatever it is we need to focus on for this particular period of our life. In short, when we focus on our inner life—our emotions, how we show up each day, how we feel about ourselves and others— we are free to fully experience the joy in life and, often, results emerge that we couldn't even have imagined possible.

Let me share the successful strategies that I employed to nurture and sustain my inner life. The strategies, or elements, that exist within this foundational subset are mindfulness, connection, and nurturing.

MINDFULNESS

If you're like me, it's hard to sit still. Literally. Life's distractions have a strong pull on me, often shifting my focus from one shiny object to another. Or perhaps you're quite willing and content to sit quietly, meandering through your internal world, leisurely lifting up and examining the intricacy of each discovery. Mindfulness, or awareness of the present moment, is amazing, because it can come into play no matter your ability to abide distraction or your comfort level in exploring your internal world. Here is what I mean. Mindfulness is a quality of mind that is awake, aware, alert, and knows it. When we build this muscle, it allows us to see things for what they truly are so we can respond rather than react. I think of mindfulness as the bridge between our inner life and our ability to exist and function in the world without being sideswiped by reactivity, emotions, and negative thought patterns. Meditation, such as the practice of present-moment awareness, are the planks of the bridge. It's how we construct and build mindfulness in ourselves. Meditation, yoga, tai chi, to name a few, are exercises we can engage in to build mindfulness.

Being the more hyperactive type, such as I am, presents obvious challenges to practicing meditation and developing awareness. I had to learn that being still and alone with thoughts does not indicate awareness, even though that's often the image we have in our mind. Rather, stillness can lead to quite the opposite—emotional or physical stasis or, worse, harmful thoughts and feelings, negative judgments that can lead to suffering, self-hate, or hatred of others. Allowing ourselves to drift into this zone creates painful loops of negative emotions that we relive and default to over and over and over again. Eventually, we only feel alive when in a state of emotional chaos and trauma. When author Anne Lamott said, "My mind is a neighborhood I try not to go into alone," I imagine she was referring to a time like this!

When we judge or hang on to our thoughts and feelings—artificially lengthening them beyond their intended lives—they imprison us, which leaves us bound up and unable to see other possibilities. We assume that because a thought has entered our brain—this organ believed to be so superior—that it must really *mean* something profound. Instead of letting these ripples occur in a relaxed state of awareness—dropping in and gently moving out—we throw out grappling hooks and waterski on the choppy waves of thought control and magnified emotions. Such passing thoughts were only intended to be flashed up on our mental screen, not revered behind stanchions and rope.

I remember vividly how, in acting class one day, the instructor became frustrated at our ongoing need to *push* the scene, a term used when an actor is more interested in guiding a scene to a prede- termined outcome than allowing the scene to unfold by way of riffing and surfing on what is actually happening in *each moment*. We push when we manufacture emotions out of thought or try to suspend them so we can wallow in them.

> "Rather than being your thoughts or emotions, be the awareness behind them."
>
> —Eckhart Tolle

On this particular day, our instructor asked each of us to leave the classroom and observe a child between the ages of three and five. She asked us to observe how the children allowed emotions to pass through them like clouds pass- ing through the sky. It was remarkable. There's no hanging on in the world of a three-year-old. They *fully* inhabit an emotion, and as soon as it has served its purpose—to blow off steam, to express grief, to exalt a joyous new discovery—they let it go and move on. You want to learn about presence? Go to your local playground and take a page from the little ones.

By experiencing what each emotion and thought has to offer, they allow themselves to be fully available for whatever comes next. They don't allow their emotions and thoughts to overtake their lives or define them. This is awareness at an evolved level. It is noticing what is occurring in our inner life without overidentification or judgment. We allow those clouds to have their moment, yet also give them the freedom to continue moving and morphing across our sky.

I want to underline the importance of observing thoughts or emotions. Acknowledging them is *just* as important as letting them pass. This was my particular weakness. I didn't want to slow down to mindfulness when I thought I might be forced to acknowledge painful emotions and thoughts. I wanted to be done with the whole matter as soon as possible. This was largely due to my belief that if I did acknowledge them, they would somehow consume me. Yet by ignoring them, they did just that! Not only did denying them make them stronger, but they eventually ate me for lunch. I was as locked up and immobilized as an emotional hoarder. It turns out the two extremes are equally as dangerous.

The film *E-Motion* explores and affirms the popularly accepted truth that when we trap emotions by hanging on to them or when we let them go unprocessed by ignoring them, we create profound emotional and spiritual disease. When unchecked for long enough, negative emotions will often manifest into physical ailments—some mild, some chronic, some life threatening. We must first see the thing before we can let it pass. We must then let it pass before we can invite what is next.

PRACTICING MINDFULNESS

To practice mindfulness, we want to be aware, in the moment. We want to notice, allow, and embrace what is happening right now. Awareness is the ability to recognize, in any given moment, the landscape of our inner life, whether it's a wrinkle of sadness, a crease of pain, a mountain of insecurity, or a sea of joy. It is also the ability to recognize, without judgment, our thoughts for just what they are. Thoughts are not rulers over our internal domain, and they are not saboteurs or rescuers. They are the results of our brain processing a piece of our subconscious, bringing it forward and offering it onstage so we may have the opportunity to *know* of it—not *become* it. While our thoughts are real, they are often not true. Rather, they are the artifacts of all the stories we've been telling ourselves during this lifetime. They are well-worn ideas and suggestions but certainly not the *truth*.

When we practice awareness we are not there to minimize, enhance, hoard, or ignore. We are there to acknowledge and allow. If we do not, we trap our thoughts and emotions internally where they will grow and become disruptive, just as a toddler becomes agitated when repeated attempts to garner a parent's attention go unnoticed. When we attend to the need that is seeking attention, we allow it breath and space, restoring order. For me, this is akin to releasing the pause button so that the movie may play forward.

And when we are dealing with powerful emotions, as I was during my own crisis, the simple act of acknowledging them is the first step toward dislodging and unwinding them so they can move and transform into something new. This is why seeking therapy following traumatic events is so important as it, too, gives us the opportunity to tell our story and walk through the emotions instead of letting ourselves be consumed by them. When, instead, we try to hold the door against the flood of negative thoughts and feelings, we may experience a short-term gain by delaying discomfort, but we create long-term consequences. Instead of spending our days walking free and light, we lumber along dragging more and more baggage behind our already diminished selves. In addition, we develop a tendency to exacerbate the crisis and catastrophize situations that trigger similar thoughts or emotions. This Chinese proverb couldn't hit it on the head any better: "If you are patient in one moment of anger, you will escape a hundred days of sorrow."

Present-Moment Awareness

There are several types of meditation and many resources that explore how to practice each modality. The meditation practice I'll be sharing is a form of applied present-moment-awareness meditation that will help us attune to thoughts and feelings; we'll be working to loosen and release the negative emotions bogging you down. If you are completely new to meditation, I suggest beginning with a more basic practice of object meditation or sensory meditation to become familiar with the territory. Look up podcasts on meditation or download the Mindfulness Daily or Headspace app on your smart phone. I've used both of these apps myself and highly recommend them. Either way, get at least five days under your belt of practicing focused-breathing, sensory, or object meditation before stepping into our work here.

To begin, find a place to sit where you are comfortable and where distractions (noise, light, etc.) are minimal. Relax your gaze, or close your eyes, and begin by focusing on your breath. Take three deep breaths, breathing in through the nose and pushing out through the lips. Then turn your awareness to your body. Feel the sensation of where your body presses against the floor, the chair, or the ground. I find that connecting with my body first is the most efficient and easeful way to usher me into the *now*. If at any time you feel a loss of presence or you begin to spin into uncontrollable thoughts or emotions, bring yourself back into your body. Bring focus to your breath, to the feel of the ground, to the weight of your torso—any element of your physical self.

Once you have established presence, allow your thoughts and emotions to walk across the stage. As each comes, notice and breathe into the bodily sensations—such as tightness in the chest or ache in the throat—and identify the emotion or thought while resisting the urge to grab on to the thought or emotion itself. For example, if the thought, "I feel anxious about dinner tonight" were to occur, simply label it "anxious." If the sensation of sadness wells up inside, label it "sadness" or "hurt." Use whatever word connects with the emotion you are experiencing.

After giving the thought or emotion a label, imagine it being enveloped by a loving presence. This could be a physical manifestation of someone or some figure that represents love to you, or it could be a nondescript energetic field of love—whatever resonates for you. Then invite the next thought or emotion onto the stage. It may sound something like this (although I speak these words silently to myself): "Nervous. Anxious. Anxious. Anxious. Letting that pass. Relaxing. Distracted. Focusing on breath. Calm. Amused. Alive. Feeling present. Content. Relaxed."

You'll notice that I repeated the word "anxious." When a thought, emotion, or sensation lingers on the stage, simply repeat what it is until something new comes along or it dissipates. Again, mindfulness is not about forcing. It's about allowing and attending to what is in front of you in any given moment. Let the flow of your thoughts and emotions be just that—a flow.

In the beginning, practice this for five minutes each day. You'd be surprised how much internal life can happen in a few minutes! And when you encounter persistent emotions or negative thoughts, give yourself the grace and compassion to go back to simply focusing on your breath. And, again, if you have been through something traumatic, please seek therapy as your starting point. Mindfulness is a powerful add-on both during and after therapeutic interventions, but it is no replacement.

When I was engaged in intense therapy, my mindfulness exercises went something like this: "Anger. Anger. Rage. Hurt. Hate. Drowning. Grasping. Unlovable. Unwanted. Alone. Hurt. Hurt. Hurt. Broken. Grief. Trash." My inner life had little conventional beauty to offer. In fact, it was unbelievably difficult to experience! But even amid the pain, I was able to recognize the stunning beauty of tearing down, sifting through, and clearing the stage. With each meditation and word spoken, I could sense the movement. I could sense my jammed-up emotional life begin to stream away. Sometimes, on difficult days, I could last no longer than two minutes before shifting focus to my breath. But the commitment I made to myself, and the one I'd like you to make, is to practice some form of mindfulness every day. Whether it is through this particular form of meditation or another modality entirely, make it a daily practice. Instead of evaluating yourself on how long you are able to practice mindfulness, be pleased with yourself for practicing each day. Eventually, you will be able to practice mindfulness for a full ten minutes or longer or while in motion, like I often do now when I'm on my bike. But first things first—get centered and commit to becoming familiar with the practice.

CONNECTION

Let's bring our attention back to the notion that, try as we might, we cannot achieve happiness by pursuing it as a goal nor by boxing up and setting aside everything that makes us uncomfortable.

Happiness—and all of life for that matter—occurs at various points along our journey and can easily be missed if our focus and attention is predominantly on the future or what's in the rearview mirror. Sadly, many of us (myself included) have bought into the idea that we can hit the happiness jackpot via buying some shiny piece of merchandise or by knocking down a flag as we attain yet another one of our lofty goals. As much as I secretly love that idea and kind of wish it were true, the reality is, we can't. If you want pure joy, don't look for a bar code. Look within. It is there, but you must connect with it to experience it.

Tara Brach, a prolific author, psychologist, and leading Western teacher of Buddhist meditation, often uses the phrase "attend and befriend" in her teachings when it comes to healing deeper levels of fear and emotional pain. (I highly recommend her book *Radical Acceptance*, in addition to her podcasts, for anyone who is in the process of overcoming difficulty, interested in exploring inner life in depth, or curious about expanding their mindfulness practice.) While Brach associates "attend and befriend" most often with healing negative thoughts and emotions, I would also apply it to experiencing happiness and joy. Too often, we focus our energy on what is negatively affecting us and completely skip over the positivity that may be waiting to be released or simply observed. This is a natural and human thing to do, because our brains are geared toward problem solving and survival as opposed to basking in a relaxed, blissful state. To fully experience all of life's ups and downs and infinite possibilities in appropriate doses, we need to learn to flex our brains in new ways.

Thanks to research into positive neuroplasticity—a fancy term that refers to our ability to establish new neural pathways and synapses via changes in behavior, environment, thinking, and emotions— we now know that we can train the brain to learn new tricks. For the purposes of cultivating a healthy and thriving inner life, it means we can resume the controls from our caveman ancestors and our overly intellectualized egos and steer our inner life toward emotional, spiritual, physical, and intellectual health. It also means that just because we've always struggled with something or reacted in a certain way, we are not doomed to this fate forever. By transforming our relationships

with the internal demons we struggle with and by regularly noticing and appreciating the positive emotions that often sit secondary to
the negative ones, we can sink our rudder deeper into the waters and
experience a richer life. As Donald Hebb, a Canadian neuropsycholo-
gist, said in his 1949 book *The Organization of Behavior*, "Neurons
that fire together, wire together."

Welcoming positive thoughts and emotions while transforming
negative ones can be a game changer for our brains and, thus, our
lives. To do this, we need to recognize that working with both sets of
thoughts and emotions is essential if we want to enhance our inner
life, including this big muscle sitting in our craniums. But *how* we sit
with each as we work to transform them is where the difference lies.
With negative thoughts and emotions, we befriend them by sitting
side by side—showing openness and a desire for connection without threat, avoidance, or judgment. And with positive emotions, we
befriend them by sitting across from them as one would when enjoying the company of favorite friends—fully available to allow their
light and energy to pour into us. Let's begin with the former and work
on the emotions and thoughts that plague us.

Healing Negativity

I don't know about you, but I have a strong tendency to beat myself
up. I beat myself up if I fall short of expectations. I beat myself up
if someone says something negative about me. I beat myself up if
I coulda/woulda/shoulda made a better choice. I beat myself up for
beating myself up. You get the idea. It's somewhat predictable and
highly annoying.

When Deli saw me engaged in yet another epic beatdown of
myself after my emotional trauma and subsequent internal implosion,
she looked at me sweetly and gently asked, "Why are you so hard on
yourself?"

To which I responded, "Because!"

I then rattled off a million reasons why I sucked and how I had
screwed up: "I should've seen this coming. I let myself believe a fantasy.

I'm a pushover. There must be some reason I deserve this pain. I'm worthless now." On and on I went.

When I finally paused for air, Deli asked, "If Niko [our son] or Uma [our daughter] experienced what they deemed as a failure at school or with friends, would you come down on them like this?"

"Of course not!" I replied.

"And if you saw them being as hard on themselves as you're being on yourself, would that be okay with you?" she asked.

"No!"

"Then why treat *yourself* so poorly? Where is the compassion for *you?*"

I had no answer. There was only silence as I grasped how abusive I had been to myself.

Then she said, "I want you to speak to yourself the same way you would speak to one of your children. *That* is the voice and *those* are the messages of love you need to hear."

In an instant, my old systems for dealing with negativity were irreversibly jammed. By shining a light on the reality of what I was doing (harming myself), Deli helped me leave behind my penchant for practicing such violence on myself. While, yes, I managed to still do slight harm to myself from time to time after that revelation, I learned how to escape the pattern of negativity. That room could no longer hold me. I had outgrown it; I had seen the truth of it. That day, I dove headfirst into identifying a new approach, a new strategy for dealing with the unprocessed and *highly* avoided themes of negative thoughts and emotions that had infected my inner life and made me a monster unto myself.

When we deal with negativity in ourselves or others, there are typically two types of responses: phobic and counterphobic. To have a phobic response is to cower, like a dog, tail tucked between its legs, that is avoiding eye contact and trying to disappear into a corner. A counterphobic response would be more outwardly focused, like an

> "The mind creates the abyss, the heart crosses it."
> —Sri Nisargadatta Maharaj

aggressive dog lashing out in fear, confusion, or a show of dominance. I was more like the counterphobic dog, attacking myself because of my inability to deal with my perceived enemies—feelings of fear, shame, and worthlessness.

Whether phobic or counterphobic, there's an element of holding with each response that is caustic to us. Instead of transforming the negativity into something new, we confine it to an unending loop where it builds upon itself until the momentum is so strong that we snap. We either hide out, avoid the negative feelings, and stomach the intolerable as we corrode from the inside out. Or we lash out at ourselves, our circumstances, or those around us. Then we self-medicate with excuses, substances, or old patterns that temporarily soothe until we complete another lap around our toxic loop and snap again. And then we wonder why the cycle keeps happening over and over and over.

The reason our harmful loops remain intact—our negativity unchanged—is because we have forgotten or abandoned the practice of love and compassion for ourselves. The more I live and the more I interact with others in my work, the more I understand that these are the two most critical components that we all need and desire yet fail to ask for or deliver. Instead of sitting side by side with the pain, we either clash with it head-on or avoid it entirely. Before we can give to others, we must first give to ourselves. If we wish to give love, then we must first love ourselves. If we wish to forgive, then we must first forgive ourselves. There's no hacking that basic tenet. It's an unbreakable equation.

So how do we offer love and compassion to heal negative patterns within ourselves? Let's first define the terms in the context of practicing connection. Love is the appreciation and care for what is here, in this moment, just as it is. There are no caveats, no conditions. It is a fullness that is all-encompassing and extends beyond judgment and attachment. In short, there is no need for the term "unconditional love" because love *is* unconditional. Compassion is the deep place of knowing and the tenderness within us that awakens in the presence of struggle and desires to ease the suffering. It, too, is without judgment as it seeks to deliver peace to those without it.

For us to practice love and compassion on ourselves, we must embrace these terms and connect them to ourselves. We must wake up the desire to ease our own suffering, understanding that we deserve a healing and compassionate presence. And we also must envelop ourselves in love, our *whole* being—the good, the bad, and the ugly—as we appreciate, *unconditionally*, the beauty of who and what we are right now.

As Thich Nhat Hanh suggests, we must understand that beauty does not come free of decay. In fact, jaw-dropping, heart-stopping beauty—such as the lotus flower arising from the mud—often emerges in the most unlikely environments and under the harshest conditions. But our lotus, our ability to see our own beauty and worth, can be stamped out if we stifle it with our own incessant mudslinging. Tenderness is what the heart calls for, and compassion can transform the pain.

> "No mud, no lotus."
> —Thich Nhat Hanh

This was my first bridge to cross in my spiritual awakening. I had to lay planks from my isolated control tower of self-abuse to an interconnected highway of love and compassion so that no matter what negative thoughts bombarded me or what abusive patterns began to replay, I could immediately access that tender place within myself and practice the same loving-kindness I practiced with my children. It wasn't easy at first. Nothing is. But I found that taking time to visit my inner demons each day and offering them love and compassion was critical to unbinding and transforming the negative patterns into something freer and more positive. I call this time Visiting Hour, which, in reality, was more like twenty minutes, but I liked the name, so it stuck.

Visiting Hour

To hold your own Visiting Hour, find a comfortable place to sit that is free of distraction. Relax your gaze, or close your eyes, and take a few deep breaths to focus your awareness on your body, creating space in your thoughts, grounding in the present moment. When you are ready, bring to mind something that's currently causing you pain or that is difficult for you. It could be the loss of a relationship, a fear that is troubling you, a situation where you feel wronged or hurt, a concern for someone, a difficult dynamic with a friend or loved one, anything that is causing you angst. Once you have the situation in mind, name (silently or aloud) the emotions and sensations passing through you, much like you did in the exercise about cultivating present moment awareness. For example, you might identify feelings of anger, worthlessness, hurt, or abandonment. Name each emotion or sensation as it comes up, allowing it to change and move; resist the desire to hold on to it. Give permission to whatever wants to come forward to do so, allowing yourself to feel these feelings, think these thoughts without judgment. Continue doing this for a minute or two.

Create a visual of yourself in your difficult situation and become curious; inquire. What sensations do you feel in your body as you're experiencing these thoughts and emotions? What do you feel in your throat? Your chest? Your stomach? Are you restless or still? You may be curled up in a corner like the phobic dog. Or you may be so full of rage that you're pulling at the end of your chain like the counter-phobic dog. Whatever you're doing, just see yourself and notice the physical sensations. Do this for another minute or so.

Keeping the visual of yourself intact, call to mind someone who has been a loving force in your life. For me, it's my grandmother on my father's side. Even though she's been deceased for many years, her kindred spirit and the way she loved me has far outlived her physical body. Call up your own loving force, whether living or deceased. Now look at the image of yourself struggling through the eyes of this person while continuing to speak (silently or aloud) the emotions and sensations that are passing through you. But this time, speak in the voice of your loving force. How would this person say these emotions and sensations? Remember that this is someone who would not want you to struggle and who does not judge you. Allow your loving presence to see and name what is occurring for three to five minutes. Allow yourself to hear and *feel* this person's voice.

This place of loving-kindness, this voice, is one we don't often use on ourselves. Rather, we pollute our environment with the nagging of our internal critic or the browbeating of our self-appointed bully. When I first did this exercise, the difference between the tone and tenor of my voice and the voice of my loving force was striking. The energy emanating from my voice was harsh, pointed, tightly wound, and aggressive. I could feel the negative energy spiraling up as I progressed through naming each sensation and emotion. But when I shifted to my grandmother's voice, the voice of love and compassion, there was a peacefulness and ease. There was a knowing and understanding that made me feel that I was really seen in each moment of struggle so that I did not hold on to any shame or negativity. At the same time, I was free to release each moment, each emotion and sensation, *because* I had been seen.

If you want a deeper experience of this, try Tara Brach's Yes Meditation practice, which can be found on her website, www.tarabrach. com. This meditation can either be used as a container to get yourself out of an agitated or negative state or as an add-on to the previous exercise. To break out of a negative current, name the source of aggravation followed immediately by the word "yes." This is the only word you're allowed to say after each thought. It might look like this:

> I feel worthless. Yes.
> I'm hurt. Yes.
> How could she do this to me? Yes.
> I want to feel loved. Yes.
> I want to be enough. Yes.
> This feels silly. Yes.
> But this is my life . . . Yes.
> Maybe I'll be okay. Yes.
> I'm okay. Yes.

You'll notice as you progress that tension often dissipates, and on some occasions, a smile may develop as the negativity transforms into either a state of letting go or fully transforms into positivity. At other times, the sensations are much more subtle as a knot of anxiety begins to loosen its grip. To bring the Yes Meditation into the Visiting Hour exercise, ask your loving force to say yes after each emotion, sensation, or thought that is named. That powerful yes will help you further accept and embrace all that is while allowing new oxygen to unlock those trapped patterns of negativity. Our loving presence brings with it a safe container in which we can dance with our emotions so as not to relive the trauma but, rather, experience it in the context of love and compassion.

While I practice other tools and strategies, Visiting Hour was the oxygen mask I relied on most heavily in the weeks following my emotional trauma. At least five days a week outside of my therapeutic process, I would hold Visiting Hours to attend and befriend whatever was troubling me. Rarely did the same visuals come up, and the source of my angst would shift as well. Some days I was full of rage, and others I was nostalgic and misty eyed. But after each session, I could sense those emotions unlocking and moving. Eventually, they no longer held reign over my inner life, and my emotions became single waves moving through the sea, not representative of the entire ocean. This is a practice I continue to use even well beyond the initial trauma. It's a tool I turn to whenever I sense that I'm turning on myself.

Elevating Positivity

Now that you have a way to attend and befriend what ails or diminishes you, let's move to the other side of the spectrum and work on your relationship with happiness and joy. Some of us have a distant relationship with positivity because we were trained out of it. For example, Liz, a highly accomplished woman I have known for decades, grew up with a mother who was quite abusive, both physically and emotionally. After a particularly nasty episode, her mother would shower Liz with gifts and accolades—a dynamic that exists in many abusive relationships, no matter what age they occur. This pattern was consistent throughout Liz's childhood even into her adult years, so Liz learned that feelings of joy were, at best, temporary Band-Aids or empty gestures. At worst, experiencing happiness was an indicator that another course of pain was waiting around the corner as her mother would often "knock her down a peg" after showering her with affection. Over many years of growing up in this environment, Liz was conditioned out of connecting with happiness and joy. For her, it was unsafe.

On the other hand, sometimes we keep ourselves on the periphery of experiencing joy in ways quite opposite to Liz's situation. Instead of avoiding it, we welcome joy and positivity, but we rush right through the experience, barely letting the emotions land on us. We are so consumed with *doing* and *achieving* that the addiction to chasing after a new goal outshines our ability to bask in the joy we experience in the journey. This gets into the "more, more, more" addiction that is so rampant in our society today. Since when did more come to mean better? It doesn't. In fact, quite often, it's far less than better.

Similar to a junkie chasing a first high, we have a strong tendency to return to the well of what makes us feel good. We collect cars, shoes, electronics, and mortgages out of a primal desire to feel accomplished, to gain a sense of belonging, or to experience joy. But we don't recognize the prices we pay for chasing material goods. We increase our stress as we take on more expense, and then spend more time at work to pay off our hobbies. We find that it takes more and more to make us happy. But, again, we've fallen into the seductive cycle of trying to purchase happiness, gaining it from the outside rather than cultivating it from within. When we do this, we set ourselves up for failure. Remember love and its freedom of conditions? Love what you have, what you are, what you feel right now so that you can open up and receive joy.

Calling up happiness can often be more of a struggle than calling up pain or sorrow. We have a stronger inherent connection to pain, whereas happiness and joy tend to be more ethereal in nature. To elevate positivity, we need to heighten our awareness to it, overcoming its weaker signal. If I were to be totally cheesy, I'd suggest we put our joy on blast. That's kind of what I recommend you do.

Use any number of Visiting Hours to focus on the happy, joyous you. Follow all the same steps but replace negativity with positivity. Call up a time when you felt amazing, proud, happy, complete, joyful, or loved. Find where in your body this feeling emanates from, and then visualize yourself in that state of positivity. Then begin naming the thoughts, emotions, and sensations that you experience. Add your own yes after each statement, this time embodying the Buddha's half smile as you do so. Take time to connect to and remember what positive feelings *feel* like. Get to know how *you* experience them so that in your daily life you can recognize those moments as they happen, especially the smaller ones, which tend to get overlooked—like taking the first sip of coffee or tea in the morning. Or watching a squirrel outfox the neighborhood dog, *again*. Or drawing in a crisp breath of fresh air on a spring morning.

> "Find out where joy resides, and give it a voice far beyond singing. For to miss the joy is to miss all."
> —Robert Louis Stevenson

Each day, raise your antenna and place intention on experiencing positivity—contentment, joy, waves of happiness, aliveness, vitality, and thankfulness. Or simply flex your capacity for joy, making it more a part of who you are. In a moment when you've managed to turn off your "thinking" brain and can sense a pause, let your eyes go soft and scan your emotions. Where are you right now? If you land on negativity, practice present-moment awareness and simply name what is happening in order to allow the sensation to pass through you. If you land on a positive moment, savor it. Breathe it in for ten breaths; let it infect you. The more moments you identify, the more you will become aware of them and train your brain to notice them. Eventually, your channel for positivity will become as strong if not stronger than your channel for negativity.

NURTURING

In her book *The Writing Life*, Annie Dillard nailed it when she penned, "How we spend our days is, of course, how we spend our lives." At first glance, this perception seems rather obvious, but I find that we need this reminder on a consistent basis. This life was not intended to be a treadmill, but we can surely make it one if we aren't present and intentional with how we seed our inner life. There are plenty of us who have become complacent about letting the outside world determine the landscape within. I also believe that our attention has become more and more dissected as the world becomes more and more instantaneously responsive; endless alerts flood our phone screens and laptops. Because of this, we need to drop Dillard's premise down one more level and focus on how we *begin* each day. For how we begin a day is likely how that day will end.

Anything is possible each day, and it is us who gets to decide how that day unfolds. Will we be enough to find happiness within ourselves? Or will we want more? Will we choose curiosity? Or will we choose judgment? Will we embody the wholeness of our being? Or will we hide behind a mask of what we assume others desire? These choices are incredibly powerful; they affect our experience of life. The gift of each day is the opportunity to set the tone and be intentional with what we wish to experience and manifest. But when we fail to grab the wheel, we allow others to determine the nature of our day. We get swept up in their drama, we lose our center, and we become susceptible to getting carried away with whatever or whoever comes our way. We turn into a careening snowball of loose emotions barreling down a mountain, completely out of control and at the whim of a landscape determined by others.

How many of you have woken up in a bad mood and then made sure everyone knew it? How many of you have begun your day without any clear vision, only to find that at the end of the day you have nothing to show for your existence? Or how many of you have woken up and nonchalantly gone about your day only to be sideswiped by an unexpected email that lands you on your back until the rooster crows again? How many of you have had all of these happen on the same day? (Raises hand.)

When we fumble through life like this, we become disconnected and untethered from our inner life, and we are easily hijacked. When we open our eyes, check our email first thing, and we instantly get caught up in the hustle and bustle of activity. Our minds are off to the races before our feet have even hit the ground. We lose our ability to experience time as something that can expand and belong to us when we chase our days instead of dictate them. One of my favorite poets, David Whyte, opens his poem "What to Remember When Waking" with these lines:

> In that first
> hardly noticed
> moment
> in which you wake,
> coming back
> to this life
> from the other
> more secret,
> moveable
> and frighteningly
> honest
> world
> where everything
> began,
> there is a small
> opening
> into the day
> which closes
> the moment
> you begin
> your plans.

When we take the time to truly meet and greet each day—instead of allowing our days to be hijacked by others' needs and ruled by our ruthlessly overbooked schedules—we pour possibility into the content of each day.

Being a bit of a computer geek and recognizing the real possibilities of system overload in our lives, I believe we need to give ourselves the opportunity to reboot. I think of my Mac and the little spinning icon that appears in times of trouble. I've termed it the "lollipop of patience," choosing a positive association. For others, it's the "spinning beach ball of death," perhaps a more accurate albeit fatalistic description. For PC users, I believe the popular phrase is "blue screen of death," another rather bleak term of endearment. No matter what your term or operating system is, the concept is the same: the indication that performing a system restart is right around the corner as we maniacally commence hitting "Ctrl+s" to save our precious work before the screen goes black and all hope is lost. Once the panic wanes and the system restarts, it generally performs as good as new.

This opportunity to perform a power cycle is as important to us humans as it is to our electronic counterparts. It allows us to pause and restart. However, for us, I suggest we not wait until we are frozen or barely lurching along. Rather, I suggest we take the opportunity to reboot each day, giving ourselves clarity and vibrancy during our "uptime." Being intentional about how we begin each day allows us to run our own power cycle or system flush, emptying anything that may be running in the background, so to speak, and not serving us well. Then we can fill up with new, fresh energy that sets the tone for a positive outlook on the day. For those of you who have professions that have you hitting the pavement in the wee hours of the morning, move this practice to the evening where it can be just as effective.

"Each morning we are born again. What we do today is what matters most."
—Jack Kornfield, *Buddha's Little Instruction Book*

The Emptying Process

The process of emptying is a cornerstone of meditative practice, and it can take dedicated students years, if not decades, to perfect. For them, it's the ability to reach a state where thoughts completely disappear or no longer arise. That isn't the level of emptying I'm referring to. In this practice, our desire is to eliminate or at least thin out the herd of negative thoughts or emotions in order to create stillness.

There are many ways to go about the emptying process, and while

I will share a few, you may have your own practice that creates the same result. The first suggestion is meditation: Simple mindfulness of breath, object meditation, or present-moment awareness are great exercises that can help you reach stillness. Meditation is so effective and so efficient—taking as little as five minutes—that I highly recommend pairing this with the other ideas for emptying. Taking the time to create inner stillness and calm before engaging in anything physical is always a great way to begin a practice.

Another avenue for emptying is freewriting. This is Deli's preferred path. She wakes up and after a few focused breaths, puts pen to paper and pours her thoughts onto a page. No editing, no holding back, just free-flowing thoughts penned exactly as they occur in her head. For anywhere from five to twenty minutes, she allows her thoughts to flow onto the page, stopping only when the last one has been entertained.

A third approach to emptying that I tend to gravitate toward is physical exercise. Physically explosive movement provides me a tangible way to experience the release of leftover, stale, pent-up energy and thoughts. It is also a great contrast to the softness and ease of meditation that I do upon waking. I can use my outward breath during anaerobic exercise, the cadence of each footfall during a run, or the thrust of each rep while lifting weights as the trigger for release. I walk into the gym with the intention to work through anything remaining that has its hooks in me, and I walk out feeling physically and emotionally lifted.

For others, twenty minutes of humming or half an hour of knitting or five minutes of visualization or ten minutes of focusing on breath is their best process for emptying. No matter how you approach the emptying process or how much time you spend on it each day, simply be mindful that the intention is to clean the slate so you can color it anew.

The Filling Process

This next step in the process could be categorized as the "yang" to the "yin" process of emptying. In Chinese philosophy, yin represents the feminine, dark, contracting, and passive force, and yang represents the masculine, bright, expanding, and active force. It is here in the filling process that we can make those active deposits, providing our mind and body the aspects we desire as we look ahead to our day. Similar to the emptying process, there are several approaches to the filling process; I'll provide some ideas so you understand the intent. Then you can either adopt one or adapt an approach to suit you.

Now that we have emptied, we are ready to seed our inner life, setting the tone for each day. In doing so, we need to be mindful and intentional about what those seeds are. Remember, what we focus on grows!

If you practice meditation, incorporating mantras is an excellent way to program positive support. A mantra is a sound, syllable, word, or phrase that many people consider capable of creating transformation in the chanter. There are multiple sources of mantras—one such source is Bija—one-syllable mantras that activate a particular chakra. (Chakras are energy nodes that correspond to massive nerve centers in the body and also affect psychological, emotional, and spiritual states of being. Keeping each of the seven chakras open and flowing with energy is critical to overall well-being.) For example, chanting "Ram" activates the solar plexus chakra responsible for power, purpose, and self-esteem. One of my favorite mantras, "Sat Nam" comes from the Kundalini yoga tradition. *Sat* means "truth" and *Nam* means "name," whereby chanting this mantra brings into vibrational awareness and calls into the power the truth of oneself. There are also phrased mantras intended to bolster whatever the chanter chooses. For example, chanting the phrase, "I change my thoughts; I change my world" would reinforce the power that positive thoughts can have in your life. Perform an online search for mantras to learn more about each one.

Another approach to the filling process involves reversing the focus on breath work. Place your attention on the inhale and inspire what you need for the day—for example, strength, joy, calm, groundedness, or creativity. Make a wish for yourself upon each inhale, and exhale the energy on the out breath.

The practice of visualization has the same reverse ability. Where prior you were visualizing the emptying of emotions, thoughts, and stress, now visualize your day ahead. What do you want it to look like? Feel like? End like? Conjure up the images and see it in your mind's eye! Imagine placing these feelings and sensations in a pool of water where they can be released into the day.

One of my favorite ways to seed a positive outlook is through Metta Meditation, also known as Loving-Kindness Meditation. Its intent is specific: to program positive emotions, such as love, and to develop compassion. To practice Metta Meditation, find a comfortable posture and place your hand on your heart. Take several deep breaths in and out and focus your attention on your heart. Feel a sense of deep, all-encompassing love begin to manifest in and emanate from your heart. Once you have a sense of this, breathe in the first intention of happiness. Next, on the exhale, speak or think the following phrase: May I be happy. Then continue on to the next. The four phrases are as follows:

> May I be happy.
> May I be kind.
> May I be safe.
> May I be peaceful and at ease.

Repeat this sequence three to five times. I typically do this in the morning while still in bed with my hand on my heart. On tougher days, I do it at night as well, when negative chatter tends to escalate for me.

After you have focused the mantra on yourself, gift it to others by visualizing someone else and offering them the phrases, like this:

> May you be happy.
> May you be well.
> May you be safe.
> May you be peaceful and at ease.

Some suggest a specific sequence when doing this meditation: beginning with someone you feel deep love for, then moving on to someone you feel more neutral about, and lastly ending with someone you feel negatively toward. Others recommend you treat your focus more as a sphere and begin widening your sphere with each repetition, encompassing all living beings as you do so. No matter your preferred approach, you can deliver this to as many people as you like, but always start with yourself.

Other ways to program and manifest positivity is through the art—although I'm tempted to call it the science—of gratitude. Making gratitude an actual practice—committing to it daily and wholeheartedly—has been shown to have a profound effect on lives. Best-selling author and researcher Brené Brown, in her Power of Vulnerability course, shares this: "I have never in twelve years interviewed a single person who describes themselves as joyful, their lives as joyous, or described the ability to lean into joy who did not actively practice gratitude." Gratitude is the differentiator between joy and no joy. These are incredibly powerful findings, and thankfully, gratitude practice is easy to integrate into our lives.

One way to practice gratitude is to write down ten things you are grateful for along with *why* you are grateful for them for twenty-one days in a row. I promise you that if you do this, you will notice a shift. Energetically, we attract more of what we acknowledge and show appreciation for. It's like sending a love letter to the universe and having it respond directly to you.

In her book *The Magic*, Rhonda Byrne provides gratitude exercises for an entire month for those looking to cultivate joy or shift their outlook; it's a great resource for forming your own daily gratitude practice. One practice that I've maintained from her book is to think through my day and decide which moment or occurrence I am most grateful for. Then I vocalize a thank you. It takes all of about sixty seconds and is very simple, but simple can be powerful. This exercise forces you to focus on all the *positive* things that happened during your day. Remember positive neuroplasticity? You'll not only be improving your outlook, asking for what you need by naming it, but also creating new neuropathways in your brain. That's not bad for sixty seconds.

Affirmations—the seeding of positive thoughts like gratitude—are also incredibly powerful because they take advantage of a freeing "limitation" of our brain: it believes what we tell it. If we make it real in our inner life, then it is capital *R* Real to our brains, and we get the benefit of having the conductor upstairs on board for the journey, rather than hemming and hawing about all that could go wrong. In this way, we can use visualization and affirmations as the mechanism for bringing all our systems online, working in unison for what we desire. A few examples are "Today, I abandon my old habits and take up new, more positive ones," "I love and accept myself for who I am," and "May whatever arises serve the awakening of wisdom and compassion." There are great resources, including apps, to assist in locating more. For example, Louise Hay, a thought leader in self-help and author of *Heal Your Body*, developed an app called Affirmation Meditations that provides affirmations based on your specific focus.

Taking the time to fill our inner life with positivity doesn't limit us to our current capabilities but provides an opportunity to begin preprogramming the new beliefs, thoughts, and behaviors we would like to adopt. Affirmations are a powerful vehicle in which to do so. We get to mute the negative chatter and give the floor to the compassionate, loving voice that is often silenced for too long.

No matter your methods or practice, the intention of nurturing is to seed what you wish to create and then cultivate those seeds through constant daily interaction. We can practice mindfulness and connection all we want in order to attend to our sources of pain and joy, but we must also be proactive in what we manifest for our future. This is where nurturing comes in. This is the daily practice that allows *you* to drop rudder and aim your inner life to your own pot of golden light.

CONCLUSION

I've been asked if we need to practice all three elements of inner life—awareness, connection, and nurturing—each day or if we can stagger practicing them throughout the week (practicing awareness on Monday, connection on Tuesday, etc.). My response is that you should adopt the frequency and cadence that suits your schedule and serves you the most. Each practice requires a minimum five- to ten-minute commitment. It'd be unwise to consistently short-circuit the length of each practice in order to fit them all in; although in the beginning, you may need to build the muscle to sustain a full ten minutes for each practice.

I practice nurturing and awareness every morning and often every evening. I like to bookend my days with stillness, gratitude, and positivity. When I began my healing, I practiced connection every single day for three weeks. I found that when I tried to skip a day, the negativity would regain momentum and overtake the domain of my inner life. A solid three weeks of unbroken practice in connection is what it took to shift the tide enough for me to spend some days outside this practice. Now that I'm in maintenance mode—sustaining the health of my inner life and strengthening my relationship with positive and negative emotions—I practice connection at least twice a week, three times if I'm lucky, and more than that if needed. As a result of remaining diligent with my inner-life practices, people no longer have to worry about walking on eggshells when I come through the door. Ten out of twelve days I have inner peace. The other two? They may be crowded with anxiety or clouded with negative thought patterns, but the difference now is that they no longer derail my day—or my relationships. Because I'm in tune with my inner life and have developed mindfulness, I recognize the instability and fortify my well-being with heightened practices and the knowing that this, too, shall pass. I take baby steps, which lead to more confident strides.

For the beginner, I suggest doing ten minutes of awareness, ten minutes of connection, and ten minutes of nurturing every day for three weeks. Get all cylinders firing while also educating yourself on the intricacies and landscape of your unique inner life. After your initial three weeks, set a new plan for yourself that includes at least one, if not more, practices per day. Remember that a tree rots from within. Strengthening the inside is the most important work. If you skip this work, you will pay a price. Not today. Perhaps not tomorrow. But someday. Give yourself the insurance and assurance that your foundation is solid at its very core by attending to your inner life each day!

PHYSICAL WELL-BEING

*"Take care of your body.
It's the only place you have to live."*

—Jim Rohn

Physical well-being is the second element essential to our foundation, and it provides an opportunity to reflect the health and vitality of our inner life. For me, physical wellness does not have a specific look. I find the images of men and women sold to us in most magazines unreflective of how diverse health can appear in different individuals. To think health comes only in a size 0 or with bulging biceps is narrow minded and, quite frankly, offensive. I have seen many body types and have learned time and time again that you cannot judge a book entirely by its cover when gauging physical well-being.

How you decide to move and exercise each day is an individual choice, and how that effort manifests in your appearance—soft, supple, hard, or sculpted, for example—depends on that decision. If you lift heavy weights all day, then your high muscle mass will be visible to others. If you, however, practice yoga, the strength that lies within may not be so easily revealed.

That said, when it comes to our physical well-being, we tend to focus on our outward appearance as the indicator of health and, therefore, target exercise as the first strategy to achieve this. But I contend that movement is not the place to start. The most important strategies for creating physical well-being are properly nourishing our bodies followed by allowing our bodies to recover from stress. I thank my wellness coach, Debbie, for bringing these elements forward so I could achieve optimal well-being in my own life.

The three elements nested within physical well-being are nutrition, sleep, and movement and exercise. How we fuel and prepare our bodies each day directly connects to the level of energy available to us for output as well as our ability to quiet our systems and recover with sleep. As the saying goes, garbage in, garbage out. It's a bit obvious that if we eat crap and skip sleep, we can expect low to zero ability to have a meaningful workout.

The less obvious yet just as relevant truth is that just because you *can* muster up a hard training session on a day fueled by garbage and on the back of an overstressed body doesn't mean you should—it's not likely you will do yourself any good. In fact, you may do just the opposite. A term commonly used for wasted efforts like these is "junk workouts." If you're overstressed and underfueled, then odds are that you'll do yourself more harm than good. In severe cases, you may end up on your way to adrenal fatigue, America's new epidemic. Adrenal fatigue, a condition marked by chronic fatigue, forgetfulness, physical weakness, and an inability to focus, occurs as a result of stepping on the "adrenaline pedal" too often as we career through our high-stress, nonstop, no-sleep days, weeks, and months. The incessant overstimulation of our adrenal glands over time can leave us low on energy and unable to keep up with our demanding lives.

Thankfully, many practitioners within the vast wellness industry are now coming to understand the dangers of adrenal fatigue and that focusing on just one piece of the picture—lifting as many weights or doing as many reps as you can—isn't necessarily helpful for their clientele. A personal trainer, for example, needs to look beyond how hard to push clients and assess their entire physical well-being, including stress levels and quality of sleep, before dialing up the ensuing week's training plan. I'm thankful and fortunate that my trainers have always held this holistic view, keeping me both healthy and functioning at optimal levels.

We have to be vigilant not only about how we treat our bodies physically but also about what we put into our bodies, because the truth is there's a lot of misinformation and garbage being thrown at us every day. We were told that foods high in fat are evil and that low fat is the way to go, period. Not so, it turns out. We were told that twenty minutes a day on the treadmill is the best form of exercise. Nope, not true either, as we're likely overworking the same muscles and doing more damage than good. Now we're sold energy drinks or herbs that are supposedly a healthy option for fighting fatigue! Nope, not a wise choice if you're looking to resolve the root issue. And we have far too many physicians relying on prescriptions to address symptoms and prop us up so we can stagger through another day. Meanwhile, sugar, a drug that comes in many forms, shapes, flavors, and colors, is one of the most destructive and overlooked addictive substances. It's the little white lie that wreaks havoc on our bodies.

I could seriously get on a soapbox and *preach*, but the fact is, we are always learning new theories about what is contributing to our wellness (or lack thereof). There's so much research out there I could write three or four books apiece! Rather than take that approach, my intention in this chapter and for the purposes of this book is to share the discoveries that have made the most remarkable transformations in my own journey to physical health. And as I learn about new scientific discoveries regarding wellness, I will update my website with this information. As Maya Angelou said, "I did then what I knew how to do. Now that I know better, I do better."

When we know better, we can do better.

NUTRITION

I have all but removed sugar from my diet after completing a twenty-one-day sugar detox back in 2014. Why? Because when I *finally* managed to last twenty-one consecutive days without sugar (fruits, white carbs, cane syrup, agave nectar, etc.), I made several discoveries. First, I realized I was an addict. Prior to this successful attempt, I'd tried and failed to complete the cleanse five times. I don't like anything having that kind of power over me. Second, the seemingly incurable adult acne that had been plaguing me for years disappeared like magic once I dumped sugar. Third, I discovered that I was a happier, nicer person when I wasn't consuming sugar. There were no longer any sharp edges where one might get randomly and needlessly nicked. And, finally, the bloat that I had unknowingly been carrying around melted away. Lo and behold, lying underneath the excess fluid lived a lean and muscular body. I could finally see the results of all my time in the gym and on the trails. Turns out, I wasn't "big boned" as my family says in the Midwest; I was just unhealthy. So you can see that with results like these, I'd have been a fool not to stick with it and leave sugar where it belongs—in the baking supplies cupboard, to be used intentionally and sparingly.

In keeping with the universe's twisted sense of humor, the day I was to begin writing this section of the book also happened to be the day after a major binge on my drug of choice: sugar. At the time, I felt quite deserving of my annual splurge on a doughnut. I had just completed a really tough Olympic-distance triathlon in Oregon. The run course was particularly gnarly. There was no flat terrain. Just rolling hill after rolling hill, a course I ran after a half-hour swim and ninety-minute bike ride. When I crossed the finish line I was feeling super proud of myself, and I already had it in my head that I would treat myself to one of the doughnuts we had picked up from the Voodoo Doughnut shop in Portland on our way to the Willamette Valley, where the race took place and where we were staying.

Willamette Valley, it just so happens, is wine country. And it also just so happens that the vineyard we were staying on grows Pinot Noir grapes, and a bottle of said Pinot Noir was left for us as a welcome gift. Guess what? Pinot Noir is my favorite wine. So it was a date with a bottle of wine, a doughnut, and my gorgeous little family.

That evening we ate a healthy dinner. I barbecued steak and roasted vegetables, and my wife threw together a delicious salad. We enjoyed the bottle of red wine with our meal. Even though all of that was yummy, I couldn't *wait* for dessert! When the time came, I opened the doughnut box as if I were lifting the lid of a treasure chest to peer at the wondrous ornaments inside. After assessing my options, I carefully made my selection: the Old Dirty Bastard, a raised yeast doughnut with chocolate frosting, peanut butter, and Oreo cookies. I savored every bite. Ten minutes after my brief encounter with the doughnut ended, I had a sugar headache like no one's business. I had expected it, so I tolerated it.

Fast-forward to about midnight. After tossing and turning for hours, I suddenly had a deep, dark craving for another doughnut. I had gotten two old-fashioned glazed doughnuts to give to friends. Unfortunately, my friends never got them because I ate both. I fell asleep on the couch where I had indulged myself and then woke up around four o'clock in the morning and snuck back into bed. As soon as Deli woke up, I told her what I had done, and we both laughed. But it wasn't long before I began paying a heavy price for my late night shenanigans.

Within an hour of waking up, I had stomach cramps and some pretty violent digestive issues. Enough said. I also felt nauseated, and for the next two days I was in a fog that I could *not* cut through. No amount of coffee could sharpen my senses. And I went from being testy and cranky on Sunday to depressed and crying on Monday. I was a mess and all my loved ones had to deal with it, which made me feel even worse. To top it off, I couldn't put one coherent sentence together, and I lost an entire day of writing (about nutrition!) thanks to my sugar hangover. There was nothing to do but wait it out. None of my inner-life practices were formidable enough to surmount the chemical changes in my brain, thanks to sugar. After my hellish forty-eight-hour detox, I was reminded, once again, of the power of addiction and that a substance such as sugar—perfectly legal and natural—is truly as powerful as heroin in its ability to get its hooks in us.

Eating the 80/20 Way

I'm an 80/20 person who doesn't appreciate black-and-white, hard-and-fast rules. I like to have options. So I follow my healthy eating plan eighty percent of the time; the other twenty percent, I treat myself to something equally tasty but perhaps not so healthy. For me, that might be a glass of Pinot Noir on a Friday or Saturday night or *one* doughnut as opposed to three. But never both. Even eating one doughnut *with* a glass of wine was enough to set off the chain of events that culminated in the wicked physical and mental distress I experienced after my binge. The culprit was the amount of sugar I poured into my body that night, which then led to an overwhelming craving to eat more. We receive a *massive* reward message when we consume sugar. We could step on that pedal a hundred times a day and each time receive the same powerful reward message: "I like that! Do it again!" With other drugs, such as heroin or nicotine, the reward levels drop off over time, so users require more and more to satiate their addiction. They are forever chasing that first high. With sugar, you get that first high every single time.

When I consumed that insanely good but insanely sugar-loaded doughnut along with a glass of wine, my brain shouted at me to do it again. And, like a fool, I obeyed. The chemicals rushing through my body were too formidable to ignore.

Here's the takeaway: Just because something feels good doesn't mean it will lead to any good. And just because you *know* what you should do, doesn't mean you will be able to control your impulses and override the chemicals coursing through your body. To stave off cravings requires an act of willpower that few of us possess. And to put yourself in harm's way day after day by having a small taste of your favorite thing is to essentially load the chamber, cock the gun, and then aim it at your foot. My Achilles' heel is sugar. It is hard for me to eat just a little without going overboard.

Your Achilles' heel may be something else: A Big Mac? Soda? Alcohol? Tortilla chips? Chocolate? A box of Voodoo doughnuts? All of the above? Get to know your enemies so you can be strategic and out-smart them. To be in denial or to downplay and ignore their control over you is foolish. There's no shame here. Our bodies consist of complex chemical and hormonal systems so, of course, it would make perfect sense that we could be manipulated by what we feed those systems.

> "The food you eat can be either the safest and most powerful form of medicine or the slowest form of poison."
> —Ann Wigmore

Exercise: Know Your Dietary Demons

Make a list of foods that are toxic to your health and well-being. We'll call them your dietary demons. These are foods that you crave, that you indulge in daily or weekly and that, to an objective bystander, would hold more power over you than you hold over them. Here is my list: cupcakes, doughnuts, chips, buttered popcorn, cereal, crois-sants, salted caramel ice cream (actually, anything with caramel), cof-fee, margaritas, peanut butter cups, and blueberries. I'm sure there's more, but this captures the main offenders and is enough to indi-cate the root of my weakness. Everything on my list, save coffee, has high sugar content. Even my beloved blueberries. Rich in antioxi-dants, blueberries are a healthier source of sugar because they are not injected with man-made chemicals, if grown organically, but they still have high sugar content. And sugar is sugar; it wreaks the same havoc on our bodies regardless of the source.

I have to be especially mindful of the amount of sugar I con-sume. It's an incredibly powerful substance that is injected into way too many of our foods. Food scientists and executives working for major corporations are no dummies. They're absolutely aware of the powerful effect sugar has on us, and they are placing it in foods that don't even need it! Read food labels and you'll find corn syrup lurking among the first ingredients. Bottom line: If I'm working in the food industry and am solely motivated by profit, then I want you to keep coming back for more. The ticket? Sugar. It's sad, but true. And now *you* know.

What are your dietary demons? First, list those out and then see if you can identify the core of your main addiction(s). Is it sugar? Caffeine? Salt? Unhealthy fats? Alcohol? Use your list of dietary demons to identify your Achilles' heel.

Dietary Demons

_____

_____

_____

_____

_____

_____

_____

_____

_____

Achilles' Heel

_____

Be hypervigilant about how often you consume your dietary demons and, perhaps more importantly, how easily you can access more. The only offender I keep in the house is coffee. I've made a conscious choice to allow myself two cups in the wee hours of the morning (I'm an early riser) and a latte in the late morning/early afternoon.

I do not drink caffeine after 2 p.m. This routine is easy to manage; it's more difficult to control consumption of my sugar-loaded offenders. Unlike coffee, these little devils transform me into a ravenous, bottomless pit. If they were around, I would eat them all up, or I'd habituate to using them every day. I'd end up moody again, with acne, completely bloated, and eventually unable to engage in the physical activities I've come to love. Since my health and happiness aren't for sale, I won't allow myself to sell out.

Keep in mind that the 80/20 rule isn't meant to be applied to every hour or every day! If it were, we'd most likely remain stuck where we are and far too vulnerable or, at worst, fueling our bodies with way too much sugar, caffeine, alcohol, or unhealthy fats, such as fried foods. This rule should be applied to the entire week where twenty percent equals one serving. One cookie (not the ones that are the size of your head!). One glass of wine. One ice cream scoop. One, okay maybe two, handfuls of chips. But only one of these items in a set week. I won't break it all down here, but you get the gist. I believe we all have a pretty good inner guide who knows when we're reaching in one too many times or have poured a bit too generously. Listen to that voice. It's your best self watching out for you. To reiterate, keep those dietary demons out of your house so that when the inevitable chemical reaction occurs and the craving for more begins, you'll be in a safe harbor, far away from the sirens coaxing you back for another ill-fated encounter.

The 80/20 Rule and Grocery Shopping

Finally, in terms of what you should be eating, I'm going to keep this pretty high level, relying on the *Life, Incorporated* website (www.lifeincorporated.co) to share the most current, in-depth information. For the book, here is what I have to offer: Eat real food. Try to avoid food that has been created in a manufacturing plant and requires a bar code. Opt for organic food you can buy at a farmers' market: produce and dairy products and meats from humanely raised animals. If you do buy packaged foods, make sure you can pronounce every word in the list of ingredients, and triple check that sugar isn't one of the top ingredients. If farmers' markets aren't an option for you, shop the outer perimeter of your grocery store. This is typically where you find produce, meats, eggs, and dairy. These are generally the better choices. I say "generally" because you'll still run into flavored milks, margarines, processed meats, and nonorganic or inhumanely farmed products in these areas. Learn about your food, and be mindful of what you're picking up.

Try applying the 80/20 rule here: Fill your cart eighty percent with items found on the outside perimeter and only twenty percent with items found in the inner aisles. There are healthy foods to be found in these aisles, too, such as coconut oil, almond butter, olive oil, flaxseed crackers, and the like.

One special note: the gluten-free aisle exists in almost every supermarket, but please don't be conned into thinking that gluten free automatically equates to healthy. More often than not, these products contain ridiculous amounts of sugar with little to no fiber and should be avoided at all costs. Again, read the ingredients list and beware of sugar dressed up as healthy. Cane sugar, agave syrup, Stevia—it's all the same.

I follow all the guidelines I've shared in this section while grocery shopping, and I make sure to pick out items with healthy fats as well. We've been fed a lot of misinformation about how horrible fats are for us and how low-fat food is the healthier option. Many low-fat prod-ucts have—you guessed it—sugar added to compensate for the lack of fat. Truth is, there are many sources of healthy fats out there. And, as an extra bonus, these healthy fats satiate the appetite and make us feel full. Sugar or carbohydrates, on the other hand, spark the blood-sugar roller coaster and leave us craving more.

Here are some of my favorite sources of healthy fat: Coconut oil is at the top of my list; not only is it tasty but it's also a great source of medium-chain triglycerides (MCTs). MCTs have many proven health benefits such as improving metabolism and blood-sugar regu-lation while also providing an excellent source of energy. In addition, MCTs are used to treat ailments such as Alzheimer's and diabetes.

Don't like coconut oil? No problem. You can purchase MCT oils at almost any health-food store. Another source of healthy fat is butter made from the milk of grass-fed cows. Almond milk, walnuts, wild-caught salmon, and avocados are my other favorite sources of healthy fat. As my list suggests, I include meat in my diet, but as with everything else, I make sure I know from where it's been sourced and how it's been raised.

Nutrition is a complex field, and I've barely scratched the surface here. My intention is to get you to think about what you eat and to question the status quo. Food is your source for fuel, and you need to consider what it is you want fueling your body, your brain, and your ability to manifest all that you desire. I can tell you in no uncertain terms that you won't reach any type of peak performance or even come close to your potential by choosing foods that are destructive to your body. I believe *many* of the diseases plaguing humanity today are caused by what we ingest and can also be cured by what we ingest.

Homework

Now that you know what your dietary demons are, record what you eat each day for thirty days along with your mood. There are five days' worth of journal pages at the back of the book to get you started. You can also record this information in "The First 30 Days" portion of the Life, Incorporated Journal found online at www.lifeincorporated.co.

Also record your twenty percent splurge each week, being sure to note your mood that day and the days following. (This is a good habit to maintain beyond the thirty days.) When you notice a pattern of negative effects, seek the culprit and remove it. Assign it to the dietary demons list where it's only to be enjoyed in a small portion once a week, or if it's already on the list, note it so you remember that using that particular substance comes at a higher personal price. And then avoid it. If you find that much of what you currently eat is unhealthy or suspect, I recommend doing a twenty-one-day detox or reset diet. One of my favorite books for this is *The 21-Day Sugar Detox: Bust*

Sugar & Carb Cravings Naturally by Diane Sanfilippo. It's a great way to reset your diet, and the book contains tasty yet practical recipes to support you on your journey.

SLEEP

Sleep is one of the most powerful, effective, and efficient tools for maintaining our health, yet it is also the most underutilized, overlooked, and downright abused. Hello, my name is Halley, and I've been appreciating sleep for sixteen days now. I don't say this to make light of recovery programs; in fact it's quite the opposite! I, and others like me, have become addicted to the always-on, never-sleep mentality. We tear through life at breakneck speed, all in the name of getting things done. We hit the caffeine tap throughout the day to keep us going, and when we finally consider retiring to bed, we find ourselves tired but wired. We toss and turn, and when we finally drift off, we don't sleep well. We wake up multiple times during the night, and then the rooster crows, and it's the same routine all over again. Except this time, we carry forward the added stress we never relieved and the added burden on our bodies. The snowball continues to hurtle down the hill.

In January 2014, *The Huffington Post* published an article by Laura Schocker titled "Here's a Horrifying Picture of What Sleep Loss Will Do to You."[8] The article revealed some of the more frightening effects sleep deprivation can have on our health:

- Increased risk of stroke: Adults who sleep less than six hours a night have four times the risk of stroke symptoms.

- Obesity: Stress prompts less-than-ideal food choices, including serving larger portions and choosing junk food.

---

8 L. Schocker, "Here's a horrifying picture of what sleep loss will do to you," *Huffington Post* (January 8, 2014), http://www.huffingtonpost.com/2014/01/08/sleep-deprivation_n_4557142.html.

- Increased risk of diabetes: Lack of sleep increases insulin resistance.

- Memory loss: Sleep deprivation can lead to *permanent* cognitive issues, such as brain deterioration.

- Osteoporosis: Studies have linked sleep deprivation to changes in bone density and bone marrow.

- Increased risk of cancer: Six hours of sleep or less has been linked to colorectal cancer and reoccurrence of breast cancer.

- Heart disease: Those who sleep six hours or less a night have a forty-eight percent higher chance of dying from heart disease.

- Death: A 2010 study found that men who slept less than six hours a night were four times more likely to die over a fourteen-year period.

Sleep is nature's balm. Truly. But sleep takes time. You can't short-cut it without short-circuiting your well-being. According to the National Institutes of Health, adults need at least seven to nine hours of sleep *each night* while school-aged children and teens need closer to ten.[9] If you allow yourself this gift, some pretty magical stuff will happen. Between the hours of 10 p.m. and 2 a.m., your growth and repair hormones increase in production. This means healing from physical exertion and the damage created by reacting to perceived threats too often during the day. Between 2 a.m. and 6 a.m., psychological repair takes place, soothing the effects of stress on our mental well-being. When we respect our body's needs by sleeping and taking advantage of these natural boosts in health, we wake up refreshed and reenergized for the day ahead—not to mention we extend our lives.

Make an effort to get seven to nine hours of sleep a night. Doing

---

9 Centers for Disease Control and Prevention (CDC), "Insufficient sleep is a public health problem" (Atlanta: CDC, 2015), http://www.cdc.gov/features/dssleep/index.html.

so is nonnegotiable if you want good health. Make bedtime a favorite ritual. Here are some tips and ideas for developing healthy sleep habits:

- Get clear on your bedtime. Back out seven to nine hours from your rise-and-shine moment so there's no guesswork. For example, I wake up at 4:30 or 5:30 each morning so my bedtime is 9 p.m.

- Stop intake of caffeine six hours before bedtime. This ought to be a no-brainer, but I need to be reminded of this occasionally. As a former coffee-guzzling maniac, I can tell you that you can wean yourself off, and once you do, it's not so challenging to resist the urge.

- One hour before bedtime, turn off the TV and all electronic devices (yes, including your iPhone). These devices emanate a spectrum of light that suppresses melatonin, nature's regulator of sleep-wake cycles. If you fail to shut them off, you may find yourself alert and unable to sleep. If you *must* be on your device (I confess, I like to do a crossword puzzle on my iPhone each night as a wind-down activity), install apps that block the spectrum of blue light wreaking havoc on your pineal gland, which produces melatonin.

- At bedtime, cover all flashing lights in your bedroom so it is as dark as possible. Turn your digital alarm clock so it's not facing you or drape a towel over it. After all, it's the sound you need—not the visual. Install black-out shades. And that blinking stereo light? Put black electrical tape over it. In essence, shut down your room so your body can shut down.

- Do one of your inner-life practices to program positivity and quiet the mind. I do five minutes of Metta Meditation or reflect on my day to identify the moment or experience that I'm most grateful for. Doing your inner-life practices at bedtime is a great way to not only close the day with positivity but also to transition your thoughts from scattered and frantic to calm and reassuring.

- Listen to white noise or relaxing music. Search for relaxation or calm meditation stations on your favorite music app, such as Pandora. There you'll find luscious, spa-like music that is sure to calm. I prefer white noise and have an app where I can dial up three sounds (waves, rain, and a fan) and mix them in such a way that it sends me off to dreamland. If you aren't sure what's right for you, experiment!

- In times of stress or if the music and darkness aren't enough, try deep breathing exercises, such as box breathing. To do box breathing, close your eyes, put your hands on your belly, and inhale through your nose for four seconds. Hold the breath for four seconds. Then exhale, pushing the air out through your lips for four seconds. Focus on each outgoing breath carrying away the tension or stress from the day.

- Wake up without an alarm once a week. Those of you with kids or early morning responsibilities each day of the week may not have this luxury. But if and when you can, take the opportunity to allow your body to wake up according to its own rhythm.

- If all else fails, take a nap. As multiple research studies have indicated, we need at least seven hours of sleep each night to maintain our health. In those rare circumstances when you are unable to achieve this, take a fifteen- to twenty-minute restorative nap during the day. In fact, anytime you sense a need for additional sleep—even if you got your nine hours of sleep the night before—take a nap. Your body knows what it needs.

I provide even more tips on the *Life, Incorporated* website, but there is more than enough here to get you safely on the road to dreamland. If you find yourself still struggling to sleep after multiple attempts using multiple approaches, see a sleep specialist. You may have an underlying condition that is preventing you from attaining and maintaining healthy sleep cycles. For example, sleep apnea can disturb our sleep cycles yet not rouse us enough to notice that we have experienced an interruption. By all means, if you toss and turn during the night or wake up on a regular basis feeling tired or experiencing a headache, reach out to a specialist.

For the rest of you, be kind to your nervous system; allow it time to rest and repair. This is the yin, the downtime, to the yang, the uptime. Remember, everything is cyclical. To access our highest potential in the dawning of each day, we must embrace and welcome the quiet power in the closing of each day.

Practice

Your daily practice is to get seven to nine hours of sleep, using the tips and tools as needed, and to find a way to achieve sleep without reliance on over-the-counter or prescribed assistance. Overuse of remedies, even natural ones such as melatonin, can block your body's ability to secrete the hormone on its own. If you must, use medicinal sleep remedies a night or two to get yourself back on the right sleep schedule, but then set them aside as best you can.

Homework

For the next thirty days, keep a sleep log in your Life, Incorporated Journal. Indicate how many hours of sleep you get, rate your quality of sleep, and describe how you feel upon rising. If you decide to do a twenty-one-day sugar detox, understand that your sleep may be affected the first few nights as your body rids itself of toxins.

MOVEMENT AND EXERCISE

For decades, if not centuries, humans have been aware of the importance of movement and exercise. How and when to do it changes with the wind it seems, but the underlying message remains: Do it! Nelson Mandela, who was imprisoned for twenty-seven years, spent one hour most mornings exercising in his cell. Here's an excerpt from his auto-biography, *Long Walk to Freedom*, where he speaks of his daily routine: "On Monday through Thursday, I would do stationary running in my cell in the morning for up to forty-five minutes. I would also perform one hundred fingertip push-ups, two hundred sit-ups, fifty deep knee bends, and various other calisthenics." Albeit an intense routine, Mandela knew the importance that exercise has on our physical and mental well-being.

As much as I'd like to say that we can rely on our inner-life practices to do all the heavy lifting when it comes to our outlook on life, they cannot. Our routine needs to include physical movement. Without it, we are prone to depression and a host of other not-so-hot conditions. Similar to the list of issues caused by lack of sleep, the list of maladies associated with lack of physical exercise is sobering. Here are the risks as found by Johns Hopkins University:[10]

- Less active and less fit people have a greater risk of developing high blood pressure.

- Physically active people are less likely to develop coronary heart disease than those who are inactive. This is even after researchers accounted for smoking, alcohol use, and diet.

- Lack of physical activity can add to feelings of anxiety and depression.

- Physical inactivity may increase the risk of certain cancers.

- Overweight and obese people can significantly reduce their risk for disease with regular physical activity.

This list seems light compared to some of the more in-depth research reports about lack of exercise. For example, here's part of

---

10 Johns Hopkins Medicine Health Library, "Risks of Physical Inactivity" (Baltimore: Johns Hopkins Medicine, n.d.), http://www.hopkinsmedicine.org/healthlibrary/conditions/cardiovascular_diseases/risks_of_physical_inactivity_85,P00218.

a 2012 article abstract, published in *Comprehensive Physiology*, that explores the link between exercise and chronic disease:[11]

> Physical activity/exercise is examined as primary prevention against 35 chronic conditions [accelerated biological aging/ premature death, low cardiorespiratory fitness (VO2max), sarcopenia, metabolic syndrome, obesity, insulin resistance, prediabetes, type 2 diabetes, nonalcoholic fatty liver disease, coronary heart disease, peripheral artery disease, hypertension, stroke, congestive heart failure, endothelial dysfunction, arterial dyslipidemia, hemostasis, deep vein thrombosis, cognitive dysfunction, depression and anxiety, osteoporosis, osteoarthritis, balance, bone fractures/falls, rheumatoid arthritis, colon cancer, breast cancer, endometrial cancer, gestational diabetes, pre-eclampsia, polycystic ovary syndrome, erectile dysfunction, pain, diverticulitis, constipation, and gallbladder diseases] . . . In summary, the body rapidly maladapts to insufficient physical activity, and if continued, results in substantial decreases in both total and quality years of life. In addition, physical activity primarily prevents, or delays, chronic diseases, implying that chronic disease need not be an inevitable outcome during life.

See what I mean? It makes the Johns Hopkins list seem like a mosquito bite. But did you also notice that thirty-five chronic conditions can be *prevented* primarily through exercise? Getting enough exercise isn't something you should do to appease society's wagging finger. You should do it because it brings life. It is something for you to begin leaning into all on your own, like a flower turning to face the sun. Exercise and movement are nourishing, and we need them to thrive.

Exercising has never been an area where I've struggled to get motivated. We all have our challenging areas (mine are getting enough

---

11   F.W. Booth, C.K. Roberts, M.J. Laye, "Lack of exercise is a major cause of chronic diseases," *Comprehensive Physiology* 2 (2012): 1143-1211, doi:10.1002/cphy.c110025.

sleep and tending to my inner life), and we all have areas we are naturally suited for. I've always enjoyed an active lifestyle, and I am deeply connected to my body. If I've had any struggle in this area, it was in *how* to exercise and move. As I related earlier in the book, I tend to be a "go hard" type of gal, which isn't beneficial if that's all you do. I had to learn to downshift into slower forms of exercise, such as Pilates, yoga, and low-heart-rate running, to avoid overtraining and causing my body long-term damage in exchange for short-term gain. The yin and yang is needed again here. We need to dip our oars into each end of the pool.

The authors of the study in *Comprehensive Physiology* also conclude that a mix of activity is not only necessary for preventing disease in the general population but is also needed to avoid physical frailty in the elderly. Both aerobic exercise (where you're building endurance) and resistance training (where you're building strength) are key. Further, the authors found that high-intensity interval training (HIIT) is particularly beneficial when it comes to delivering health benefits. HIIT is described in their report as "near peak performance for short bursts alternating with longer periods of low-intensity aerobic activity." I do HIIT once or twice a week.

When it comes to finding the optimal frequency, duration, and mix of exercise that's right for you, I suggest engaging a personal trainer at the onset of your fitness journey. This way you can work side by side to dial in both your current fitness level and where you'd like to be. When interviewing trainers, take the time to understand their varying approaches. First, ask them what modalities they train in. Ideally, you want someone who trains in a mixture of modalities, not just CrossFit, TRX, or HIIT, for example. Second, ask them if they consider other areas within wellness in addition to exercise. You want a trainer who is interested in your sleep patterns, diet, and stress levels, not someone solely focused on the numbers on the scale. Third, find a trainer who is still active in learning about the latest research on nutrition, exercise, and new training modalities. Lastly, if your potential trainer is eating or selling a bunch of sugar-loaded "health bars," walk away. You want a partner who can wisely advise you on the frequency, duration, and form of exercise and movement you should nest into your weekly fitness plan. Your particular needs are unique and your plan should be tailored to you.

> "I have always believed that exercise is the key not only to physical health but to peace of mind."
> —Nelson Mandela

Finally, I want to touch on what we Americans spend a *lot* of time doing that is negatively affecting our health: sitting. I am amazed each day by the latest findings on just how harmful sitting, of all things, is to our health! Here are the highlights found by Canadian researchers who gleaned their findings from forty-seven studies on the health effects of sedentary behavior:[12]

- People who sat for prolonged periods of time—even those who exercised regularly—had a higher risk of dying from all causes.

- Excessive sitting was associated with an eighteen percent increased risk of dying from cardiovascular disease and a seventeen percent increased risk of dying from cancer.

- Sitting for too long was tied to a ninety-one percent increased risk of getting type 2 diabetes and about a thirteen and fourteen percent increase in the risk of being diagnosed with cancer or heart problems.

- Among studies that looked at cancer type, sitting for too long was associated with a higher risk of being diagnosed with, or dying of, breast, colon, colorectal, endometrial, and ovarian cancers.

While no one at the time of this book's publication date knows exactly *how* sitting is causing all these issues, they do know that it *is*

---

12 A. Biswas, P.I. Oh, G.E. Faulkner, R.R. Bajaj, M.A. Silver, M.S. Mitchell, D.A. Alter, "Sedentary time and its association with risk for disease incidence, mortality, and hospitalization in adults: A systematic review and meta-analysis," *Annals of Internal Medicine* 162 (2015): 123–132, doi:10.7326/M14-1651.

causing all these issues. Prolonged sitting is defined as anything more than eight hours a day. Many researchers now suggest that you get up and move every two hours, if not every hour. To get you in the habit of doing this, set an alarm on your phone or hang a cuckoo clock on the wall to remind you to get up and move. Even simply standing up is a massively better choice than sitting.

In a nutshell, exercise and movement promote health while sedentary lifestyles steal it away. The most important thing you can do here is commit to the practice of daily movement, daily exercise. Note the word *daily*. When you're at the office or in front of your computer or TV at home, remember to set an alarm and walk around or stand. Minimize time spent folded over sitting in a chair. And work with a fitness specialist who will partner with you in your wellness goals and who can design a plan for you that isn't "one note." Committing to a more active lifestyle will not only boost your "happy chemicals" such as dopamine, serotonin, and endorphins but also likely enhance the quantity and quality of your life.

Homework

Your homework is to find a trainer who will be a great fitness partner for you. Someone who can meet you where you are in your current level of fitness and whose approach and philosophy fit the criteria mentioned previously. That's job number one.

Practice

Your first practice is to move or stand every hour during prolonged sitting. For every sixty minutes spent on a chair, spend ten minutes upright. I understand that there will be times when this isn't possible, but I think you'll find that more and more, it's not uncommon to see people stand up during long meetings. It's not disruptive as long as your attention remains where it needs to be.

Your second practice is to commit to some form of daily movement or exercise for at least twenty minutes a day, five days a week over the next thirty days, and record what you do and for how long in your journal. These don't necessarily need to be long exercise sessions, but they do need to occur. Work with your personal trainer and family to scratch out a plan that's both conducive to your wellness and your schedule. My hope is that you will remain committed to this practice well beyond thirty days because you will experience, firsthand, the differences in mood, vitality, confidence, and happiness that come as a result.

Remember, we can either place limits on ourselves and choose excuses, or we can see through perceived limitations and choose possibility. An excuse gives us a reason to fail. Possibility gives us the freedom to succeed.

CONCLUSION

As with your inner life, your input determines your output when it comes to your physical well-being. Your physical well-being requires the same thoughtful attention and positive programming as your emotional and spiritual well-being. If how we feed our mind determines our outlook for the day, then how we fuel our body certainly determines our capability for the day. It also plays a significant role in outlook as well. There's a popular saying in the fitness industry: "You can't out-exercise a bad diet." I would add, "You can't outshine a fog-induced mind-set." Even those practicing the most diligent inner-life work each day can't overcome poor nutrition choices. No matter how brightly your inner light is shining, there are some levels of haze it cannot burn off.

Speaking of burning, we have become a society trying to keep pace with the uptime and speed of technology, burning the candle at both ends, but the joke's on us. We can replace a laptop, we can replace a light bulb, and we can replace a battery, but we can't replace our bodies. We need to wake up to the essential need of sleep that all living things require.

On the opposite end of the spectrum, we should remember that our bodies are capable of so much more than simply housing our brains! If we exercised the rest of our muscles a fraction of how much we exercise our brains, we wouldn't be facing the astounding health effects that obesity and sedentary lifestyles create. You are so much more than what sits above your neck. Embrace your body, the beautiful temple that holds your life force.

ENVIRONMENT

"In the end, only three things matter:
How much you loved,
How gently you lived,
And how gracefully you let go
Of things not meant for you."

—attributed to Buddha

The third element of foundation is environment. As we work from the inside out, from inner life to physical well-being, we often take for granted or don't even consider how our environment affects us. We tend to recognize when it's beneficial—when there's a comfortable or welcoming energy or a sense of calm—but too frequently we habituate to environs that are counteractive to the health of our foundation. I am especially reminded of this as I write this chapter from a hotel room in downtown Los Angeles that is surrounded by mega-sized LED panels. The sky around these massive billboards never gets dark.

Thankfully for me and my love of nature, my trip ends tomorrow, and I will be returning to my own nurturing environment.

However, being in a new surrounding often pops open doors in my creativity that, perhaps, wouldn't otherwise have been revealed. But if I were to stay here long term, I'm pretty sure I'd have a different story to tell. The constant bombardment of advertising messages and the absence of trees would erode my foundation. A metropolis like Los Angeles or New York is, for me, what a short burst of nutrients is to a flower—sometimes needed and sometimes powerful, but unhealthy to reside in on a permanent basis. And yet, for others, this kind of environment is an ideal setting.

But environment isn't just our physical surroundings. For the purposes of this book and our focus on strengthening our foundation, environment also refers to the people who surround us as well. Therefore, the two elements nested within environment are community and surroundings. Community refers to those we keep company with—whether chosen for us (family and coworkers) or chosen by us (spouse and friends), and surroundings refers to the objects and landscape around us.

We are all made up of energy, and none of us have fireproof doors that shield us from the energy of others. We absorb the toxicity that certain people emit just as we absorb the toxins from a smoggy city. Try as we might, we may be able to minimize our intake, but some amount, some level, will always seep through. On the flip side, there is light and love to be absorbed as well when we breathe in the clean air provided by a forest of trees and draw in the kiss of a loved one.

If we imagine our life, our being, as a tree in a forest, we can understand how our surroundings and community would affect our ability to survive and thrive—or not. To be rooted in soil that is littered with toxins is a slow drip of poison. Let's be sure to set our roots in a foundation that has the capacity to infuse us with life-giving energy. By committing to practices that promote the health of our inner life and body, we are doing the work to ensure that *we* infuse ourselves and others with the same positive energy; now it's time to take stock of the people and places that surround us as we do this work.

COMMUNITY

The people we surround ourselves with—those who bring us love and joy and those who bring us pain and confusion—have a significant impact. As I write this, it feels like common sense, and we could just skip this chapter altogether. But I, along with many others, have chosen to remain in negative or toxic relationships time and time again. Why is that? Why do we keep ourselves in negative dynamics? Why don't we cut bait and keep our community circle well pruned so as to let in the sunlight? My observation is that it's usually due to one of two reasons. First, our brain *loves* patterns, and one way in which we create familiarity is by re-creating relationship dynamics we have experienced in the past, especially those toxic or volatile in nature. We revisit these patterns in the hopes of creating a positive outcome this time around but, often, we only end up digging ourselves into the same difficult dynamic. Or, second, the reason is noble in nature; as compassionate beings, we often want nothing more than to fix something or someone. But when is it time, and is it ever time, to walk away? My answer would be yes, and more than likely, sooner than we think—or should I say, sooner than we feel.

It's not easy to say good-bye to a loved one, whether this person is a member of your community by choice, such as a friend, or a member by default, such as a family member. I know all too well the pain of choosing to separate from a loved one, because my life's journey has taken me deep into this forest. And when it comes to family members, it is especially difficult because we feel a deep calling to remain that extends far beyond any sense of duty. We either feel that we can and *should* be able to make a parent or sibling happy or that *we* are the ones who need fixing. So we work to fit our square peg into their round hole day in, day out. Month in, month out. Year in, year out.

When we do this in any relationship—when we compromise ourselves, when we make ourselves small—we diminish the unique qualities that make us the loving, lovable, irreplaceable beings that we are. And then slowly, over time, our life force is snuffed out, either by someone's careless breath of negativity or by our own hand as we extinguish our flame—pinching off our confidence and joy—to please another.

Difficult as it may be, there comes a time to sail free of those relationships, to cut the bowlines and escape the current of negativity pulling us closer and closer to their shores. Who are these people in your life? You probably know or, at the very least, have a good sense. The Relationship Gauge consists of questions to help you assess whether or not that difficult person in your life comes at too high of a cost for you. Picture that person in your mind and then answer the following questions:

- Overall, does this person bring you a sense of ease or anxiety?

- Does interacting with this person leave you energized or exhausted?

- Does this person take responsibility for personal issues or blame others, perhaps even you?

- How frequently does this person reach out to see how you are? Often or hardly ever?

- When was the last time this person made a positive contribution to your life? Recently or quite awhile ago?

- Does being around this person bring out your best self or your worst self?

- How do you speak of this person to others, positively or negatively?

- After interacting with this person, do you tend to be grateful for having spent time together or regretful?

- How many character traits does this person possess that you admire? Several or very few?

- If you were to meet this person for the first time today, would you want this person in your community or would you steer clear?

- Does this person challenge you in a positive way, sparking change or personal evolution? Or does this person challenge you in a way that leaves you questioning your self-worth or capabilities?

If more than five of your answers landed on the negative side of the spectrum, then you have someone in your community who is toxic to you—a source of negativity—or someone who may not be toxic but who contributes little positivity. Neither of these scenarios is due to "bad" people in your life. I don't dare judge another's character. We are all doing the best we can given where we are today.

One of my favorite quotes that always inspires compassion in me is this line of Ian Maclaren's: "Be kind, for everyone you meet is fighting a hard battle." It's a great reminder that we each come into this life saddled with a struggle that has our name on it. It seems that at some point prior to inhabiting our physical bodies, our souls pull a card (I'm imagining a take-a-number dispenser at the dreaded DMV), and there we have it. Our particular challenge for this lifetime: self-sabotage, insecurity, addiction, isolation, self-worth, abusiveness, or mistrust. The list goes on. Some of us have the dubious honor of getting to pull down two tickets so we can double up our adventure! Oh joy! Eesh. All this is to say that I get it. We're all beautiful struggles in motion. The person causing you strife is no better or worse than you, no better or worse than those who contribute in a positive way to your life. It's more a matter of this person not being a good fit for you right now; for whatever reason, the alchemy between the two of you is unhealthy and unstable. That is what you should judge: not the person but the *influence* this person has on your life at this particular time.

I believe we forget that relationships are often transient or mercurial. They are as impermanent as life itself. Only a precious few stay with us on a consistent basis throughout our journey. The rest—the majority—are momentary or sporadic collisions in time meant to teach us something or give us something we need. These collisions can be insanely positive, insanely gut-wrenching, or somewhere in between. The purpose, I believe, is the same: to challenge or inspire us to break through whatever is holding us back. And I believe that in many cases, the purpose is also for us to serve as a catalyst for them.

To hoard our relationships, to try and lock them away, keeping them forever like Gollum and his precious, is counteractive and a bit unnatural. When we hoard relationships, we waste time trying to hang on to people that we were never intended to keep (thus the difficulty in keeping them!), and by doing so, we miss out on fulfilling our life's purpose. We become distracted by people and lose focus as we work to fix someone or settle back into old patterns that feel so good for our brain yet wreak havoc on our inner life. Relationships are impermanent. When a particular relationship has waned or turned toxic, be mindful not to judge yourself and your ability, or lack thereof, to hang on to it. That notion works well in a love song, but it doesn't play out in real life.

Instead, focus on *influence*; assess that. Is the influence a relationship is having on your life right now positive or negative? That is absolutely a call you can make without apology. You are the captain of your life; you are ultimately responsible for how you choose to spend this lifetime. There is no prize for stoicism or for allowing yourself to become distracted or taken advantage of. And we should take care to lose shame or timidity when it is clear we are in a harmful dynamic. If a relationship is consistently taking a toll, then no matter the reason, we should feel free to say a brief or final farewell. It's important to surround ourselves with influences that promote and inspire growth. If we allow toxic relationships to create deficiencies in our soil, our foundation will be compromised. We will never be able to reach our full potential by allowing the situation to remain as it is. I know this. I have lived this. If you can't give yourself permission, please accept mine.

On the flip side, there are those who pour light and positivity into our cup. Their presence makes us feel loved, seen, appreciated, and adored. Without them saying a word, we are infused with self-confidence, courage, joy, and kindness. They fan our flame when we falter and believe in our ability to shine brighter than we may even imagine. In return, we shine our light back into them, returning the life force they have so selflessly shared.

In our solar system of relationships, these people are our "suns." They are the people we want inhabiting our community. We want these people close to us, orbiting within reach so that we may always feel their gravitational pull to be our better selves. While no person can burn bright at all times, our experience with these people is generally positive. Being in a relationship with them does not come at a personal price. We are there to happily support them in their times of need because they remain steadfast in their commitment to see us, too, create a joyful and meaningful life.

Exercise: Define Your Terms

An important first step in consciously shaping your community is to define what the terms "positivity" and "negativity" mean to you specifically. For me, someone who displays positivity is honest, compassionate, daring, loving, fun, safe, and aware. Someone in my life who possesses these attributes would be a sun, a person who exudes positivity and light.

Now you define the term for yourself:

Positivity: _____

The same goes for negativity. How would you define it? For me, someone who displays negativity is dishonest, cruel, uncaring, dangerous, egotistical, shallow, and disloyal. Your turn:

Negativity: _____

Now that you have decided what positivity and negativity mean to you, you can define your kula, a term I much prefer to "family," because it gives us permission to craft our community rather than simply accept it as fate. Let's begin.

Exercise: Define Your Kula

"Kula" is a Hindu term that has been translated to mean "a community of the heart, a group coming together of its own free will, an intentional community and a family."[13] It is a community, and it is a family. But what stands out to me about this translation are the phrases "of the heart" and "intentional." Keeping these two phrases in mind, I'd like us to think of the people who make up our inner circle as our kula, an intentional community of the heart. In this way, we can be proactive about who we include in our kula, and we can be accountable for how our kula influences us. No more throwing up our hands and being victim to the Negative Nancies and Downer Dans in our lives. Now we have ownership and responsibility. And if we keep getting bombarded with negativity, then we can simply look to ourselves and make adjustments.

Your kula is not the universe of acquaintances and relationships out there in the world that are somehow connected to you: your old high school buddies on Facebook or your LinkedIn and Twitter followers or the ex-coworker you have coffee with once in a blue moon. That is your community at large. Your kula also isn't your team at work or any other team that's been crafted outside your control. That is your work community, or your church community, or your fitness community . . . you get the idea. (Though any one of these individuals may be placed in your kula.)

Your kula consists of the people you have *intentionally* placed close to you as fellow passengers during this leg of your life's journey. Imagine a series of concentric circles with yourself in the middle; your kula would be the next ring out, because it has one of the greatest impacts on your inner life, second to the impact you make on yourself. Think of the people that have an impact on you at least once a week *or* people with whom you have long-standing relationships—you may not directly communicate with them every week, but their impact and influence on you goes without saying. For example, I think of

---

13 L. Macleod, "'Kula'—community of the heart" (Kula Yoga, 2013), http://kulayoga.com.au/blog/kula-community-of-the-heart.

my dearest friend Paul. We may go weeks without talking, but we are always psychically connected. I always include him in my Metta Meditation practice, and I can sense when he needs me to pick up the phone and call him. Impact doesn't have to look like the obvious—a text, a conversation, a letter. It can be as intangible but as powerful as an open channel of energy directly connecting two hearts.

To define your kula you must clarify what you desire from it. Be as mindful about selecting your kula's attributes as you would selecting the people to include in your kula. The following words and phrases are examples of what you may choose as attributes: joy, support, trust, challenging me for the better, curious, creative, loving, compassionate, lots of laughter, rich in integrity. Now write down attributes for your own kula, perhaps borrowing some of the preceding examples or adding your own. This is very personal, so it should reflect your personality!

Attributes of Your Kula

_____

_____

_____

_____

_____

_____

_____

_____

Exercise: Create Your Kula

Now that you have chosen your kula's attributes, let's work on populating your kula. The first step is to take stock of the people in your personal community, your solar system of relationships, so you can determine who to hold on to and who to shed as you transform your personal community into your kula. Who are your suns, the people who emit positivity and light, who deserve your breath, your love, your touch, who deserve to be pulled in close to your center? Who are the "planets" in your life? Planets are people who are more neutral than suns; they don't shine a steady stream of strong, positive life force your way, but they still bring more positivity than negativity and thus deserve your attention and kindness. What about "moons"? Moons are not able to provide their own light at this time and often require an outside source of positivity to shine. Later you will have an opportunity to assess the moons in your life to determine if there is benefit to keeping them close or, perhaps, if you'd be better off placing them farther out in your solar system of relationships. Finally, are there "black holes" in your life? These are people who radiate negativity, who need to be cut loose. Their energy is likely not only affecting you but all those you keep in close proximity.

It's important to note that these categories are not set in stone. It's normal for the level of positivity a person emits to fluctuate over time. We'll talk more about this later. For now, find out how many suns and planets you have compared to the number of moons and black holes by filling out the following lists. I find it's easier when you begin with those who inspire positivity. Use the Relationship Gauge earlier in this chapter for help in categorizing your relationships when needed.

Step 1: Define Your Solar System of Relationships

1. Fill out your sun list. (Suns are people who inspire positivity.)

_____

_____

_____

_____

_____

                    `

_____

_____

_____

_____

_____

2. Fill out your planet list. (Planets are people who may not be as significant as suns but still have a generally positive effect on you.)

_____

_____

_____

_____

_____

_____

_____

_____

_____

3. Fill out your moon list. (Moons require more positivity from you than they provide for you.)

_____

_____

_____

_____

_____

_____

_____

_____

_____

_____

4. Fill out your black hole list. (Black holes emit negativity on a regular basis.)

_____

_____

_____

_____

_____

_____

_____

_____

_____

I strongly suggest that you remove from your kula, on a temporary basis at least, anyone on your black hole list. Outside of the work
we do in our inner-life practices, our kula is often the second most

significant source of energy affecting our emotional, mental, and spiritual well-being on a daily basis. So we need to be mindful of whom we allow to have that much potential impact on us. That said, those on your black hole list have a proven track record of wreaking havoc on your emotional state. Cut them loose without judgment but with concern for your own well-being. Let them know that you are not able to be in a relationship with them at this time and wish them well. If they dig for reasons, focus on what you need rather than placing blame or fault outside of yourself.

For example, you could say something similar to this: "Mary, after thinking about the dynamic I create with you, I find myself often falling short of my own expectations. I've decided to take a break from this dynamic in order to achieve the goals I have for myself. It is through no fault of your own but, rather, due to a personal choice. I hope you can understand. I wish you the best."

Keep it simple. And remember, people on your black hole list will likely respond in anger or try to reel you back in when you cut them loose. At the onset of severing the relationship or when they have not yet made the choice or had the opportunity to make necessary shifts in behavior, avoid the trap. Stay firm and keep communication brief. A nonresponse may be the best response for someone who enjoys doing battle!

Now that you've dealt with your black hole list, let's move on to those who occupy your moon list. These are individuals who have a tendency to require more attention and positivity from you than they are able to give. Because we all go through cycles—just as the moon has phases—it would be inhumane and rash to lop someone out of our lives just because their internal resources aren't as abundant as our own. Instead, we need to take a step back and gain perspective on these relationships. Temporary waning is perfectly normal and should be expected. In fact, I've been known to start off the day as a sun and end up in a darkened moon phase by lunch! Our emotions can be incredibly mercurial at times, and those emotions can have an impact on our outlook and how we interact with others. To phase between sun, planet, and moon is just downright normal. We can show compassion for those experiencing temporary waning, knowing that when we wane, we may also be buoyed by their love and compassion. It is only when the waning is constant or comes at a significant price to us that we should consider removing these moons from our kula, until their life force begins to wax again.

Here are some questions to help gauge when a moon may be detrimental to your kula:

- Has this person always represented a moon? Or does this person phase between planet and sun as well?

- How long has this person been a moon? More than six months or less?

- Do you foresee a change? If so, when? Within six months?

- How does tending to this relationship affect your ability to achieve your own goals and maintain the health of your inner life? Negatively or positively?

- If you were to remove this person from your kula, what would you gain? What would you lose?

As you might have guessed, if the cons outweigh the pros or the pattern and outlook reach beyond six months, then I highly suggest temporarily separating this person from your kula, until something shifts. I know it sounds harsh, and there's an aspect of me that cringes whenever I suggest separating from someone because it seems counterintuitive to our compassionate nature. But remember (even I must remind myself!) that most relationships are impermanent, transient, meant to ebb and flow, or meant to pass through our lives just once. We are as deserving of our own compassion as much as, if not more than, those we are in relationship with. If we fail to place the oxygen mask on ourselves, if we fail to care for the environment in which we inhabit—including all those who inhabit it—then we invite distraction, negativity, and chaos into our lives. Removing a moon from your kula is often not a permanent choice. More often than not, closing one door prompts another to open for this person; a new dynamic presents itself, and a shift in demeanor becomes possible. Then one day, you are back in each other's energetic embrace. But the letting go must happen first.

Finally, scan your planets and look for excess. This is an opportunity to do some pruning if need be. Are you carrying relationships that really don't have much of a place in your life right now? Are you that child with the Easter basket overflowing with colorful, but empty, eggs? Again, our self-worth should in no way be connected to how many relationships we have. Social media empires would have you believe otherwise because they've gamified relationships. The more friends, or connections, or followers you have, the more worthy you are. There are even algorithms that can rate your clout based on your relationships. Please don't allow a handful of enterprising CEOs to define your self-worth. Collecting relationships for the sake of having them has absolutely no benefit. That sort of grasping and clinging comes at a cost.

I believe Henry David Thoreau captures it with this quote from *Walden*: "The cost of a thing is the amount of what I will call life which is required to be exchanged for it, immediately or in the long run." We'll talk about this more in part 2, "Expression," but Thoreau's notion comes into play here as well. Whatever we engage in, whatever we take on requires energy. There is no taking without giving. And that giving—that cost—is an aspect of life itself. Whenever we pick up a new relationship or continue to carry an existing one, we are spending energy that could otherwise be spent on ourselves and our own expressions of life, whether it's more downtime, focus on our family, effort put toward our passion, or time spent imagining what's next. Anything we do—and certainly cultivating and nourishing relationships—takes time away from something else. The question is, is it worth it? Is there value in continuing this relationship?

I focus on planets here because this is where I see the most clusters of excess. Because these relationships are neutral, we keep on keeping on with them. We go on coffee dates with these people, attend their parties, or play a never-ending, open-channeled game of "We should really get together some time!" and then continue to make no plans whatsoever with them.

Here is a list of questions that can help you assess whether a planet is a contributing member of your kula, a relic of times past, or simply a member of your greater community at large:

- When was the last time you actively engaged with this person? Within the last six months?

- Does this person ever wax to a sun? If so, how many months within the past six months was this person a sun?

- Does this person ever wane to a moon? If so, how many months within the past six months was this person a moon?

- How does tending to this relationship affect your ability to achieve your own goals and maintain the health of your inner life? Negatively or positively?

- If you removed this person from your kula, what would you gain? What would you lose?

If your answers indicate a person has no impact, negative impact, or a propensity to wane into a moon, then this is likely a relationship you are simply hanging on to out of habit or a sense of obligation. I recommend allowing planets like this to simply drift off out of your kula and into your greater community, a direction they are likely already being pulled toward.

Now you've done the hard work—letting go of those you've become accustomed to even though they may have been detrimental or habitual. Humans like comfort, and sometimes the discomfort of change is more difficult to attempt than staying in the discomfort of a toxic, but familiar, relationship. By now, I hope you've come to understand the prices we pay when we act passively and tolerate. This is your opportunity to exercise compassion for yourself and others by generously cutting loose those who drag you down or heavily tax your life force.

Step 2: Populate Your Kula

Now let's create that kula! This should be a moment of celebration as you craft your dream team. For those of you who play fantasy football, this exercise ought to be right up your alley. Go back to your lists on page 90 and place the suns, planets, and moons who remain.

_____

_____

_____

_____

_____

_____

_____

_____

And there it is, your kula, your intentional community of the heart.

Your Contribution

I want to say a few words about you, how *you* show up in your own kula, or anyone else's kula for that matter. And I say this from a very personal place. It is not your kula's responsibility to rescue you or do *your* work for you. You don't get to kick back and let the suns in your kula create positivity for you. Everything in this book comes back to you and requires your full participation.

The reason so many of us go through our days unhappy or yo-yoing between feeling good, bad, and worse is because we place our power outside ourselves. Your kula requires your hands on the steering wheel—how you show up is just as important, if not more so, than how your kula shows up for you. I say this because I took my hands off the wheel once and experienced what can happen when we get lazy or decide to coast. I went from being a sun in a close friend's life to being a black hole; subsequently she placed me in a very long friend "time-out." It was incredibly painful for me, but when I realized she was simply following the advice I give in this book (hate it when that happens!), I understood. I never faulted her for cutting me loose; instead, this pause gifted me with the insight that I was re-creating old, unhealthy patterns that had been prevalent in my life. The dynamic that had been at play in my relationship with my friend mimicked enough of the attributes of a particular toxic relationship in my past to create a perfect storm. I essentially replayed old traumas, having cast her in a role she never signed up for. After I gained this clarity and realized how unhappy I, too, had become in this dynamic, I was able to heal those unattended wounds so I could once again be a healthy contributor to my friend's kula. This experience also shined new awareness on those seductive, toxic patterns that can so often get their hooks in us. Happiness doesn't occur by osmosis; we must nurture it from within by properly tending to our inner life.

We also can't share something we don't own, and I mean really *own*: ourselves. If we go around sipping from other people's oxygen masks of positivity in order to feel good and have something to contribute, we'll not only deplete the goodwill of people we love but we'll find that those bursts of positivity are short-lived. Joy, happiness, and a sense of well-being are all emotions that are highly individual and need to be cultivated and seeded by each of us. No one can do it on our behalf. If we don't cultivate our own positivity, negativity will breed like wildfire.

Our choices have a profound impact on those connected to us. For example, I happened to let go of my inner life, but your tendency may be to let go of your physical well-being and skip that cardio class for a week. It doesn't matter what you let go of, but keep in mind that if you do let go, you will devolve. Be aware of this as you make choices, because those choices will affect the people in your kula. Later on in part 4, "Impact," we'll look more closely at our intentions, how we approach others, and whether or not our mind-set will result in damaged relationships or positive, healthy dynamics.

Again, it is normal for an individual to wax and wane between different phases, a moon today and a sun next week. In fact, to stay in any *one* of these states long term would be unnatural, I think, requiring some sense of holding and controlling on our part.

What you should be mindful of is how often you spend time as a moon. If you are there frequently, then you are missing an aspect of your inner-life work. It's an indication that something internal is off, and there is healing and attending to be done. If you are being pulled into your own negative vortex, thus creating your own black hole, then you have let go entirely of your inner life and need to attend to it urgently.

The Greater Kula

Finally, let's look at the world—this planet and all that inhabit it—as our greater kula and, with that, carry a sense of loving-kindness for all the beings, elements, and organisms we share this planet with. Let us be a sun for our own planet, Mother Earth. Find a way to positively affect someone or something each month. I constantly mix this up depending on where my focus happens to be or what I notice happening around me. Some examples of my sun work have included the following:

- Leaving twenty dollars with the cashier at a grocery store to help pay the person's bill behind me
- Picking up trash on the side of the road or on a trail
- Helping cook a meal for those in need and serving it to them
- Spending an afternoon working with troubled teens
- Volunteering at an elementary school
- Making a small donation
- Helping a neighbor put out her trash
- Striking up a conversation with a stranger

Sun work can include a million different things—some big, some small—but they all have an impact on the greater kula. We'll dive deeper into this subject later in the book when we talk about impact, but for now, as you go about your days, think of how you can have a positive impact on the greater world you are a part of. How can you provide a ripple of positivity that, one day, may come back to lap against your shore? Remember, it's the smallest of gestures that come together to shift a tide. Drop your penny into the waters of possibility and positivity; contribute to the wealth of joy and love so that everyone may live in abundance.

SURROUNDINGS

If community, or kula, is the first ring in the series of concentric circles that influence our inner life, then our surroundings would be the second. *Where* we are—where we spend our days and, consequently, our lives—has an impact on us. There are many with the philosophy that if one is whole and full of positivity, then surroundings cannot have a negative impact, but I disagree to an extent. Yes, if I am doing my heart's work in a depressed area where the landscape is scorched and the people made haggard by poverty and disease, these surroundings will not diminish my inner life because it's work I am called to do, and the *place* in which I do this work is part and parcel of that calling. In other words, if my calling is to help the impoverished, then the setting in which it takes place is a given. It's wrapped up with my passion. In this way, I absolutely agree that positivity can overcome a place that seems dark and unfriendly. When I speak of how our surroundings can have an impact on us, it is not a question of beauty, or what we perceive as beauty. What I am speaking of are the positive or negative effects our environs have on us and of which we may be unaware.

As I write this section, I am sitting in an airplane. The lack of comfort is implied. I'm reminded of the lyrics of one of my favorite songs by The Postal Service, where the singer references the stale taste of recycled air.

Being stuffed in an airplane or crammed into a tiny hotel room in the middle of downtown Los Angeles isn't my normal idea of beauty. But I am in these environs because of following my heart and doing my life's work. These surroundings are transient, a brief stopover in my journey. So in that way, they are tolerable and don't work against me. In fact, they're more than tolerable—they're enjoyable. Because I am aligned and at peace, I'm able to appreciate them and find the beauty. However, if I were in these environs as a result of aimlessness or because I was just following a path that appeared to work for others and thought, "Why not me too?" my experience would be much like the handful of grumbling, irritated, and short-tempered travel companions sitting around me.

Swiss philosopher Henri-Frédéric Amiel stated it well when he said, "The man who has no inner life is a slave to his surroundings." Amen. To be a slave means to lose or give up control, to relinquish the rudder of our own vessel in life. When we cede our power, we become victims and mostly unhappy ones at that.

For me, these brief stopovers don't have a negative impact on my inner life, because I am aligned to my passion, my inspiration—*and* they are brief blips on my radar. Temporary. Just as being in a flood zone is part of an aid worker's job, being in uncomfortable places like a stuffy airplane or a smoggy city here and there is just part of getting my work done. But if I placed myself in a habitat or environ for the long term that ran counter to my internal compass, it would most certainly have an impact—and not a good one. This is what we experience when we are insanely passionate about what we are doing but, perhaps, are performing that work in a place that doesn't sing to our soul, because we find the surroundings lonely or oppressive.

For example, I spent my high school years growing up in the Midwest. There are a lot of people whom I love out there, including my father, and I absolutely adore being around farm animals. The horses alone take my breath away. But for reasons I don't fully understand (and have lost the need to try and understand), I need to be close to water—and not just a lake or river. I mean *big* water. In fact, the places I feel absolutely my best are on islands smack-dab in the middle of the ocean. But because those places would be a bit limiting for my family and me—lacking access to the other features I crave, such as mountains, snow, trails, forests, urban city life—I live in the Northwest. Here, I feel like the great outdoors mirrors the limitless possibilities in my own life. We fit like a glove, so I made a conscious choice to root myself here.

Had I chosen or felt a sense of obligation to root myself in the Midwest, my inner life may not have been fully compromised, but it would certainly have been more of a struggle to maintain. And I would face challenges in my ability to express what inspires me. Could it have been done? Sure. And in cases where we cannot change our environment, we'll discuss strategies to mitigate the impact of an adverse environment. But if the choice is available to me, why comply to a circumstance that I know absolutely makes things harder? Why stack the odds against myself? Why add one more major obstacle to an already tricky and complicated course? We need to honor our own sense of *place*, whether it's a physical landscape that beckons us or simply surroundings made positive by the energy of those who reside in it.

> "Why do you stay in prison, when the door is so wide open?"
> —Rumi

In some ways, I think we may possess the same instincts as homing pigeons who intrinsically find their way home. Whether it's an artifact of a past life or a sense of home programmed into our very DNA, we vibrate when we're in environs that speak to our soul. Conversely, we rattle when we stray too far away or remain in an inhospitable place too long.

Exercise: Find Your Sense of Home

This exercise will help you identify your ideal surroundings. If you cannot physically place yourself there due to current limiting factors, this exercise will help you find ways to bring elements of your ideal environment into your current nest.

Step 1: Describe Your Ideal Surroundings

First, close your eyes and recall a time when you felt at total peace, when you were relaxed and taken aback by your surroundings. Then, answer this list of questions:

1. Where were you?

_____

2. When were you there?

_____

3. What are the images that come to mind?

_____

4. What were some of the features that made it so ideal?

_____

5. What colors did you see? What aromas did you smell? What sounds did you hear?

_____

6. What do you feel it is about this place that made it so welcoming to you?

_____

7. Finally, is this a place you can make your home sometime in the future?

_____

Step 2: Describe Your Actual Surroundings

Now let's examine where you are now. Please answer the following questions:

1. Where are you now?

_____

2. How long have you been here?

_____

3. When you close your eyes and take in your surroundings, how do you feel (e.g., calm, chaotic, invigorated, cramped)?

_____

4. What are the features here that you like?

_____

5. What are the features here you dislike?

_____

6. When you think of remaining here for another five years versus living in your idyllic setting, how would you rate your feelings? (1: Unacceptable; 2: Tolerable; 3: Not ideal, but okay; 4: Pretty good; 5: Great, I have found my home)

_____

If you answered question 6 with a 1 or 2, it may be time to seriously consider digging out and finding a location that is similar to your ideal home. If you answered with a 3 or 4, then there are likely some modifications you can make to nudge that number closer to a 5. To do this, go back to the first set of questions in step 1, and take note of the features, colors, aromas, sounds, and other elements that made your ideal surroundings so inviting to you. And then ask yourself, is there a piece of art you can bring into your home that would reflect some of these attributes? Can you place splashes of color here and there? For example, after I visited Tuscany with my family, I introduced more pops of bright red into our home to remind me of the red poppies that carpeted the hillsides.

What about aromas? Our sense of smell is tied to memory and emotions and, according to psychologists and researchers, it is our strongest, most primal link to long-term memory. Find a hand soap, perfume, or cologne that takes you back to that place.

And what about the auditory experience? Or the culinary experience? Or the cultural habits you observed? Find pieces to braid into your current surroundings so you can knit together your very own home away from home.

Surroundings are profound in their ability to influence our focus, energy, and capability. To lock up a lion in a cage is as inhumane as it is to lock yourself up in a habitat that has you climbing the proverbial walls. This world is vast, and the organizations that occupy it are also vast. If one doesn't suit you, find another. As you go, pick up on what made one sing and what made another feel hollow. Use that information to be intentional about locating the best place for *you*.

CONCLUSION

A healthy inner life and physical well-being are two essential prongs of our foundation. Yet to overlook the power of our environment would potentially set us up for failure. In this chapter, we discussed two key elements within environment: community and surroundings. Community (or kula, our intentional community of the heart) serves as our playground and safe harbor as we express what it is that makes our heart tick. Our kula provides an opportunity to connect all the great work we do in our inner life with those we cherish. And it's also the scaffolding around us when we need to lean on another as we wax and wane through our own phases of sun, planet, and moon.

Our surroundings refer to our physical location and present an opportunity to take notice of how we are affected by where we set down roots. Given that impact, we may make subtle or not-so-subtle shifts that place us in a location that nourishes us.

To fully understand the effect of environment, let's imagine ourselves to be trees in a forest. The trees growing next to ours, *where* we have anchored, can affect our health. If we are nestled among a cluster of trees whose only aim is to nourish themselves at the cost of all others, we will forever be in their shade, unable to access the sun. Our roots will wither as invaders steal the precious nutrients intended for us. Or if we plant ourselves in an environment that is inhospitable to our nature—think of a palm tree in the hills of Alaska or a madrona in the Deep South—our surroundings cannot sustain us. In fact, our surroundings work actively against us if they do not work in natural harmony with our needs.

We must be selective about the people we include in our grove while actively pruning our environment to remove those who don't support us. People who only relate via an exchange of pain or who exhibit unrelenting negativity should be let go; the price of maintaining a relationship with them is too high. Care for yourself the way you would care for a rare and beautiful tree. For you *are* that tree, and this lifetime requires your attention. Will you wither in a pot that has become too small? Or will you venture out to where you can grow, where you can feel welcomed, held, and appreciated? As the saying goes, people will rise or fall based on what you expect of them. The most important expectation is the one you have for yourself. Set it high so you are compelled to reach the sun.

Part 2

ROOTS:

INSPIRATION

"If you don't know where you're going,
any road will take you there."

—George Harrison, "Any Road"

I love this line because of the duality of the message. In one way, it can be interpreted as a warning against being directionless, against having no aim. If we don't have our destination keyed in, we will find ourselves anywhere. And perhaps, landing "anywhere," some random place we are deposited, is less worthy than arriving "here," a precise target.

This message is often programmed into us at an early age. Throughout my childhood, my well-intentioned parents would ask, "What do you want to be when you grow up?" I remember not having a clue, which seemed to be a concern for them until I learned to appease their anxiety by throwing out some random occupation like nurse or firefighter. But throwing out firefighter seemed to create just as much anxiety. After a brief pause, as my desire to climb ladders and do what was considered a man's job at that time was processed, I'd eventually get a pat on the head followed by "Firefighter! Wow! That's neat, kiddo! But, hey, you've still got time to figure it out." Funny thing was, I didn't feel like I had time. I felt I was already late to the game.

As we mature, the questions keep coming, and there's increasingly more at stake. Our goals come under more and more pressure from not only ourselves but also our loved ones, who may grill us about the direction of our personal and professional life. Do we want to play the field? Be in a committed relationship? Or is it more serious, like getting married? Kids or no kids? If so, how many? What are our professional goals? To achieve a certain title or position? Make more money? Get a promotion?

You get the picture. The more we add to our life—for example, relationships, careers, hobbies, volunteer work—the more we feel a need to attach some sort of measurable goal or outcome to them. Time and time again, we're asked to name a destination. We decide what it is we want to *do* and then we measure ourselves against our ability to get from where we are to a well-defined and measurable "here." Usually, the fastest one to the finish line wins, or at least that's the perception of many.

Another interpretation of the quote is that we *can* get "there" (the place we are meant to be) even without knowing where we are going. True, we may not land on a well-defined, precise target, but maybe that's not the point. Maybe that's not even the purpose of our life's journey. Maybe landing "there"—wherever the hell that is—is a worthy outcome, an amazing destination, something to take pride in, and it's exactly where and what it needs to be as long as we are following our own North Star, our passion. Chasing purpose, in my mind, is unnecessary. Purpose reveals itself in the rearview mirror as a result of us pursuing our passion.

I don't think our lives and all the ways in which we express ourselves should be about the where, a specific destination. Yes, having some short-term, outcome-based goals is important, because they keep us motivated when we hit the inevitable bumps in the road. After all, it's nice to see a mile marker, cross it off the map, and know you've made some progress. But that's where it ends. Other than those mileposts, I believe our focus should be on the why, losing the fixation on a predetermined where. When we focus on the why and stay true to engaging in something that deeply matters to us, where we land takes care of itself. Where we are deposited as a result of following our passion can *only* be the right place. In other words, when we locate what drives us, the proverbial X on the map finds us.

I cannot tell you how many panels I have participated in, interviews I have heard, and stories I have read where the übersuccessful entrepreneur or innovator or artist or scientist or you-name-it has been asked, "What advice would you give others who want to achieve the kind of success you have?" Whether it's Steve Jobs, Jim Carrey, Jim Hensen, Carl Sagan, or Richard Branson, the answer is the same: Follow your passion. Do what you love to do and the rest will come.

They didn't chase the where, the outcome; they chased the why, their passion. I can say from personal experience that this advice is dead-on.

In this section, we will look at inspiration, what we are passionate about. What drives and compels us. What pours light and energy into our powerful beings. We will write our personal manifesto, identify our core values, and pen our personal mission statement. We will look at the root of our tree and identify each vein of passion so we can reach ever deeper into our foundation, become attuned to our creative flow, so that we can bring it up and out—extending our life force to ourselves, those we love, and the greater community in which we belong. This is where we become still and visit with ourselves so that we can identify and connect to what feeds our soul.

THE INSPIRED LIFE

"Become who you are."

—**Friedrich Nietzsche**

In Western society, there is a rampant fixation on *doing*. Scratch that, it's an all-out addiction. According to Brené Brown, one of my favorite researchers and authors on the topic of living wholeheartedly, we are the most obese, in debt, medicated, and addicted adults in human history.[14] Take a moment and let that sink in. It's a profound statement, and, sadly, it's true. We are overeating, overspending, overmedicating, and numbing out at historical highs. In addition to substance abuse and gambling, we're talking about addictions to email, video games, TV, sugar, work, gossip, social media, and more. At its base, addiction is compulsive and chronic numbing.

I believe that the reason the majority of us are numbing out is because we aren't living authentic lives. We are so afraid of being

---

14 B. Brown, "The power of vulnerability" (TED Talks, 2010) https://www.ted.com/talks/brene_brown_on_vulnerability?language=en.

inadequate that we live our lives on the grand, delusional stage of the world known as social media and global perception so we can feel a sense of belonging, a sense of importance. Instead of valuing ourselves by our own measure, we value ourselves by how many "likes" our status receives. How many views our profile gets. How many "shares" our thoughts have garnered. The phrase "pics or it didn't happen" has become our mantra. This everything-for-show style of living has led to the gamification of life. Instead of living a real life belonging to *us*, we live our life in a virtual reality, racking up points in a game that has no winners. We hustle away our hours, weeks, months, years, lifetimes doing, doing, doing. I have never seen Americans so busy as we are now. I often wonder if public speaking is still our greatest fear, even above death, or if our greatest fear has become sitting alone—in our own company—with nothing to *do*.

Our ever-increasing fear and all-out avoidance of stillness has to do with our own discomfort with ourselves. When we don't know ourselves—when we become a stranger in our own company—we feel anxious and depressed, and we run, fast and hard. We run to our phones, we run to our vices, we run away from ourselves in search of meaning. We forget that no one can give us meaning, that we have to come home to ourselves and find stillness to cultivate our own sense of purpose.

When we are at peace, find comfort, feel confident, and sense harmony, we lose reasons to run. In those moments, we are firmly in *our* life, living congruently with our authentic selves. I believe the antidote to living an inauthentic life is to find and embrace our passion—inspiration that can only be ours—so that our vision for ourselves is so compelling that we simply lose the need for comparison and chronic numbing. And once we find our passion, good luck moving us off it. It's akin to athletes who are clear on exactly what they need to do. Whether they're engaged in practice or competition, there is no pulling their focus. They cannot be distracted, because the calm yet powerful connection to their inspiration grounds them to the earth.

Here's a notion you may be familiar with: We are human *beings*, not human doings, human thinkings, human nothings, human everythings, human machines, or human wastelands. Being is at the heart of what we are. It's the feminine energy—the yin—the quiet but powerful center from which everything begins. Perhaps it's no coincidence then that "begin" is an anagram of "being."

But how many of us put the doing, the masculine energy—the yang—the outward expression of our lives ahead of being? In many ways, the doing is representative of the branches on our tree. It's how we show or express ourselves. I'm not suggesting that this isn't vitally important—it is! It's through expression that we often find gratification in our passion, and in part 3 we'll dive into that topic. But the outward extension is not where the intention, the catalyst for action, should stem from. If we are doing because we have nothing else to do or because we are in some kind of sick competition with ourselves or others, we are incredibly vulnerable to living an inauthentic life, someone else's life.

Our addiction to doing for the sake of numbing out of our inauthentic lives in this new culture of busyness is killing us. No joke. It is making us incredibly sick, stressed, angry, depressed, and empty, aged beyond our years, because we are not originating our expressions from the roots of our tree, our inspiration. We are operating, instead, from a shallow and unsustainable position, leaching our foundation dry as we ignore our heart center, our roots. We need to reach down into our roots, our inspiration, and lift and extend our branches, our expressions, from there. We need to begin with the *being* and allow the *doing* to come second, as a natural extension of our intention. I say all this knowing perfectly well it's incredibly difficult to do.

BREATH OF LIFE

Inspiration is, indeed, the very breath of life itself. Without our ability to inspire we cannot live, and we certainly cannot hope to *be* an inspiration or *give* inspiration. For any air-breathing organism, there is no expiration of breath (or *expression*) without inspiration. It's fundamental. Without a breath in, we have no breath to give. Should our inspiration, our breath in, be of a shallow nature—one that fills only our chest and fails to expand our diaphragm—then our expression, our breath out, will be equally weak and short-lived. But when we relax our belly and allow the breath to expand, reaching deep into the sacral chakra where creativity resides, we are able to release the breath with intention, strength, and clarity. And so it is, too, with inspiration, which inhabits our soul, compelling and stimulating us to action. Those who fail to connect with their passion, their own inspiration, live frail and shallow lives.

In our day-to-day lives, outside of a meditation practice, we don't spend a lot of time thinking about the process of breathing. It's innate, instinctual, so we put it on autopilot. But for actors, breathing is a moment-to-moment exercise that provides the fuel, the drive for the characters who live vicariously through them. When an actor is deeply connected to his instrument (his mind and body), his intention, his character, and his inspiration, he delivers a memorable performance. A great actor is subtle—he doesn't appear to be *doing* much. His delivery, movements, and actions seem unforced, easeful, and effortless. This is because of the significant preparation he has done prior to hitting the stage. He has identified the why—the inspiration, desires, hunger, passion, and driving forces behind his character. So he is able to embody fully realized, complete characters that he connects to, draws in, and re-establishes with each and every breath. This is hard, *hard* work. Don't ever let an excellent actor's look of ease deceive you. If you don't believe me, if you think it's easy, sign up for an acting class and experience this firsthand!

> "By letting it go, it all gets done. The world is won by those who let it go. But when you try and try, the world is beyond the winning."
>
> —Lao Tzu

On the flip side, an over-emoting actor comes across in exactly the opposite way: inauthentic and unconvincing. Usually, this is a beginning or lazy actor who doesn't take the time to understand his instrument and the importance of breath, nor does he dive into his character to discover what makes him tick. As a result, he lacks the ability to express himself in a meaningful way, and his performance is grounded in nothing substantial. There are no roots anchoring him to his character's motivation or purpose. There is no connection to his body. Instead, the delivery of each line is a shallow mechanism to move the story forward. To pass as the craft of acting, this actor layers on thick coats of manufactured emotion to convey meaning, but the emotions are often overwrought and grasping. He flails and distracts while the professional actor seamlessly flows through the script.

The over-emoting actor lives out his purpose on stage by showing, the other by knowing. These are two wildly different approaches with two wildly different outcomes, both for the actors and for the story lines they play out. The over-emoting actor saturates the boards with sweat as he struggles to make meaning of something he doesn't understand. He leaves the audience bewildered when his only goal is to please. The professional actor, anchored by breath, spills his heart on stage as he navigates the intricacies of living in all dimensions. He leaves the audience moved, inspired, when his only goal was to *be* inspired. And in the process of being fully engaged and connected to his passion, the accolades, the awards, and the recognition simply come. In our lives, too, the same scenario and results occur as we tread the boards on the stage of life. When we connect, the universe responds, and we live an inspired and inspiring life. When we don't, we live a life of grasping and reaching that leaves not only us but also our audience, our relationships, exhausted.

INSPIRATION VERSUS ASPIRATION

Most of us have been caught up in aspiration, the want to have or achieve something. Sometimes we mistake this desire for inspiration. I know I have. Aspiration and inspiration are a tricky pair, one that has given me much pause for thought.

As I stated earlier, goals are a worthy endeavor. We need outside feedback to understand if we're moving closer or further away from whatever progress looks like. Also, our hearts and our egos yearn for the recognition, the universal pat on the back that says, "You're right where you need to be. You matter."

To think that I, for example, could live a totally fulfilling life without those signposts would be fantasy. It's part of what makes me tick.

I *like* achievement, and I honor myself by foregoing judgment and embracing that about myself. I know of no other way to truly understand the impact I have. That said, I place achievement—aspiration—at the bottom of the deck. It lives underneath my inspiration. Every day, I reshuffle my deck to keep it there.

If I allowed aspiration to guide me, I'd be living someone else's life—and probably not all that well because all my time would be spent trying to cross a finish line that doesn't exist in the first place. I'd always need more things, more recognition, more approval, more love, more accolades, more money, more comfort because I would be attempting to fill a pit that has no fill line. A vacuum.

When we lose our inspiration—when we become untethered from our own why—we are at sea. We are lost, adrift in a constant struggle, grasping, reaching, searching for some*thing* to fill us up. The punch line to this twisted joke is that no*thing* can fill us up. No one, no thing, no place can act as a surrogate caretaker for our souls. Nothing—and I mean *nothing*—can replace inspiration or passion. Without this, we become black holes, living life from the neck up with broken or brittle hearts, sucking up everything in our path and needing more, more, more with each passing day. Nothing is ever enough, because we haven't been enough to ourselves. We haven't found our own infinite well of life-affirming sustenance.

As you can probably guess, I've lived other people's lives when I got caught up in replicating someone else's definition of success. For example, I lived a shallow, albeit exciting, life in my early twenties when I held the attitude that this world was here to serve me. I lived an intensely melancholy life when I realized I was empty and hadn't yet learned how to nurture myself. I have been on and off this balance beam throughout various stages of my life, and there's no shame in that. In fact, there should be no shame in anything, just acknowledgment of the lessons gifted to us through living each day. It wasn't until my early thirties that I really got the importance of identifying and following my passion.

I've always been a passionate person, meaning whatever I'm engaged in I attack (key word) with a passion. It took me some time to differentiate between doing something *with* passion and doing something *out of* passion. Once I understood this, every life decision became that much easier. Instead of getting locked up in my head over whether to do this or that, I found myself operating from my gut. The decisions seemed to make themselves. And when I followed my North Star, success followed me.

It became so important to me that during interviews I questioned job candidates more about their passion than anything else. I could sense almost immediately if they were at my doorstep due to following their passion or if they were there to find their next paycheck. Not only was it important to me that they land wherever it was they were meant to be, but it was also important that all the employees at my company were there out of a strong connection to their passion. It felt good to have that kind of passion existing within the walls, and as a business owner, it was good business sense. Just like how success followed me when I followed my passion, success found them when they followed theirs. And when we were all successful together, the company, too, was a glowing success.

When I speak with others about passion, I often refer to how the universe (for lack of a better term and wanting to remain agnostic) seems to reward us when we are involved in pursuits that are anchored in our true passion. But when we engage in pursuits for other materialistic or ego-driven reasons, the universe lets us have it. We get our proverbial backsides booted as we are nudged back on course. It usually starts as a whisper (an uncomfortable thought, a tug at your psyche, a second guess about what it is you're doing), steps up to a tap on the shoulder (things become difficult, we battle uphill, we are easily knocked off center), until we get the all-out collar pull where the message is so strong, it sends shock waves. Our current landscape shifts in such a way that it can never be as it once was. This upheaval may come in the form of a divorce filing, financial devastation, loss of a job, loss of a home, or the unbelievable void of anything positive occurring in our lives.

This is not to say that bad things only happen to people who are disengaged from their passion. It would be disrespectful and entirely small minded to think that we can control everyone and everything on this planet. I have a healthy ego, but I'm not that egotistical. Wars happen, natural disasters occur, markets collapse, and innocent people are sliced through in the process. Those events don't occur because people live half-hearted lives. Those events happen because *everything* in the universe is impermanent and swings toward chaos. Sometimes we can help mitigate this chaos by negotiating a peace treaty, heeding the whistle-blower's call, or adjusting how or what we consume from the planet. But other times, it's beyond our control.

I believe the universe catapulted me out of the company I once ran because it proved impossible for me to fully engage with my newly emerged passion of healing the disconnection in lives while also running my existing business. As much as I tried to make these pursuits mutually sustainable, they were not, even though I felt as if I were still engaged in my passion given the kind of training work my company did. But over time and at the end of a laborious struggle, it became clear that my driving passion had shifted and my heart was now with this work—bringing connection back into our lives.

As I am in the process of writing this book, I really don't know how this new chapter in my life will play out. I may publish this book and sell three copies. I may publish it and sell over a million; who knows? The thing is, it isn't about the outcome, the aspiration; it's about the intent, the inspiration. I feel called by a powerful desire, grounded in something bigger than myself, to write *Life, Incorporated* and offer it to the universe. No matter what the physical outcome is, I know that I will experience my own version of success because I followed my passion, because I'm fully connected to my inspiration. Success may be that I've navigated my own life, healed from pain, and have reconnected to what matters most to me. Success may be that I experience a sense of calm as a difficult chapter in my life closes. Success may be that others identify with my story and find a way out of their own personal prisons. That would be the best. These are aspirations that I hold, but they do not *lead* the work. My inspiration is what pulls me forward.

Before we go any further, let's take a look at how aspiration and inspiration differ, because they can feel much the same. The easiest way to put it is this: Inspiration typically takes no physical form; it's energetic, a desire to *be* in some way. It isn't something to have or to get but more of an impression you want to make on yourself and the world. To *inspire* is to draw out, to exert animating, enlivening, or exalting influence on. To identify inspiration, we should ask ourselves, "What is it that I want to *bring forth*, *draw out*, or *exert influence on* in myself? In others? In my community? On behalf of animals and humans alike? For this planet?" Inspiration often begins with you, because it is a way you've personally identified to *be* due to factors particular to you, but its ultimate intent is for others. Inspiration exists in order to benefit someone or something else, not solely yourself. Inspiration lives *inside* of you and *for* you with the purpose of positively affecting those *outside* of you.

"Your work is to discover your work and then, with all your heart, give yourself to it."
—attributed to Buddha

Aspiration, on the other hand, often does take physical form because it is the desire to *do*, to have an impact on yourself and the world. Aspirations take on a physical representation so that we can identify when we've achieved them. While we have inspiration *for* something, we aspire *to* something. This usually means there are mile markers or a finish line along the way to measure progress. That said, we typically have multiple aspirations tied into a singular inspiration. While inspiration lives *inside* you for the purpose of positively affecting those *outside* of you, aspiration lives *outside* of you for the purpose of positively affecting what is *inside* of you. It's the warm fuzzy, the pat on the back, the great feeling we get when we can truly see that we've done something good, when we've made a positive impact on others. You can think of this as a loop, an element of flow. Our inspiration emanates from within, is expressed in a tangible way outside of ourselves, and is then drawn back inside and reinforced when we realize our aspirations. See table 4.1 for examples of inspiration and aspiration.

Inspiration	Aspiration
Heal the human condition of striving and surviving; demonstrate how to lead a life from the inside out.	• Reach over a million people with the message in Life, Incorporated. • Participate in conversations that evolve the epidemic of stress and failing health in America. • Transform lives—in some small way—each and every day.
Cure the epidemic of obesity in children.	• Reduce the amount of sugar placed in foods. • Fund healthy lunch programs in public schools. • Lower the rate of child obesity by 10% within 10 years.
Create moments of joy that inspire.	• Produce quarterly art festivals in inner-city neighborhoods. • Offer art programs to youth. • Delight the public with random flash mobs of art installations.

Table 4.1. Examples of Inspiration and Aspiration.

As you can see, what inspires one person can be similar to or very different from what inspires another. What makes your inspiration unique is that it is yours and only yours. Where it comes from, how it flows through you, and the ways in which you will express it are a combination no one else can match.

INSPIRATION LEADS, ASPIRATION FOLLOWS

Identifying your inspiration is a unique experience. At times we may be incredibly conscious of our passion, running alongside it. Other times, we feel lost and ready to simply adopt a cause to help us feel that our time on earth has at least been of some use. We'll work through some exercises in this chapter to help you hone in on what fires you up, what makes you want to reach beyond your comfort zone, but first I want to share a few last reminders about inspiration and aspiration.

First, inspiration isn't static. It shifts, mutates, transforms, evolves. We have got to get out of this mind-
set that what we were fired up about in our college
years will remain our passion for the entirety of
our lives. If there's any species more susceptible
to change and changing their minds, it would
be us humans. We change *everything* in our
world at a breakneck pace, from the societal to
the individual level. We change the car we drive,
the place we call home, the way we style our hair,
our favorite food, the way we feel about aging, anything
and everything on a frequent basis. So why the heck do we cement our
vocation (one of the main avenues in which we can express our inspiration) in stone and then leave it there to bake in the sun for all eter-
nity? I often feel that we outgrow our vocation, breaking the mold that's
formed around our feet, but we feel so obligated to remain committed
to it that we piece the clay back together and throw some duct tape
around it, daring it to disintegrate. We're almost defiant in our desperation to cling to what we've known and done for so long. And over time,
the inspiration that was once our calling becomes an iron ball and chain
keeping us anchored to something that no longer rewards us. This is the
gateway to a life of grasping, clinging, and denying joy.

Second, inspiration can only remain front and center if we *keep* it
front and center. Remember that deck I mentioned earlier and how
inspiration has a tendency to sink to the bottom? When we don't find
ways to reconnect with our inspiration on a fre-
quent basis, bringing it to the top, one of two
things happens. We either wake up one day
to find ourselves totally uninspired with a
lot of wasted time clocked in (see the preceding paragraph!) or our aspirations take
over, controlling us like a squirrel pulling Fido's attention away from what was
supposed to be a serene stroll through the
woods. Our Zen and good intentions fall to

> "There is no passion to be found playing small—in settling for a life that is less than the one you are capable of living."
> —Nelson Mandela

> "If one advances confidently in the direction of his dreams, and endeavors to live the life which he has imagined, he will meet with a success unexpected in common hours."
> —Henry David Thoreau

the wayside as, like Fido, we chase squirrel after squirrel in a manic pursuit that leaves us more exhausted than anything. The phrase "hamster on a wheel" applies here. We get so caught up in being busy that we forget why we're on the damn wheel in the first place, and we wouldn't know fulfillment if it hit us in the face! If all we're doing is striving, then we are forever arriving, never knowing the bliss that only occurs in the moment of now, in total presence.

When it comes to aspiration, I adopt Albert Einstein's approach to intellect. In one of his more well-known quotes he states, "We should take care not to make the intellect our god; it has, of course, powerful muscles, but no personality. It cannot lead, it can only serve." Replace the word "intellect" with "aspirations" and we arrive at an equally important piece of advice. Aspirations are, indeed, incredibly powerful muscles that can keep us moving and engaged, especially when we need some added fuel to stay focused on our inspiration. Let's face it, not every day is easy when you're traveling your own path, the road less traveled, the one that is yours and yours alone. In fact, there are many challenging days in store for us when we opt into this kind of life and out of mainstream Life, Inc. I know that I've had more than my fair share of breakdowns and breakthroughs in the process of fully engaging in my passion and writing this book. So to lean into an aspiration of transforming lives came in handy time after time. Even achieving goals of completing a chapter gave me immense satisfaction along the way. Without those aspirations, then I may have given up . . . or gone berserk. At times, my inspiration felt like a cross to bear, and I was ready to throw it down and burn it in one magnificent spectacle! Think Burning Man–level of magnitude. So it's okay to rely on your aspirations in times of duress or insecurity. It's also perfectly fine to celebrate the realization of one! By all means, let's recognize how good it feels to receive outside acknowledgment of our efforts. Too much navel gazing or time spent on or with ourselves is never a good thing. We get weird. We just do.

But back to what I was saying about Einstein's altered quote. Aspirations have their place . . . and it isn't at the front. They serve as the engine that powers the boat, but *we* are in charge of plotting the course. We must set sail toward our North Star, our inspiration, and remain steady as it pulls us forward, our engine, our aspirations, supporting us. So let's dive in and begin. We'll start with one of my favorite exercises, writing a personal manifesto.

PERSONAL MANIFESTO

I'm often asked why we begin with a personal manifesto. I'll tell ya why: It has attitude. Yes, personal mission statements are great, and we'll pen one, but I find those are a tough place to begin. Instead, I like to begin with something that feels freer, that gives us permission to dare speak courageously and invites passion. In a guest post for the blog *A Man's Life*, Zach Sumner put it this way: "A personal manifesto functions as both a statement of principles and a bold, sometimes rebellious, call to action." Okay. He had me at "rebellious." The word "manifesto" comes from the Latin *manifestum*, which means clear or conspicuous. Rebellious, bold, conspicuous—these are all words I like, and it's not because I'm some diva. I'm not. I'm a card-carrying introvert who shudders every time I'm told I have a dinner party to attend. I like those words because they're evocative, which is *exactly* what your personal manifesto should be. If it doesn't get you fired up, if it doesn't resonate with you, then you haven't allowed yourself to reach far enough. This is an exercise where you get to seriously play, and it is for your eyes only, unless you choose to share it.

To get you in the mind-set for creating your own, read the following manifesto by Seth Godin. Other good examples include the manifestos of lululemon, Expert Enough, and the organization (RED). No matter what type of entity or whether the manifesto matches your personal beliefs, you'll notice one thing in common: They went there. Each manifesto is passionate, specific, personal, and bold. Here is Godin's:

> I am an artist. I take initiative. I do the work, not the job. Without critics, there is no art. I am a Linchpin. I am not easily replaced. If it's never been done before, even better.

The work is personal, too important to phone in. The lizard brain is powerless in the face of art. I make it happen. Every day. Every interaction is an opportunity to make a connection. The past is gone. It has no power. The future depends on choices I make now. I own the means of production—the system isn't as important as my contribution to it. I see the essential truth unclouded by worldview, and that truth drives my decisions. I lean into the work, not away from it. Trivial work doesn't require leaning. Busywork is too easy. Rule-breaking works better and is worth the effort. Energy is contagious. The more I put in, the more the world gives back. It doesn't matter if I'm always right. It matters that I'm always moving. I raise the bar. I know yesterday's innovation is today's standard. I will not be brainwashed into believing in the status quo. Artists don't care about credit. We care about change. There is no resistance if I don't allow it to defeat me. I embrace a lack of structure to find a new path. I am surprising. (And often surprised.) I donate energy and risk to the cause. I turn charisma into leadership. The work matters. Go. Make something happen.

There is no right way or wrong way to create your own manifesto. No statement is too soft, too strong, too compelling, too flat, too clever, or too mundane to include in your manifesto. Send your inner critic down to the river to collect rocks and allow yourself to relish the opportunity to connect with what turns you on. I use a simple construct to get us from a blank sheet of paper to a full-fledged personal manifesto. I find having a little structure *incredibly* helpful for us process-loving people, especially during creative exercises. It gives our left brain something to do (which keeps it out of the way) while our right brain sneaks off to play. Ready? Let's go!

> "Be yourself; everyone else is already taken."
> —Oscar Wilde

Exercise: Write Your Personal Manifesto

In this exercise, challenge yourself to come up with ten statements about what you believe, three statements about how you want to change the world, and five statements about what you know to be true. You will then combine these statements to create your personal manifesto. Writing these statements isn't easy—I got stuck on a couple myself, but it was the challenge of being required to dig deeper that landed me on some of my most powerful statements.

I'm a rule breaker, so if you want to do more or less of any type of statement, that's okay. All I ask is that you don't lessen the amount because you've chickened out or because you can't seem to come up with as many as have been asked. Try to do what the exercise asks and then if you want to pare back, you can. On the flip side, having twenty statements about what you believe may demonstrate a lack of focus. Twenty is fine, but only if each is laser focused and absolutely one hundred percent true for *you*. Again, I suggest seeing if you can work within the numbers asked of you. Then, if you want to create more statements or break them into smaller pieces, go for it! At the end of the day, this exercise is for you. So I want you to do what is necessary to make it useful. Hopefully your manifesto will be something you'll want to hang on your wall so you can bask in just how powerful you are.

Step 1: State What You Believe

Write ten statements that complete the sentence "I believe . . ."

Examples

- Love is the answer.

- Comfort is dangerous.

- Making the world a better place starts right here, with me.

- The impact we have on others is breathtakingly profound.

- The worst thing anyone can do is give up.

- Our bodies deserve as much attention as our thoughts.

- Our thoughts are more powerful than we know.

- To create a new belief, we must first let go of an old one.

- The only thing standing between you and your dream is you.

- Every life is precious and every soul deserves to be seen.

Step 2: State What You Want

Describe how you want to change the world by writing three statements that complete the sentence "I want . . ."

Examples

- To end the debilitating struggle of "I'm not enough," "I don't matter," and "Someday . . ."

- To teach others how to self-generate self-worth

- To demystify what stands between us and our ability to experience long-term, sustained fulfillment and happiness

_____

_____

_____

Step 3: State What You Know to Be True

Write five wisdom statements that complete the sentence "I know this to be true . . ."

Examples

- One cannot pursue happiness. Happiness occurs in the pursuit of one's dream.

- No *thing* will ever be "enough"; being "enough" is an inside job.

- Greed leads to bankruptcy; generosity leads to wealth.

- How we treat others is a direct reflection of how we feel about ourselves.

- The solution to most of what ails us is human connection, beginning with our own connection to self.

_____

_____

_____

_____

_____

Step 4: Revise

Step back and evaluate each statement. Does it resonate? Does it have its own energy? Does it evoke something within you? Each one should provide its own "moment" for you—that inner fist pump, a stirring of emotion, the unshakable urge to get up and get to it. Refine each statement until you find that energy. And if you find yourself struggling with a statement, be open to the idea that perhaps this one sounded like a good idea or feels like something you should have passion for—maybe you even did at one time—but now, where you are today, it is no longer relevant for you.

For example, I felt like I *should* have something in my personal manifesto about conservation or trying to somehow turn back the clock on climate change. It is something I'm keenly aware of and genuinely concerned about. But every time I wrote a statement around this cause or idea, it fell flat. At first I thought there was something wrong with me, but then I realized that I cannot be *passionate* about everything. I have a great deal of interest in the issue, yes, but it isn't mine to take up and carry in my arms. I have other issues that compel me, like the one I write about in this book—helping people heal their minds, bodies, and spirits by showing them how to live from the inside out. If you find yourself struggling with the same problem, take my example as an invitation to question where your passions and beliefs really lie.

Step 5: Organize

Now, arrange the statements in any order you want. Once you have refined your personal manifesto, put it somewhere it can be top of mind. For example, mine hangs in my bathroom, because I start and end my days there. It's one of the first and last things I see. And being reminded of any one of my phrases can not only put a little pep in my step but also remind me of why I'm here, keeping me connected to my inspiration. My personal manifesto also reminds me to have courage, one of my core values, to get out there each day and live fully. I hope your manifesto does the same for you. And now since I mentioned values, let's move on to that exercise. Because we need some guideposts in our view when living out loud. Off we go!

CORE VALUES

I sometimes feel bad for the term "core values." It's about as nauseating a term as one can find. In fact, I'm willing to bet you are stifling a yawn at the mere mention of core values. I get it. I've worked in corporate America and have witnessed the abuse of the term. Company executives trot out their core values on a piece of foam board during some awesomely boring presentation and spout off about how important their values are; then, in too many cases, their behavior indicates the exact opposite. We tune out because it's all just a bunch of corporate speak, and we know it's wasted time.

> "Be faithful to that which exists nowhere but in yourself."
> —André Gide

Now that I've depressed everyone, let me try to wind this back into something positive! Core values don't deserve that kind of bullshit treatment nor do they deserve the negative associations we may have with them. That belongs to the individuals and corporations who use them as a gimmick. We've got to take back core values and put them in the positive light they deserve! Our values aren't too terribly far away from the statements we made in our personal manifestos. They can (and should) be just as evocative and inner-fist-pumping-ish as their manifesto counterpart. The difference between core values and a personal manifesto is that core values are more focused on guiding principles—they determine *how* we interact with the world. They guide our behavior, actions, choices, priorities, and ethics. If we wrote our personal manifestos correctly, we've got some stuff we want to get done. Our core values answer these questions: What is it going to take to get those things done? And how do we want to accomplish them? Another way to approach core values is to ask yourself what adjectives you would want others to use to describe you. That's how you want to live your life and do your work.

Similar to your manifesto, these are very personal and there's no right or wrong way to do it. You get to be Goldilocks and decide what's "just right" for you. Let's begin!

Exercise: Choose Your Core Values

Define your core values in this four-step exercise.

Step 1: Reflect

Read your personal manifesto three times and then reflect on these questions:

- When I read my personal manifesto, what do I notice as a common thread?

- What is important to me?

- What is nonnegotiable in how I live my life at my most abundant and happiest?

- What are the elements that make me unique, that make me tick?

- What is important to me in how I carry out my life?

- What do I want to be able to say about myself and how I behave?

- What do I want others to notice about how I behave?

Spend a few minutes writing in your own journal to get your thoughts down.

Step 2: Create a List

Based on your answer to the questions in step 1, create a first draft of a list of values. They should reflect the common themes or threads you found in your personal manifesto. Don't worry about nailing it here; this is more about teasing out those values so you can look at them on paper. Choose ten to begin with. Here are some examples of values: adventurous, generous, accountable, passionate, trustworthy, and daring.

_____

_____

_____

_____

_____

_____

_____

_____

Step 3: Refine Your List

Now is the time to refine. Narrow your list to five by determining if there is any overlap between your core values. For example, "generous" and "charitable" are similar enough you could choose one or the other, same thing for "authentic" and "transparent." Only you know what you intend with each word, so I'll leave it to you to determine which have the potential to overlap. Listen to your gut. Words are *very* powerful and mean different things to different people. Go with the word that immediately struck you as *yours*. We want these to be evocative.

_____

_____

_____

_____

_____

Step 4: Finalize Your List

Define your five core values. What do they mean to you? Different words have different definitions depending on the person. I want you to always remember exactly what your intention was when you chose the word you did. If you share your core values with others close to you, they will benefit from learning your dictionary as well. Here are my core values and their definitions:

1. Adventurous: To explore the unknown with curiosity and compassion as a means to better understand the world and my role in it.

2. Passionate: To live my life fully and purposefully, with no holds barred.

3. Courageous: To embrace what makes me unique, stand up for my beliefs, and speak up about issues important to me, regardless of judgment.

4. Connected: To remain grounded in myself while building and nurturing deep, meaningful relationships with those important in my life.

5. Generous: To view this world from a mind-set of abundance and treat myself and others in ways that support and sustain living a fully realized life.

1. _____   _____

2. _____   _____

3. _____   _____

4. _____   _____

5. _____   _____

If you really got in there, dug deep, and connected to what is essential for you in *how* you show up in this world, your core values ought to excite you and freak you out a little, too. Our core values are what we aspire to at all times, and they may present us with moments of struggle. For example, as "luck" would have it, I had literally just finished writing this chapter when I received an exciting email. It was from a former business associate who knew of my speaking abilities and wanted to know if he could recommend me to a friend who was looking for someone to speak at a women in leadership event. I was *thrilled*! It had been six months since I changed careers, and since then, I'd spent most of my time focused on writing this book. I desperately longed to connect with others and get back out there on the stage. It also felt wonderful to be thought of and asked. My spirits (and ego) were soaring.

I immediately wrote back: *Heck, yeah! Let's do it! What are the next steps?*

He replied just as quickly and said that he'd introduce me to the CEO of the company, but first, knowing I'm an animal lover, he wanted me to be aware that I'd be speaking on behalf of a pharmaceutical company that conducts animal testing.

Now, I've had animals since I was little—cats, dogs, bunnies, parakeets, guinea pigs, horses, even a goat with whom I had a somewhat contemptuous but respectful relationship with. Growing up on a farm, I would look in on the barn cats and take special care of each new litter, celebrating each day as the kittens grew and reached another level of cuteness. I'd also deeply mourn those that didn't make it; their little, fragile, lifeless bodies would haunt my thoughts for days.

I reread my business associate's email several times. The next five minutes were excruciating and beyond manic. I couldn't believe it. Here was an opportunity I was dying to take advantage of and then *this*! In all my years speaking, never, and I mean *never*, had an issue of animal testing come up. And now? What was with the timing? My first invitation in months with this kind of monkey wrench? I went back and forth—picture a devil and an angel on my shoulder. The internal chatter went something like this:

DEVIL: Oh my god. It would be so great to get back out there and speak!

ANGEL: Yes, but, Halley, *animal testing*.

HALLEY: I know . . . but what if I say no?

DEVIL: You may not get another opportunity! I mean it's been *months*!

ANGEL: Yes it has, but, Halley, *animal testing*.

HALLEY: Oh man. Geez. I know. That's bad, right?

ANGEL: *Halley!!!!* See it in your mind's eye, the lab-
oratory, the animals, the experiments, the
side effects. Tell me, what do you believe?

HALLEY: (sigh) I believe that every life is precious
and deserves to be seen.

ANGEL: And your values?

HALLEY: To be courageous. To speak out and stand
up for my beliefs, regardless of judgment . . . shit. I guess it's a no.

At that moment, there was no turning back. I had to follow my value of courage. It was intrinsic to me—part of my fabric—and to go against it would be to act against or outside of myself. Not possible. I respectfully declined and expressed my sincere gratitude for not only the invitation but also the thoughtfulness of giving me a heads-up on the situation. Not everyone would think to do that. I asked if he thought I was being foolish.

He wrote back: *Not at all. You have to follow your heart. Oh and by the way, there will be more opportunities coming your way.*

Done, easy as that. He was supportive, and I got the very real sense that our connection had just deepened. On top of that, I felt as proud of myself as I could possibly be. I had lived my value of being courageous and the sensation was as good as if I had won the lottery. My spirits (and confidence) were once again soaring.

Admittedly, I was fortunate in this example, because the universe hired an understanding person to test me on my values. That isn't always going to be the case. Sometimes we'll be tested and there won't be a mutual high five for us adhering to those values. Sometimes there will be disgust, ridicule, judgment, or rejection. That's the way it rolls when dealing with our values or anything else that we hold dear or believe in wholeheartedly. It takes courage, and this is exactly why I chose being courageous as one of my core values; it's *way* less likely that I will default on any of my values. Because if I were to default on one, I'd be automatically defaulting on a second: courage. So know this: As soon as you commit wholeheartedly to something, the universe will conspire to test your resolve. My advice? Hold true. Suck up the nerve, ask for support, and greet the challenge. Believe in yourself enough that the universe will believe more in you. Be mindful of how you operate and what you operate with. Your personal manifesto is your rocket fuel propelling you forward while your core values provide sure-footed guidance in *how* you approach your life and everyone in it.

The last exercise in this chapter provides the opportunity to pen a personal mission statement. This is where we can create a more concise "banner" that will serve us well as we launch forward into part 3, how we express our inspiration.

PERSONAL MISSION STATEMENT

A personal mission statement, while perhaps sounding broad, is in reality a statement that provides focus. It's an exercise in identifying what kind of impact you want to have on your own life and on those in your world. If you turn back to page 122, you'll notice that the examples of inspiration are similar to a personal mission statement. The emphasis is on *being*. Something that exists deep in your cells and isn't for show. It's part of the fabric of your very soul, the deeply personal, unique sense of *why* you are here. On this planet. Right now. I don't believe in happy accidents; I think everything happens for a reason. So the fact that you are *here*—alive, in existence, in full color—must be an indication that there is an intention for bringing you forth. But as with all things, the answer won't fall in your lap. You must discover this intention for yourself. Creating your personal manifesto and choosing your core values have provided the groundwork for writing your personal mission statement.

> "The two most important days in your life are the day you are born and the day you find out why."
>
> —Mark Twain

Exercise: Write Your Personal Mission Statement

There are, it seems, about a hundred different varieties of mission statements out there. An online search yields overwhelming results, many of them verbose and lacking in thrust and clarity. So I'm going to be specific about how I'd like us to construct ours.

Our formula for creating a personal mission statement requires a shout-out to William Arruda and Deb Dib, authors of *Ditch, Dare, Do: 3D Personal Branding for Executives*, for coming up with this snappy equation (with a slight tweak from yours truly): the *value* you create + *who* you're creating it for + the intended *impact* = your personal mission statement. I want to remind you that the word "value" doesn't refer to what you can *do*. We often mistake what we do for our value. Heck, that's how I went through half of my life—thinking my value to the world was based on what I could produce. Wrong. So wrong. That's how we, myself included, end up overstriving and grasping, trying to fill that bucket that has no bottom.

What I mean by "value" is the way you want to *be* in order to have a positive impact on your chosen target. A simple tool to help us stay focused on this is to use the word "be" in your mission statement when you're naming your value. If that word doesn't rock your world, then choose other like-minded verbs: for example, live, embody, serve, remain, commit, or embrace. These are all verbs that imply a sense of ownership, and there's a certain quiet strength to them. There are other options but those are just a few to give you an idea.

Speaking of ideas, here are some examples of personal mission statements that model the one I'd like you to construct. Notice how each one follows the equation: value + who + impact = personal mission statement.

To be a teacher. And to be known for inspiring my students to be more than they thought they could be.
—Oprah Winfrey

To be a thrilling writer who is a companion to many.
—Anonymous

To use the power of connection, wonder, and growth to
light people up to their full possibility and
create their most authentic self.
—Jen Fowler, yoga instructor

To be a great competitive athlete who
makes the competition evolve.
—Anonymous

To live life with integrity and empathy, and be
a positive force in the lives of others.
—Amy Ziari, founder of Pasta

To be an explorer and find something wonderful
to share with the world wherever I go.
—Anonymous

To be whole. And to encourage mindfulness, awareness,
compassion, connection, and joy in all aspects of the
lives of others.
—Halley Bock, author of *Life, Incorporated*

As you can see, these mission statements run the gamut. Some
are more specific, like Winfrey's, which identifies a role to embody—a
teacher. Others choose to embody the role of an athlete or a writer.
And there are versions that don't include a specific role but, rather,
describe a particular state, sensation, or feeling. For example, I desire

to be whole while others desire to explore, be a positive force, or shine light into people's lives.

Find *your* value. What is your gift to yourself and the world that no one can express quite like you? Review your personal manifesto and core values for clues and then use the formula to draft your personal mission statement: the *value* you create + *who* you're creating it for + the intended *impact*. Give yourself the freedom to write whatever comes to mind without editing. Create as many mission statements as you need before you sense you've hit on something. Then start playing with that until it is absolutely, unequivocally yours. May your personal mission statement be as limitless, unique, powerful, and moving as you!

_____

_____

_____

CONCLUSION

First of all, let me say thank you for doing the work. Completing these exercises can be exhilarating at times and anxiety inducing at others—not because it's necessarily hard work but because the work requires us to focus solely on ourselves. My hope (and not-so-hidden agenda) is that the reaching in you did gives you even more cause and excitement to continue (or begin!) your inner-life practices. We need to constantly find ways to come home to ourselves and reground in *us*. Not in what others think, do, or desire, but in the rich, diverse, endless expanse that is our inner world, what it is that makes us tick.

"You were born an original. Don't die a copy."
—John Mason

In this chapter, we accomplished three significant goals. We wrote a personal manifesto, we identified core values, and we penned a personal mission statement. All three of these exercises are designed to get you back in touch with you and your intentions for this period in your life—what fires you up and what matters to you. Your manifesto is the fuel, the emotional spark that compels and propels you forward. Your core values are the rudder that keeps you steady, helping you navigate the turbulent waters to come. And your mission statement is your North Star rising above the land, where you aspire to reach as you glide through life. This alchemy of inspiration is a combination that should stir something deep and profound within you—breathing new life and sparking new flames.

Remember, we are allowed to change. To shift, mutate, mature, do an all-out about-face. In fact, we *will* change. It's part of that whole human condition thing I mentioned earlier. So please don't set your manifesto, core values, or mission statement down in stone. Nothing in life should be in stone. Keep transforming and allowing yourself to shift. If and when one of your core values or a statement from your manifesto no longer rings true, change it! Tend to your inspiration just as you would your foundation. Everything must be revisited and touched on again and again if we wish to maintain awareness. And avoid falling back into the all-too-easy, mundane routine of sleep-walking through your days or engaging in the gamification of life—striving, struggling, and grasping for self-worth.

Touch on a piece of your inspiration every day. Hang up your manifesto, core values, and mission statement where you can see them. Use a website to create word art out of one, or all, of your pieces! Create a password—especially on a site that requires multiple log-ins each day (i.e., it boots you out every two hours or so)—that speaks to a component of your mission statement. If there's one thing I've learned in being as physical as I am, it's that our body follows our head. We look somewhere, and our body follows. We think something, and our cells believe it. Use this power for good, and create opportunities to consciously remind yourself of where you're going. Your body, your thoughts, your gut will begin to take you there in ways you won't even be aware of. But you'll be on your way.

Now that we've created a healthy and meaningful root system for our inspiration, let's now move onward and upward to our expression. How do we begin to take what lives in our roots up and out to the world? Let's find out.

Part 3

BRANCHES: EXPRESSION

"Let the beauty of what you love be what you do."

—Rumi

And now we have finally arrived at the *doing* part of things, the branches of our tree. Up until this point, we have intentionally spent a significant amount of time on everything *but* doing because I know all too well how hardwired we are to begin there, only to realize one day that all we're doing . . . is doing! We get caught up in activity and achievement, lulled by stockpiling physical or imagined trophies on our mantle. We plant ourselves at the front of the line and gobble up everything in sight, or we do the opposite and strand ourselves on an island after giving too much of ourselves away. Either way, we wake up to the realization that our lives have passed us by.

We think that by doing—whether it's on behalf of ourselves or others—that we'll get what it is we seek. Nothing could be further from the truth. Instead, we must find comfort in *being*, in truly connecting to ourselves and nourishing our inner life before we even think about lifting a finger. When we first ground in our foundation and inspiration, any action that follows—any doing—is simply a natural expression as opposed to a parade of superficial or careless deeds. There's an easefulness to it as opposed to a forcefulness. Such action represents thoughtful generosity as opposed to perpetual self-sacrifice.

That said, I believe it's just as dangerous to do nothing as it is to overdo it. No good things can be found in extremes. One of my fundamental beliefs is that few things are more dangerous than the busy hands of an idle mind, except perhaps the busy mind of idle hands. If we only live in our head and find no way to express our inspiration, then we fall victim to the trappings of our thoughts. We start overanalyzing, we lose touch with reality, we lose our sense of belonging, we become paranoid, we start to see everyone else as other, and we become toxic unto ourselves and to our community. Finding ways to express our inspiration is as fundamental to our well-being as nurturing our foundation and identifying our inspiration. As I said in chapter 4, inspiration is the breath of life, but we cannot draw another breath if we do not find a way to expire, or express, first. Maintaining this cycle requires both the inward filling up of inspiration and the outward letting go of expression.

Expression is the outward, physical pressing out, or action, of making your thoughts, beliefs, and feelings known by whatever method required. And because we have multiple beliefs, feelings, and desires, we need multiple, diverse ways in which to express them. One of the hang-ups I find in Western society is the belief that what we do for work, our vocation, is the one area in which we can live the life we were meant to live. Like it's the be-all, end-all of life purpose and inspiration. Like if our inspiration isn't earning us money, then we haven't quite figured it out yet, or we need to get on it and live a nobler life.

That's horseshit. We can't all be so lucky as to have a vocation that allows us to fully express our inspiration. On top of that, I don't think it's possible to fully express the entirety of our inspiration via one expression. You know why? Because I believe in multiple things, I have multiple sources of inspiration. Some are related to one another like my core value of generosity and the statement in my personal manifesto: "Everyone deserves to be seen, to belong." And some of my sources of inspiration have nothing to do with each other, like my desire to "end the debilitating struggle of 'I'm not enough,' 'I don't matter,' and 'Someday . . .'" and my equally strong belief that "Our bodies deserve as much attention as our thoughts." These two very different statements are both driving factors in what inspires me. One inspires me to pay attention to my thought processes and beliefs, often prompting me to be still, to take stock of and nurture my inner life, while the other inspires me to leave all those potential trappings behind and fully inhabit the rest of my body, from the neck down. So I'm not going to simply chase one slice of the pie and call that "enough." If I did, I wouldn't be happy. I wouldn't be complete.

And neither would you. To live a fully inspired and fully expressive life, we need multiple avenues in which to express the vastness of our inner light.

Your expressions are the branches of your tree. What extends up and out of your well-rooted inspiration. These expressions represent the ways in which you can live your manifesto or actualize your personal mission statement, and these branches also represent the key relationships, or roles, we are committed to. Because expressions signify any and all physical manifestation—the *pressing out*—of our doing, then we need to have all of them represented here so we can view them in their entirety and understand our intention with each. I don't know about you, but I found that in the absence of doing this work and being mindful of my tree and the number of branches extending out, I had a freakish-looking tree—one of those dark silhouettes of a tree you see on a spooky late October night. All twisted, full of dead wood and confused growth, reaching out but also growing back in as if to strangle itself. Come to think of it, that describes how my life felt at the time. So if you have twenty different spindly branches jutting out of your tree, like I used to, then this is a wonderful opportunity to do some pruning. We can only be as much to others as we are to ourselves, meaning our resources are finite. So let's choose our battles, so to speak. Or as I prefer to put it, choose our life—with intention.

In the following chapters, we will explore four categories of expression: play, avocation, vocation, and key relationships. If you do not identify with one of the expressions—if it simply doesn't pertain to you—then don't force it upon yourself. You may have no vocation but two avocations! You may have one or three key relationships. Or you may not have any. Whatever the case may be, your life—your tree—should accurately reflect what you *desire* to have on it. As I said earlier, now is the time to either do some pruning or add new growth—an interest that you've always desired to explore. There may be a little bit of both to do as there was in my case. We will then go through some exercises designed to help unearth ideas about how you can express yourself in ways that are tethered to your inspiration. Are you an unfulfilled writer who's never had the courage or taken the time to pursue writing wholeheartedly? Are you owning your days or are they owning you? How can you live a meaningful life that represents you at the deepest level? These are all questions we will address as you work through the exercises and then birth the tree—the life—you desire for yourself. Let's begin.

EXPRESSION 1: PLAY

"We don't stop playing because we grow old;

we grow old because we stop playing."

—George Bernard Shaw

The first expression is play. It is the expression that is *all* about us. It is activity that we do purely for enjoyment. It is, without a doubt, the most important expression we can undertake, yet it is *the* most forgotten or misunderstood. Play is often at the bottom of our list, if it's there at all. In a society that is all about outcomes, it's increasingly hard to justify, or even recognize, the importance of play in our lives. If there's something that needs doing at the office, or an item we can knock off our to-do list, or an extra errand we can squeeze into our day, we'll do it. Give us an extra five minutes and we'll spend it on anything but ourselves, because we have become a society obsessed with pleasing and showing. If an activity doesn't move something or someone forward and culminate in concrete results that we can display, then we consider it frivolous and irresponsible. Or worse, self-indulgent and hedonistic.

After all my years speaking with, working with, and listening to successful individuals—those who have found happiness and a sense of "balance" in life (they are driving their life instead of life driving them!)—I have learned that to *not* participate in play is the most irresponsible thing we can do. Here we go again with all the age-old adages of putting our oxygen mask on first. Of filling our cup first. Of giving to ourselves before we can give to others. We hear these words of wisdom over and over again, yet we still don't associate them with play. We either dump that advice into the category of "Oh, I should get more sleep tonight so I have more energy to give to my kids, my spouse, my job, my community . . ." or we think we have to spend our free time engaged in some super self-enlightening or self-enhancing exercises to make sure we're filling our cup with something worthwhile. We are always, always, always on the move to up our game. Hear me when I say this: Relax! Play and the activity of filling our cup have absolutely *nothing* to do with an outcome nor do they deserve to be measured. Let go of the need to derive meaning out of every little thing. Or to be your best self every moment of the day. The art, the act of play gives us the much-needed white space we need in our lives. Without it, we lose perspective, we lose our sense of self, and we lose the ability to adapt and create. Let me throw in some research to bolster my passionate pleas for play.

Thanks to Brené Brown's work, I was introduced to Stuart Brown, an unlikely hero in play research because his career began in researching violence. After the world came to a standstill on August 1, 1966, when Charles Whitman climbed a tower at the University of Texas and opened fire, killing sixteen people and marking the largest mass killing in the United States at that time, the governor of Texas, John Connally, pulled together the most extensive and comprehensive group of researchers, psychologists, and experts he could find to understand how something like this happens. He wanted to know what it was that could incite such violence in an individual. His hope, of course, was to lessen these occurrences by understanding the factors that conspired to create a Charles Whitman and other violent offenders.

Included in that team was Stuart Brown. At the time, Brown, a psychiatrist at Baylor College of Medicine, was put in charge of analyzing the data. The team was concerned about whether such an extensive, broad study could yield any conclusive findings. It was the first large-scale study of its kind, and the potential for data overload was high. Would there—could there—be any significant takeaways from so many experts looking across so many spectrums? The answer turned out to be a resounding yes.

The first pattern that emerged was that every subject in the study had a history of restricted play. Whitman, for example, had not been allowed to have unstructured time. His overbearing, controlling father simply had not tolerated play. The findings were so significant to Brown, the implications of losing play as an element in childhood and adulthood were so strong, that he eventually left clinical medicine and founded the National Institute for Play, a nonprofit corporation committed to bringing the unrealized knowledge, practices, and benefits of play into public life.

This isn't to say that if we all stop participating in play we'll end up morally depraved and homicidal. To make a blanket statement like that would be a leap of epic proportions. What Brown's findings do indicate is that the expression of play is essential to our ability to regulate emotions, to create, to adapt, to forge and reinforce bonds with one another, to develop compassion for ourselves and others, and to ease stress.

> "The opposite of play isn't work. It's depression."
>
> —Brian Sutton-Smith, developmental psychologist and educator

It was Brown who introduced me to one of my new favorite terms, "psychological neoteny," the retention of immature qualities into adulthood. Yeah, let that one sink in. There's actually a term for that! Contrary to its association with immaturity, psychological neoteny is actually a fairly evolved and special trait. Humans are one of the most plastic and neotenic species on the planet, which gives us a huge leg up on adaptability because these immature traits include affection, sociality, playfulness, and curiosity. These qualities are essential and powerful when we are faced with change; they allow us to break up the cement around our feet and look for new solutions, new possibilities. This is why humans have evolved to the extent that we have. Our ability to play, to retain some "immaturity," has real benefits! Any self-critical naysayers who believe, as I used to, that play is a waste of time have an opportunity here to shift a belief. To engage in play is to build and maintain an important muscle in our evolutionary progress, not to mention our much-needed, day-to-day ability to adapt to change.

WHAT IS PLAY?

If we understand that play is important—that there is a real cost when we don't participate in it and substantial benefit when we do— we need to understand what, exactly, play is. In his book *Play: How It Shapes the Brain, Opens the Imagination, and Invigorates the Soul*,[15] Stuart Brown defines play through the following seven properties:

1. Apparent Purposelessness: Play is done for its own sake, with no apparent survival value.

2. Voluntary: Play is not obligatory or required by duty.

3. Inherent Attraction: It's fun. Play makes you feel good.

4. Freedom from Time: We lose a sense of the passage of time.

5. Diminished Consciousness of Self: We stop worrying about how we are perceived. We are fully in the moment.

6. Improvisational Potential: We aren't locked into a rigid way of doing things. We never really know what's going to happen.

7. Continuation Desire: We desire to keep doing it, wish to extend it.

---

15 S. Brown, C. Vaughan, *Play: How It Shapes the Brain, Opens the Imagination, and Invigorates the Soul* (New York: Penguin, 2009).

So according to Brown, we engage in play out of our own free will, and it is time spent without purpose. It's time we wish we could extend and time we lose track of. Play is adventurous, and it's something that makes us feel good—when we are engaged in play we don't care about how we are being perceived. Gosh! When was the last time you did something like that? Something that had absolutely no purpose? Something that you enjoyed so much you didn't give a rat's ass about what others thought of you while you were doing it?

When I was first looking at play in my own life, I initially thought that participating in triathlons—swimming, running, and cycling—were my expressions of play. I hung on to this notion for quite some time. In fact, it wasn't until I thoroughly reread my research on play that I realized I had gotten it backward. While those activities all have the *potential* to be play, how I engage in them most of the time doesn't fit the criteria for play after all. Yes, those activities make me feel good. Yes, I often lose sense of time. And yes, I wish I could stop time so I could continue to do them. But there is a purpose to engaging in those activities, a clear purpose. The time I spend training is time spent to improve upon something, whether it's my speed, my form, my tempo, my endurance, my strength, or my flexibility. And because those activities are often scheduled according to a training program, there can be a sense of duty or obligation to complete them. As much as I wanted to think of my training as play, turns out it isn't. It's an avocation.

That said, if you dropped me in the ocean with a pair of goggles I would be at play. You can forget your plans for me, your expectations, your whatever. When I'm in the ocean, I'm there to do one thing: Be one with the ocean and my body. I float on the water, rolling with the waves, and I search for sea turtles and shiny things on the ocean floor. I get distracted by groups of fish darting by, often following them to see if they'll lead me to a magical fairyland of sea turtles. I'm not kidding. As serious as I can be in life, I still believe in magic, and the ocean is often where I connect with my neotenic characteristics. Hours can go by without me knowing it. And I become that kid who finds excuse after excuse to spend just one more minute in the ocean before finally being dragged out by my family. That is play.

Dancing is another form of play for me. Others are hiking, playing beach volleyball, taking spontaneous bike rides, and hopping into the car with good friends and good music and driving until we're lost while singing at the top of our lungs. During a recent date night, Deli and I discovered another expression of play. After dinner, we were strolling through a neighborhood when we found a dive bar packed full of pinball machines. We tentatively crept in, and, before we knew it, we were both slamming on pinball machines while feeding the old-fashioned change machine dollar after dollar. We laughed, we were appalled by our lack of pinball skills, we high-fived, we had an amazing time, and I still have no idea how long we were there. All I know is that it didn't matter. All of a sudden, getting back to the babysitter became a lost thought and we were twentysomethings again. That was play.

> "What did you do as a child that made the hours pass like minutes? Therein lies the key to your earthly pursuits."
>
> —Carl Jung

EXERCISE: WHAT IS YOUR EXPRESSION OF PLAY?

The reason I begin with play is not only because of its importance in our life but also because numerous clues and untold stories lie buried within what we define as play that can help guide us in uncovering what our avocation and vocation could be. So if we begin here, then we will have not only done the work for this expression but we'll also have begun the important work of building a base for some of our other expressions.

In his Ted Talk titled *Play Is Just More Fun*,[16] Stuart Brown drew the parallel between play and vocation this way:

---

16 S. Brown, "Play is more than just fun" (TED Talks, 2008), https://www.ted.com/talks/stuart_brown_says_play_is_more_than_fun_it_s_vital?language=en.

So what I would encourage on an individual level to do, is to explore backwards as far as you can go to the most clear, joyful, playful image that you have, whether it's with a toy, on a birthday, or on a vacation. And begin to build from the emotion of that into how that connects with your life now. And you'll find, you may change jobs—which has happened to a number people when I've had them do this—in order to be more empowered through their play. Or you'll be able to enrich your life by prioritizing it and paying attention to it.

Step 1: Explore Past Images of Play

I want you to do what Brown suggests and think back to your earliest, most profound image of play. Then, we'll explore how to incorporate that image into your current life. Here are some questions to help you identify those initial images:

- What images come to mind when you think back to your earliest memories of clear, joyful play?

- What activities did you do as a child where the hours passed like minutes?

- When you were given the luxury of free time, what are the things, activities, or people you would run to first?

When I think about these questions, these images and experiences come up for me:

- Climbing the big oak tree in our front yard

- Riding my yellow mountain bike through the forest between my street and the next block

- Floating down the creek that ran through our backyard,

past my best friend's house, and into a park that kept horses, goats, sheep, and bunnies

- Volunteering at that same park and taking care of the animals

- Mashing the buttons on my Atari joystick in a rousing game of *Space Invaders* or *Donkey Kong*

- Telling stories to my sister at bedtime and seeing how hard I could make her laugh

Your turn. What are some images that come up for you? List at least seven images.

_____

_____

_____

_____

_____

_____

_____

_____

_____

Step 2: Explore Present Images of Play

Next, let's fast-forward to present day. Here are some questions to help you identify your current images of play:

- What images come to mind when you think of what now represents clear, joyful play in your life?

- What activities do you engage in now that make the hours pass like minutes?

- When, or if, you are given the luxury of free time, what are the things, activities, or people you run to first?

Here's what comes up for me, some of which I've already touched on:

- Swimming in the ocean

- Taking leisurely bike rides on quiet, country roads

- Going on short road trips with friends, getting lost while singing our hearts out

- Playing arcade games in dive bars with my family and friends

- Searching for sand crabs at night with my family on the beaches of Maui

- Going for long walks in nature with music as my companion

- Having great conversations over a glass of wine

Your turn. What are some images that come up for you? List at least seven images.

_____

_____

_____

_____

Step 3: Compare the Past to the Present

Now answer the following questions to look for similarities between your past and current images of play:

- What common themes do you see between the images of play from your past and your current images of play?

- When you think of those themes in terms of emotions, what feelings do these images consistently evoke?

- Are there similarities between the environment, activity, people, or sensations of play that have spanned across the decades?

Here is what I found when I answered these questions for myself:

- The element of water has always played an important role in my life.

- I love being on two wheels.

- The uninhibited joy I experience while playing arcade games lasts to this day.

- Finding moments of lightheartedness and creating laughter is important to my soul.

- The sense of adventure—of being challenged or going outside of what's familiar—is a common thread from childhood to adulthood.

- I have always had a connection with animals, and I continue to seek out ways to connect with them whenever possible.

- Being in touch with nature is a balm to my soul.

Your turn. List at least seven commonalities, themes, and patterns between your past and current images of play.

PULLING IT ALL TOGETHER

Now that we've done our research on play, let's bring this all together to identify your individual expressions of play. Play is its own branch, or expression, on your tree but can be expressed in many different ways. Your goal now is to identify all the ways in which you can play so that when you're in the thick of life, brain racing and to-do items piling up, you can review your list and make play as accessible as possible.

We want to make sure that your expressions of play fulfill Brown's seven properties. If they don't, then you've either identified an avocation, like I did when I considered my athletic endeavors to be play, or perhaps you've hit on something that is more of an obligation than play. I know that as a mother I often feel that I *should* view certain activities with my children as play. Shouldn't I find reading to my daughter at night utterly blissful and want time to stand still? Is there something wrong with me if playing *Uno* with my son feels like an obligation rather than pure fun? Is it bad that doing certain activities with my kids can feel like work to me?

These are judgments that are easy to make about ourselves. Let's face it, we don't spare ourselves much when it comes to criticism, and we rarely miss an opportunity to beat ourselves up a bit. But hear me when I say that it is okay—in fact, it's *really* okay—if your expression of play doesn't match someone else's expression of play. Yes, it's important that you engage in the expressions of play defined by your loved ones—we'll explore that more in depth when we dive into key relationships—but someone else's expression of play in no way needs to define yours. Your expressions of play should be unique to you and free of judgment from your inner critic and the voices of others. This *has* to be a self-indulgent exercise that fully embraces *you* That is, after all, what play truly is.

> "Play is the highest form of research."
> —Albert Einstein

You may have already identified many of your expressions of play in the second step of this exercise, but see if you can identify some new possibilities to explore based on the overlapping themes you found when comparing your childhood joy to your adulthood joy. We'll split the list into expressions of play (actual activities or how you can "do" play) and elements of play (the feelings, emotions, components, and motifs of play).

Here are my expressions of play, some proven and some newly discovered thanks to reflecting on the commonalities between what I loved as a child and what I still enjoy as an adult:

- Being in the ocean (snorkeling, swimming, floating, bodysurfing, boogie boarding)

- Doing free-range exploration (unstructured cycling, running, driving with loved ones)

- Retro rollicking (playing arcade games in dive bars, singing and dancing to '80s music)

- Communing with nature (hiking, exploring tide pools with the kids, horseback riding)

- Engaging in wholehearted connection (having conversations with close friends, going on date nights)

- Listening to live music (attending outdoor concerts, riffing on the piano or guitar)

- Doing Sunday morning crossword puzzles

- Binge watching my favorite shows

And here are my elements of play as identified by recurring and strong themes:

- Adventure (at least one element of the unknown or an element of risk)

- Lack of inhibition (in an environment where anything goes)

- Relaxation (no pressure of time)

- Nature (outdoors, on an island or in the sea)

- Creativity (watching or taking part in the live creation of art)

- Spontaneity (freedom to take a "left turn")

- Intimacy (with myself, family, or a close circle of friends)

Now it's your turn. First, list your expressions of play.

_____

_____

_____

_____

And now, list your elements of play.

Thanks to the work you just did, you should now have a list of play expressions along with your elements of play. If you started this chapter feeling a bit cynical or perhaps having lived without much play in your life, I sincerely hope that you have come to understand the importance of play and have identified some ways in which you can start exploring play for yourself. If you desire to be creative, innovative, adaptive, connected with yourself and others, resilient, malleable, and plastic, then play is your new best friend. We need it as children and we need it, perhaps more, as adults. The goal is to express play at least once a week as we work through the rest of the expressions.

"Whoever wants to understand much must play much."
—Gottfried Benn

Now that we have spent time mining for what brought us some of our earliest and recent images of joy, let's dive into the next expressions: avocation and vocation.

EXPRESSIONS 2 AND 3:
AVOCATION AND VOCATION

"Twenty years from now you will be more disappointed by
the things that you didn't do than by the ones you did do.
So throw off the bowlines. Sail away from the safe harbor.
Catch the trade winds in your sails.
Explore. Dream. Discover."
—attributed to H. Jackson Brown,
P.S. I Love You

While avocation and vocation are two distinct forms of expression, I've combined them into one chapter for practical reasons and ease of use. First, in determining these two expressions, there is a lot of overlap in the exercises. Instead of having you perform these exercises twice, you'll do them once. Second, the primary difference between a vocation and an avocation is whether or not it provides you a necessary source of income. You may be in a situation where you do not require a vocation. In that case, an avocation will be your primary focus. And, finally, I want you to keep an open mind as you explore these two expressions, so first we will explore them without the labels of avocation or vocation. Later on in the process, we will determine whether or not an expression could be a potential source of income. With that said, let's begin.

EXPRESSION 2: AVOCATION

The second expression, avocation, includes activities we do for pleasure first, rather than to earn money. While avocations can be a source of income, we don't engage in them for that reason alone. Earnings are a bonus, not an expectation. An avocation is the next extension of ourselves as we work out from play, which is our center, our fully self-focused expression. Avocation moves one step beyond that center, often affecting others. If I had to put a percentage on the weight of intention, I would say that play is a hundred percent focused on benefitting self with zero percent obligation to benefit others. However, avocation would be around seventy-five to one hundred percent focused on benefitting self and zero to twenty-five percent focused on benefitting others, although these numbers can certainly range well beyond that. Avocation is where we can regularly participate in activities and efforts that we're passionate about without the concern of how much we earn while doing them.

These activities can also be opportunities to help others in ways that our vocation doesn't allow, such as mentoring, volunteering, coaching, participating in a group effort (such as a quilting bee or fund-raiser), or endeavoring on our own to create what we feel compelled to express. It could be stretching ourselves in some capacity, seeding our own future and our next vocation by way of entrepreneurial efforts, or simply putting our talents and gifts to good use. An avocation is where we find a way to express elements of our inspiration, core values, and personal manifesto without the pressure of outcome.

Avocation could also be thought of as a "slash career," a term Marci Alboher popularized in her book *One Person/Multiple Careers:*

The Original Guide to the Slash Career. She found that more and more people were looking for ways to either boost their income, find greater fulfillment in their work, or simply make a difference. Instead of relying on one main source for this, such as a single vocation, many of us are building more creative and fulfilling lives by braiding together multiple expressions to create and complete our own tapestry of a fully realized life. This thinking is right up my alley because I've always been baffled by the prevailing belief that our vocations should reflect our inspiration, values, sense of purpose, and passion in totality. While it's possible to strike this kind of luck, it's incredibly rare. More often, we catch glimpses of this kind of epic synchronicity in short stretches of time, but it's difficult to sustain because what drives us continues to shift as we experience life and are in turn shaped by those experiences. We are much more able to adapt to shifting desires if we can add or replace an avocation or find a new source of play instead of having to drop our one big thing, typically our vocation, and exchange it for another of equal importance and weight. There's more ease, flexibility, and responsiveness in the former approach.

Some examples of people with slash careers that Alboher interviewed in her book are lawyer/minister, nurse/photographer, and teacher/decorator. For some, the left side of the slash was their left-brained activity while the right side represented their opportunity to be creative. For others, the left side represented plan B in case their riskier right side was still under development or simply unreliable and ill-suited as a full-time career. In both cases, having a slash career gave these individuals the opportunity to find passion and meaning in their work.

> "The life you have led doesn't need to be the only life you have."
> —Anna Quindlen

For the purposes of crafting our tree and its branches, which represent our key expressions, I want us to frame avocation as an opportunity to express an element of ourselves that we feel compelled to express in a greater way than we're able to do through play or a vocation. Vocation has pressure associated with it because it generally represents our earning potential and is our lifeline to sheltering and feeding ourselves and our loved ones. Play, on the other end of the spectrum, is completely without pressure—totally free of expectation and purpose. Avocation sits somewhere in the middle, straddling an element of purpose without fear of results or the lack thereof. Again, your avocation (or avocations) may be a hundred percent focused on benefitting yourself or it may have an aspect of benefitting others. However that percentage falls for you is spot-on as long as your avocation scratches that itch you've been unable to reach through your vocation or other endeavors in life.

EXPRESSION 3: VOCATION

The third expression is vocation. Here, the ratio of intending to benefit ourselves versus others might be closer to 50/50; we look to benefit others as much as we look to benefit ourselves. With a vocation, let's face it, the focus on benefitting others *has* to be a significant component, because this expression is typically based on an exchange. We give our talents, our time, our energy, and our expertise to another entity so that we will benefit in some way, typically in the form of a paycheck. The more we contribute, the more we are monetarily rewarded for those efforts. Or at least that's the way it's supposed to work.

Hopefully, you're also getting other benefits such as a community of like-minded rebels or a tangible sense of changing the world or a flexible environment that allows you to live an easeful life or opportunities to stretch yourself and expand your horizons or, even better, all of the above! The real danger lies in allowing the scales to tip beyond 50/50 into the self-flagellating, victim-y, or downright abusive territory of 75/25 and beyond. That's when we know we've got a problem, and we need to examine how we're spending our days.

The way I used to frame vocation was as a job. You punch in; you punch out. You get what

> "Live like someone left the gate open."
>
> —Anonymous

you need whether it's status, money, accolades—some sort of compensation we dream will fill us up only to find it's a hollow promise.

Vocation, instead, infers a kind of calling, a *strong desire* for doing the work one *should be doing*. It's not trying to gobble up self-worth at some job while bleeding ourselves dry. It's not defaulting into a career because we found we're good at it and so, hey, let's stick with what's working. It's not mindlessly flitting about, hopping from one short-lived position to another.

A vocation in its truest and best form is an intentional trajectory mapped intimately with our inspiration. And while a vocation may shift or change from time to time, the one through line that remains consistent is its marriage to our calling at that time. As we shift, all the unique strands that make up our life also shift. If we feel a pull toward something new, we might introduce a new avocation to explore it. If and when it sustains over time, we find a way to transform that new avocation into a vocation.

Let's look at what those potential threads, or strands, can be for us. The reality is, we may not find our most inspiring work in our vocation at this point and time. As much as I'd like to say that our ideal path is always lined with bright lights and welcome signs, it isn't. There's often some searching, exploring, and navigating we must do before we can make our way to the next oasis beyond the mirage. Because of this, it's important that we not only define what it is we're seeking—become intentional with our lives—but also explore both areas of vocation and avocation to find where it is we can pick up a thread in this moment to begin seeding and manifesting the life we desire. Let's get started with honing in on what those opportunities may be for us.

WHAT ARE YOUR EXPRESSIONS OF AVOCATION AND VOCATION?

I often find that the biggest limits in our lives are the ones we place on ourselves. We box ourselves in, saying things like: "I'm a terrible artist," or "I'll never be as good of a writer as Susie, so why even try?" or

"That works for John because he's a natural innovator," or "I'm forty-something years old, why bother?" These beliefs are all ways in which we impose limits upon ourselves. Limits that we either have fully bought into because of a bad experience, sharp criticism, or the need to protect ourselves from taking a risk. None are good enough reasons to hold back from pursuing that *one thing* we've always secretly fantasized about. The good news is that we can gently reach out and braid in that which we've dreamt about. We no longer have to think of these pursuits as an about-face or complete career change. Instead, they are facets of ourselves that we can incorporate into our life.

Exercise: What Are Your Special OPS?

The first step in locating potential expressions of avocation and vocation is to revisit the work we did in inspiration and then find our opportunities, passions, and strengths, known as our special OPS. We want to remind ourselves what makes us tick, what strikes a chord in us, what fires us up, why we feel we've been placed on this planet.

Step 1: Discover Your Opportunities, Passions, and Strengths

First, reread your personal manifesto, core values, and personal mission statement. Then answer the questions that follow. Many of these questions are similar to ones you've already answered; the goal is to draw out your strengths more and more. By answering them you will eventually arrive at the core of what makes you unique. If your answers overlap, phrase your responses differently. Force yourself to provide a unique answer to each question, because it will uncover nuances that may be helpful. For example, if I am identifying my strengths, I might answer, "Building relationships." I could easily provide the same answer when identifying my natural talents. I want to dig a little deeper, so instead I might say, "Creating strong connections with people by tapping into what they're passionate about." Identifying your OPS is a process similar to Michelangelo's process when he sculpted David. As he put it: "I saw the angel in the marble and carved until

I set him free." These questions are meant to act as chisels to knock away everything superficial until your angel is revealed.

Opportunities

- What is a struggle for me, yet worth persevering through?
- What is difficult for me, yet highly rewarding?
- What would I like to learn more about?
- What would I like to master?
- What have I always wanted to be, say, or do but have never had the courage to pursue?

_____

_____

_____

_____

_____

_____

_____

_____

_____

Passions

- What am I drawn to?
- What brings me joy? (Revisit your expressions of play and elements of play.)

- What are my interests or areas of interest?

- If I could make a positive impact on the world, how would I do it? (Revisit your personal mission statement.)

- If I were to say that I had a passion for something, it would be . . .

_____

_____

_____

_____

_____

_____

_____

_____

_____

Strengths

- What are my strengths?

- What are my natural talents?

- What comes easily for me?

- What do others say I excel at?

- What makes me great?

_____

_____

_____

_____

_____

_____

_____

_____

_____

_____

Step 2: Connect the Dots

Now scan your answers. Do any of these OPS currently show up in your daily life (e.g., through work, hobbies, books, or clubs)? If so, list them. Next highlight the answers from step 1 that connect with a current form of expression in your life. The nonhighlighted items represent OPS that currently lack expression; you might investigate both expressed and unexpressed OPS for possible avocations or vocations.

Example

- OPS: Building Relationships
- Expression: My work in consultative sales

_____

_____

_____

_____

_____

_____

_____

_____

_____

Step 3: Ask Others

Let's now invite the perspectives and thoughts of others. Choose three people whom you trust wholeheartedly and admire. Explain to them that you are examining your life and taking inventory of all the ways in which you express your potential and inspiration. Let them know that you value their perspective and that there are no wrong answers. What you truly seek is their unadulterated view of you so that it might provoke new discoveries about yourself. You can ask the questions in person or through email. I think there are potential benefits and downsides to each, so I don't see an issue with doing this either way. If you opt for email, please remember that we each possess our own internal dictionary, and without the in-person cues, it's easy to ascribe the wrong meaning to a line of text. That said, if you need or desire clarification, ask for it. Here are the questions:

Opportunities

- Where do you see my greatest opportunities for growth?

- What obstacles have you seen me tackle that bring me a sense of pride and are highly rewarding, even when difficult?

- What do you hear me speak about doing yet take no action to accomplish?

- When you imagine me mastering an art or skill, it would be . . .

_____

_____

_____

_____

_____

_____

_____

_____

_____

_____

Passions

- What do you see me gravitating toward?
- When do you see me at my happiest?
- What do you perceive as my interests or areas of interest?
- If you were to guess my passion, it would be . . .

_____

_____

_____

_____

_____

_____

_____

_____

Strengths

- From your perspective, what seems to come easily for me?
- What would you say my gifts are? My natural talents?
- Is there an ability in me that seems innate?

_____

_____

_____

_____

_____

_____

_____

_____

Step 4: Connect the Dots Again

Now, again, do a quick inventory and scan for answers from Step 3 that currently show up in your life (e.g., through work, hobbies, books, or clubs). List them and then highlight those OPS that you are able to currently express. The nonhighlighted items represent OPS that lack expression; you might investigate both expressed and unexpressed OPS for possible avocations or vocations.

_____

_____

_____

_____

_____

_____

_____

_____

_____

_____

Exercise: Identify Your Potential Avocations and Vocations

Taking what you learned in the preceding exercise, the highlighted items you're currently expressing and the nonhighlighted potentials, explore whether these items could be expressed as avocations or vocations that aren't currently in your life. For instance, if I had listed "natural comedian" as one of my strengths and "to make people feel good" as one of my passions, then I might come up with the following ideas:

Potential Avocation(s)

- Stand-up comic (Take an acting or clowning class; participate in open mike nights; join Toastmasters.)

- Goodwill ambassador (Volunteer at children's hospitals and retirement homes.)

Potential Vocation(s)

- Client relations or customer service role (Work for progressive company who cherishes their clients.)

- Trainer in the power of laughter (Develop course and market to businesses who are focused on culture.)

You get the idea. And that's just taking two prongs. Let your imagination run wild; let there be no limits to the audacity in which you dream up possibilities. No one will make you commit to any one of these, but you sure as hell will get a lot of great ideas and potential clues. And, hey, if you do follow one of these on your list, would ya let me know? I love hearing your stories. Okay, it's your turn. Go! Follow my example and list a few potential avocations and vocations based on your OPS lists.

OPS Aspects

_____

Potential Avocation(s)

_____

_____

_____

Potential Vocation(s)

_____

_____

_____

OPS Aspects

_____

Potential Avocation(s)

_____

_____

_____

Potential Vocation(s)

_____

_____

_____

OPS Aspects

_____

Potential Avocation(s)

_____

_____

_____

Potential Vocation(s)

_____

_____

_____

OPS Aspects

_____

Potential Avocation(s)

_____

_____

_____

Potential Vocation(s)

_____

_____

_____

OPS Aspects

_____

Potential Avocation(s)

_____

_____

_____

Potential Vocation(s)

_____

_____

_____

I hope you thoroughly enjoyed this exercise. Dreaming up possibilities has always been a favorite pastime of mine, because it activates the creative brain while also bringing what's in our subconscious forward, where the universe can conspire to help us manifest our greatest desires. As a result of this exercise, you should have a list of potential avocations and vocations. In the final section of this chapter, I'll ask you to identify one to three avocations (currently being expressed or newly discovered!) and commit to pursuing at least one of them. But before we get too far ahead of ourselves, let's dive deeper into our current work situation. We need to take a peek under the hood to see if the time spent here is well worth it. Or if we might be due for a change.

Exercise: Job or Vocation?

If you're currently employed, go through the steps that follow to determine where you are on the spectrum of being employed in a job versus engaged in a vocation. The closer you are to vocation on the spectrum, the more aligned you are in this expression with your inspiration. Conversely, if you're tending toward the job end of the spectrum, it's an indicator that some shifts need to take place in order to get you better aligned.

Step 1: Analyze Your Workweek

First, let's break down a typical workweek. In table 6.2, list the tasks, activities, and responsibilities involved in a typical workweek, along with the percentage of time you spend performing them, the primary feelings you experience when performing them, and whether or not they connect with an element of your OPS. If tasks, activities, and responsibilities repeat throughout the week, there's no need to list them more than once. Simply estimate the total percentage of time you spend doing them over the course of a week. Our goal is to capture all the pieces that come together to reflect what a normal week consists of. In table 6.1, I've provided an example of how a typical workweek could be broken down.

Tasks/Activities/ Responsibilities	Percentage Of Time	Primary Feeling(s)	Connects w/OPS
Submitting Expense Reports	10%	Bored	No
Client Calls	45%	Invigorated; Connected	Yes
Team Meetings	20%	Engaged	Yes
Data Entry into CRM	15%	Flatlined	No
Fulfillment Tracking	10%	Agitated	No

Table 6.1. Example of Tasks, Activities, and Responsibilities in a Typical Workweek

Tasks/Activities/ Responsibilities	Percentage Of Time	Primary Feeling(s)	Connects w/OPS

Table 6.2. Your Tasks, Activities, and Responsibilities in a Typical Workweek

Step 2: Tally It Up

Now tally up the percentages of positive versus negative feelings. (I would say "bored" and anything to the left of that should be considered a negative feeling. Anything to the right of "apathetic" I would consider a positive.) Give yourself a point for each percentage. In my example, my positive feelings totaled sixty-five percent, so I would write sixty-five in the Positive Feelings field. The remaining thirty-five percent would be written in the Negative Feelings field.

POSITIVE FEELINGS: ___ %
NEGATIVE FEELINGS: ___ %

As you may have guessed, the percentages speak for themselves. If you're weighted primarily in the negative, then you have a job. If you're weighted on the positive, chances are good you've got yourself a vocation. But being a loophole kind of person (as in, if there's a way around an argument or equation, I'll find it!), what if my positive feelings only account for thirty percent of my experience *but* those positive feelings are shot-out-of-a-rocket amazing? Kind of like really good sex? Should I still be concerned about the seventy percent mundane negative feelings? As I pose this question to you, I think of the years I spent in high tech experiencing massive waves of unbelievable excitement, adventure, and pure adrenaline. When things were good, man, they were *good*. And then there were the off days or weeks that, in comparison, were a total letdown. The culture was sick, the egos unchecked, the technology more important than humanity. It was a series of steep highs with cascading lows.

If I had done this exercise during that time in my life, I might have easily ended up with that 30/70 ratio. So is it okay to stay? Does it mean I'm "happy" and "good" if the highs are so epic? My answer is no. I don't care how you classify the highs compared to the lows, if you're in the negative spectrum longer than you are in the positive, you're playing to something smaller than yourself. You're making yourself small or you're compromising too much or you're chasing the next high like a junkie needing a fix. My advice to you would be the same advice I give all my kvetching-but-still-gonna-stay friends in high tech: Get what it is you need and then leave. And in the meantime, stop giving those negative feelings so much attention. You're there by choice, so while you are there, feed what is positive. At the very least, you can still work to protect your inner life.

Step 3: Discover If Your Work Connects with Your Inspiration

So down off my soapbox and back to this exercise. For those of you on the positive end of the spectrum, your vocation may well remain a great match for you. But let's check in with how it connects to your inspiration and how it's affecting you and those in your life. This next set of questions is for everyone, no matter where you fall on the positive versus negative feelings spectrum.

I now want you to total up your positive and negative points to find the net effect. A percentage point in the Positive Feelings column equates to a +1. A percentage point in the Negative Feelings column equates to a -1. So, for example, if I had 65% positive feelings and 35% negative feelings, my total would be 30 points (65-35). Now you do the math and write in your totals using the following formula:

POSITIVE FEELINGS: ___ POINTS
NEGATIVE FEELINGS: (___) POINTS
TOTAL: +/- ___ POINTS

Now use the following formula to overlay components of your OPS (opportunities, passions, and strengths), personal manifesto, and personal mission statement to find how inspired the work is. For every yes, where a task, responsibility, or action from step 1 connects to an element within your OPS, manifesto, or mission statement, give yourself 5 points. Subtract 5 for every task, responsibility, or action that does not connect. For example, I listed three items that don't connect to my inspiration (submitting expense reports, performing data entry, and doing fulfillment tracking) so I would give myself 15 points in the Uninspired column. I would then give myself 10 points in the Inspired column to reflect the items that do connect—participating in team meetings and making client calls. Here are my calculations:

INSPIRED: 10 POINTS
UNINSPIRED: (15) POINTS
TOTAL: - 5 POINTS

INSPIRED: ___ POINTS

UNINSPIRED: (___) POINTS

TOTAL: +/-_____ POINTS

Finally, determine the overall impact by bringing the two totals down (the net effect of your positive versus negative feelings and the net effect of your inspired and uninspired work and calculating the sum. Here are my calculations.

POSITIVE/NEGATIVE TOTAL: + 30

INSPIRED/UNINSPIRED TOTAL: -5

OVERALL IMPACT: + 25

POSITIVE/NEGATIVE TOTAL: +/- ___

INSPIRED/UNINSPIRED TOTAL: +/- ___

OVERALL IMPACT: +/- ___

If your total is 100 or more points, congratulations! You are likely in a fairly ideal situation—one that is not only creating joy but is also allowing you to exercise your strengths. But if you're in the red, you're in need of a major overhaul. And if you're somewhere in the middle, a closer look is needed, as you are likely running into obstacles when it comes to your happiness or your ability to exercise your natural talents and strengths. In these cases the reasons for our frustration or lack of long-term fulfillment can be a little harder to spot. We need to look beyond the surface.

Sometimes coming home week after week in a crappy or blasé mood isn't the whole story. To add insult to injury, we can find ourselves not only feeling like shit but completely devoid of purpose. Redundant. Empty. Disposable. Irrelevant.

Or maybe we come home from work feeling like a hero on a regular basis! Ego stroked, chest puffed out, accomplishments garnered, the bad-assery looming large in us. We level *up*. And up. And up. But does it have meaning beyond making us feel good? Beyond making us money? Is there a point to our current existence? Are we a polished trophy for others to admire? Or are we stockpiling trophies? Where is the inspiration in all this effort?

Of these two scenarios, I find the feeling-like-a-hero situation to require the most amount of digging deep. In the first scenario, we can't feign comfort. We're already uncomfortable, so taking a risk and seeking out an actual vocation versus the job we have is a step we're more willing to take. We are already closer in proximity to risk, so whereas this might seem like a leap to some, it's more of a small stretch to this group.

However, if we've become conditioned to an abusive environment, then there is work to be done in our inner life. We need to find a different way to exist, a way to leave behind the drama and trauma, if we wish our next step to move us into a positive direction versus only sidestepping into a different version of the same hell. If this is you, and you haven't already done the inner life work, I encourage you to flip back to chapter 1 and dive in. I can attest, from personal experience, that you have to value yourself first before you can receive the value others see in you. So go back and get cracking.

If you're in that second group, racking up accomplishments and feeling comfortable, but your job has no connection to your inspiration, change is usually a tougher road. Let's face it, it's easy to get used to a certain kind of living, especially when you have all the creature comforts such a life can afford. You likely have decent compensation, status, perks, plaques on the wall, and the admiration of others. Those are nice things to have! I know. I had them. But if you aren't rooted in inspiration, then you will someday reach the end of that road, paved with all your perks and accolades. You'll reach either a spiritual dead end or a professional one as long as *you* remain out of your own future—content to travel on autopilot in shallow waters.

When we disengage with life, it eventually disengages with us. It gets what it needs and then moves on with no remorse. We're not so lucky. We get hammered when we are proverbially kicked to the curb. We feel used up, unappreciated, confused, defeated. We wonder where karma is hiding out. Didn't we just give the best of ourselves to this career or organization or boss? Where then, exactly, is the universal justice that says the world owes us what we put forth? Ahhhhhh, it's because we've forgotten about dharma. There is no positive karma when one is living outside their dharma.

Dharma, in Hinduism, is an organizing principle that all existing beings must accept and respect to sustain harmony and order in the world. In the context of our discussion, dharma is the pursuit and execution of our true calling. Only then are we playing our unique role in cosmic concert with the universe. For example, it is the dharma of a bee to make honey, of a cow to give milk, of sun to radiate sunshine, of a river to flow. We each must discover our own unique dharma, but the through line for all of us is that following our dharma connects us to each other and to the essence of what sustains life and this universe.

PULLING IT ALL TOGETHER

When I first began dreaming up this book, I was still in my previous career, running a training company. As much as I wanted being an author and getting this work to readers to be part and parcel of that job, it wasn't. It couldn't be; the responsibilities and volatility of that career weren't welcoming to any new pursuits. If I had sketched out my avocation at that time, author would've been my expression for that, with my vocation resting as CEO. As fate or fortune would have it, being an author shifted from an avocation to my vocation when I finally trusted myself, followed my dharma, and wholeheartedly committed to writing this book. Today, my vocation is author, educator, and provocateur, and my avocations have become athlete and advisor/mentor. When I completed the exercises in this chapter, my answers revolved around similar themes: my passion for resolving the stilted and disjointed lives I feel we're living, my passions for leadership and building businesses, and my passion for athletic endeavors, such as triathlons (and sometimes even actually participating in a few races a year!).

With my new rearranged avocations and vocations, I am now able to focus on what I am passionate about and in the appropriate amounts. Because authoring this book has become my North Star, I have made a shift so that it can pull as much focus as it desires from me. By making it my vocation, it naturally gets a healthy front-row seat in my life. But I still get to flex my other muscles literally and figuratively. My avocation of being an advisor and mentor to others allows me to keep my knives sharp and play in the leadership and business world, which I absolutely adore doing. I can also exercise my other passion by continuing to train in the sports I enjoy because being an athlete is my second avocation. The essence of the braids in my life hasn't shifted dramatically, but how I express them has.

> "If you don't make the time to work on creating the life you want, you're eventually going to be forced to spend a lot of time dealing with a life you don't want."
>
> —Kevin Ngo

This process of refining and shifting our vocations and avocations is alchemic in nature. We can shut something off completely or add something new, resulting in a drastic transformation, or we can adjust the pressure or output of each, refining our evolution so that what's needed now can emerge. Whatever the process required, the desire is to achieve the alchemy that sings to your soul and your soul alone.

With that said, let's determine what shifts may be appropriate for you. This is where *you* will play with the braids available to you and craft your ideal scenario. In this way, we will go from current situation to ideal situation and then make a plan for today and the near future. Let's begin.

Current Situation

My Avocation(s)

_____

_____

_____

My Vocation(s)

_____

_____

_____

My Ideal Situation

My Avocation(s)

_____

_____

_____

My Vocation(s)

_____

_____

_____

Take a look at the gap between your current situation and your ideal situation. If the leap seems tremendous, please know that we can pick up each strand, one at a time, and braid it in. I am not always a believer in flushing everything out before beginning anew. In fact, when we're dealing with expressions such as avocation and vocation, that have so much impact on some pretty important aspects of our lives, I think testing our theories is a good approach. Something may look great on paper or in the moment, but will it sustain us? To find that out, choose one shift at a time. In the last chapter of this part of the book "Expression," we will piece together a game plan to do just that.

Let's now move on to the final expression, key relationships, where we join with others while embodying a full expression uniquely our own.

EXPRESSION 4:
KEY RELATIONSHIPS

"Remember that the best relationship is one in which your love for each other exceeds your need for each other."

—attributed to the Dalai Lama

Here we are at the fourth and final expression, key relationships. As with so much in this book, I really struggled with the order of each expression, as no matter how often you say that order doesn't matter, some amount of importance is still assigned to the number in which they appear. I will tell you that the *only* reason key relationships comes fourth is simply due to the fact that the progression of exercises from play to avocation and vocation made the most sense when laid out sequentially. I'm a big believer in momentum. I've seen it do its thing in sports, work, relationships, and habit-change, taking us on a quicker and quicker track to success or utter failure, so I wanted to use momentum to my advantage when building up to our avocations and vocations, because these two areas often command the majority of our time. Had it not been for that, key relationships would've come second. Aside from the necessity of play to fill our own cup, I believe those who are key in our life are second to none when it comes to living and expressing ourselves fully.

WHAT ARE KEY RELATIONSHIPS?

Key relationships speak to the significant relational roles (often familial) that exist outside of any vocation or avocation. These are relationships we have deliberately signed up for and are committed to at a deep level. We also spend a significant amount of time engaged in them, whether that deep, emotional, and spiritual connection allows for physical presence or is nurtured across space and time due to a temporary physical separation of some kind. Here are the three criteria for a key relationship:

1. It is by choice. *You* desire the relationship; it hasn't been thrust upon you, and it is free of obligation.

2. You are highly engaged, highly committed. You give four or more hours a day to this relationship.

3. It stands alone. This relationship exists outside of any other role (coworker, business partner, boss, etc.).

Let me expand on each because I know we could interpret these a lot of different ways!

By Choice

With "by choice," I mean not under duress or obligation. Okay. So I know that not *every* day you're thinking, "Man! I have the most perfect partner/spouse/child/BFF/whatever in the world! Not a day goes by that I wouldn't choose to have this awesomeness in my life! Especially when they're making my life fucking hell!" If you do think that every day, you're not human. Or at least I'm highly skeptical of your genetic makeup. Even with my own kids, I often find myself wondering, "Why me? Why did I get this particular combination of highly emotional, hardheaded, who-needs-common-sense, my-way-or-the-highway bundle of DNA?" On those days, which are at least one out of thirty, I feel as if one or both of my kids has been thrust upon me. The only thing keeping me from running out the front door like a lunatic is a sense of obligation mixed with deep maternal love—that and Child Protective Services showing up on my front door. Some days, I have those moments with my wife, too. I know I said, "I do" all those years ago. Sometimes I forget why.

Does that make me a bad person? Hope not! It certainly makes me honest, but, more importantly, it makes me human. It's what makes all of us human. To worry, to fret, to have our ups and downs, and then to work our way back to one another in the end. Or at least give it one helluva shot. What makes my relationships with my kids and my wife key relationships is that I am in them because I choose to be. At this moment, I wouldn't want it any other way. Aside from the not-quite-ready-for-prime-time moments when one or more of us is in an individual or collective mess, I desire these relationships wholeheartedly. The sporadic moments of feeling obligated are just that—*feelings*. The truth is, I'm there by choice, and happily so. That said, my two key relationships are with my wife and my kids.

What *doesn't* make a key relationship are the relationships that we participate in primarily out of a sense of obligation. The ones we are paid to be in or would flee and never choose if we felt like we didn't *have* to be there. Being a caregiver could be a prime example here, because it is a relationship often born and continued out of duty.

Another example would be a codependent relationship where the need to feel worthy and useful is tied up in another's need to be taken care of. Whether it's helping someone get off booze, get off welfare, or get out of another abusive relationship, basically out of a personal hell, whatever that may be. We tell ourselves that if we leave, this person will fall apart when the truth is, we'll fall apart. We say that we stay out of guilt, but the sense of shame we have for ourselves is the real reason we stay.

The former example, the caregiver, while not a key relationship (one made out of delight and free choice), is certainly an important aspect in our overall ecosystem. Instead of being a relationship that extends from our own tree, it is its own tree, tightly situated against ours. The latter example, the codependent relationship, when chosen with delight by us, can represent a key relationship, albeit a highly toxic one. Should we allow any extension or expression of ourselves to be toxic in nature, it will poison our entire tree, making us sick. In these cases, with these "black holes," we must untangle ourselves from them and, instead, set them aside to anchor in their own soil—not ours.

For the caretaker who feels strangled yet obligated to provide support or the adult child who has to feign love for a detached, uncaring parent who has long since ceased contributing anything meaningful to the relationship, put those individuals in perspective. They live *outside* of you. As important as those people will always be in your life—love 'em or hate 'em—I understand that for many, there needs to be a constant "tending to" of these relationships. That's okay, if it's okay with you. And while no one can remove the burden that comes with situations of that nature, remember that these people in no way need to be *attached* to your tree. They may sit close to you, five feet from you, or a hundred yards away. Whatever distance you need to keep safe from any toxicity they produce. Just like with your kula, you can decide the impact they have on you. Limit them or welcome them in appropriate measures.

Your key relationships are the ones that bring a grin to the corner of your mouth when you think of them in your mind's eye. You aren't there due to any moral, material, or monetary obligation or because you'll receive anything (sex, drugs, free rent, etc.) in exchange for spending time with this person. Nope. This person is in your life simply because you desire it. The only expectation is that you bring your best self to the relationship every single day.

Examples of a key relationship could be your spouse, partner, coparent, mother, father, soul sister, brother, daughter, son, BFF, my one and only—you get the idea. Anyone, and I mean anyone, can be a key relationship as long as it meets the three criteria. The first of which is a relationship you walk into with eyes wide open and of free will.

Let's explore the second criterion, significant interaction for four or more hours a day.

High Engagement/High Commitment

What do I mean by "high engagement"? I mean that this relationship is one in which you are truly *actively* engaged for at least four hours a day, maybe more. Yes, I know, this much time can make achieving the first criterion of "by choice" a little more difficult. Let's face it—the more time we spend with people, the more likely they are to get on our nerves. This is exactly why a high level of engagement and commitment is one of the criteria of a key relationship. It sort of separates the boys from the men or the dilettantes from the connoisseurs; key relationships aren't the easy-peasy, coast-along relationships that make us feel awesome all the time because we get to have *major* distance from them whenever we want. Nooooo. A key relationship is one that is a bit more challenging, requiring us to dig deep on a regular occasion to remain deeply connected in spite of our day-to-day demands.

That said, high engagement does *not* necessarily require physical presence. Sometimes physical separation is part of a key relationship. For example, after my parents divorced and my sister and I would spend time with one parent, such as our mother, it did not mean that my dad didn't have us engaged in his heart for several hours each day. I know that if I were physically separated from my children I would still have a tight tether on their hearts, actively thinking of them and imagining what they were doing with each hour. For others, it's a spouse who has been temporarily relocated for work reasons. Or a service man or woman deployed to some far-off land. Or, perhaps, a couple in a tenuous place in their marriage, hoping to work things out but not sure how—or if—it's possible.

The factors that create the physical separation are not important. What truly matters is your ongoing level of engagement and commitment. For example, if you've separated from your spouse and have moved beyond reconciliation and into envisioning a new future that does not include them, yet your spouse has not, then this person is

no longer a key relationship for you. You may still be a key relationship for the spouse or partner you've separated from, but that doesn't
mean you have to mirror someone else's tree. On the other hand, if
you are physically separated from your children, your best friend, your
partner, or your beloved, and you actively cultivate a relationship with
them through shared spiritual connection, active communication, and
a deep-seated commitment to loving each other to be your best selves,
then they are absolutely key relationships. In fact, I have seen divorced
couples, often who have children together, remain key relationships
because of the way they continue to care for and nurture one another
beyond their previous roles of spouse. When that happens, let me
tell you, it's a beautiful thing. It's the depth that matters here, which
underscores the second component of this element, a high level of
commitment.

We can't be in a key relationship and not have the dedication
required to navigate our fair share of rapids. If we weren't in it wholeheartedly, then we'd probably bail after the first or second wipeout.
To be committed means full presence on a daily basis while projecting a long-term vision. We aren't just hedging our bets based on this
moment; we're investing in the future. By attaching this relationship
to our tree, we are symbolizing our desire to *be* in this relationship.
Not just have it. To exist in the present moment, just as it is now. And
to reach and strive for growth. There's an intertwinement, a sense
of giving deep love while embracing deep love from another. In that
way, we can experience the raw, tender, powerful, and transformative
essence of love itself.

Stands Alone

Finally, our key relationships need to be able to stand alone outside
of any other roles they may occupy in our life, meaning they aren't
duplicates we've copied over from an avocation or vocation. Here's
what I mean: My wife and I met while working for the same company, then we worked together at another company, then we worked
together at a third company, and now we're working together again.

I know. Crazy. Working with a spouse, best friend, or family member is *not* asking for the easy road, and it introduces a whole new layer of complexity and hazards into a relationship. In one case, I have a happy ending to share—Deli and I continue to thrive in our relationship while enjoying collaborating together. And in the other case, I have the epic, disastrous, planets-colliding ending to share—two of my familial relationships were, at least temporarily, decimated thanks to the intermingling of family and business ownership. These two endings are exactly why it's so important to distinguish a key relationship and the role that accompanies it from an avocational or vocational relationship and the role that accompanies it. Being able to stand on its own is the single most effective tool in maintaining the health of those more complicated relationships, no matter where they sit on your tree.

For example, Deli currently occupies a facet in two branches on my tree. She is woven into my vocation of author, educator, and provocateur because she and I collaborated heavily in bringing this book to life. We could often be found huddled together, penciling out new concepts for retreats or challenging our current beliefs and finding new tidbits to share with each other. Collaborator, or coworker, is one kind of relationship I have with her as it relates to my vocation. But she also fully occupies another branch on my tree—as my wife she represents a key relationship that is of great importance and significance to me.

Collaborator and wife are two distinct roles that deserve distinct means of nurturing. How do I know this? Recall my stories about two different endings resulting from mixed business and familial relationships. I've seen it over and over again: Misunderstandings about the family business erode trust between a father and son. Or a nasty divorce between a once-affectionate couple destroys goodwill between them. I, too, have pressed my nose close to the pavement, nearly losing it all with Deli, when one or the both of us were too focused on our work, allowing our relationship to career out of control.

It's for these reasons that we need to categorize the people we love deeply as key relationships. If we don't, then we run the risk of only relating to our husband, wife, son, daughter, or whomever on the transactional, matter-of-fact plane of business, and the personal aspect of the relationship begins to wither. It becomes lost. Where we spend time and focus are the areas of our tree that we flood with sunlight. We feed and nourish the areas we cultivate.

If we are always hanging out with a loved one in the context of vocation and not in the context of a key relationship, then those relationships atrophy, sometimes beyond repair. The reason we are tethering these people to our tree as a key relationship is so we are less likely to drift away from them over time. When we turn toward a branch such as our vocation and remain there for any length of time, it's akin to being in the sea with our back to the shore. We don't realize we're drifting. We can only sense the shift in our position when we turn around and see the shore. If we let our relationships drift for too long, we'll have a *lot* of ground to make up, especially when the currents become stronger. Remember momentum? The longer we remain in a current that pulls us away from something, the freer and faster it carries us away. This means much more effort is required on our part to not only shift the tide but to pull ourselves back to our loved ones. Our key relationships will always require a certain mindfulness from us, and that is why it's important they are visible on our tree.

And now that we understand what a key relationship is, let's move on to identifying the key relationships on our tree.

EXERCISE: WHAT ARE YOUR KEY RELATIONSHIPS?

Let's begin by listing the key relationships in your life. After you've written them down, we'll check each against our criteria.

_____

_____

_____

_____

Criteria 1: By Choice

1. Are you in this relationship solely because you choose to be?

2. Are you receiving any compensation (materials, money, favors, or otherwise) for being in this relationship?

3. Is there an expectation that this person will receive something from you in return for your company?

4. Do you feel obligated to this person in any way?

5. Are you in this relationship due to feelings of guilt or fear of what will happen should you leave?

If you answered yes to questions 3, 4, and 5, this is not a key relationship. Draw a line through the name. If you answered yes to question 2, make note of that. (If you answer yes to question 1 in Stands Alone, then this person may remain a key relationship. If the answer is no, then draw a line through the name.)

Criteria 2: High Engagement/High Commitment

1. Do you spend more than four hours a day actively engaged with this person, whether in a physical or spiritual manner?

2. Are you looking at this relationship as a short-term escapade or temporary union?

3. Do you remain committed to this relationship largely because this person has professed a commitment to you?

4. During periods of physical separation, do you find ways in which to communicate with this person on a fairly frequent basis?

5. When this person is not around, would you say the phrase "out of sight, out of mind" applies to your feelings?

If you answered yes to questions 2, 3, and 5, this is not a key relationship. Draw a line through the name.

Criteria 3: Stands Alone

1. If you have a relationship with this person through another area of your tree (play, avocation, vocation), does this person hold a distinct role outside of that (such as partner, spouse, child, parent, etc.)?

2. If you are a caretaker for this person (which would live in avocation or vocation), would you still desire a separate and distinct key relationship with this person?

3. If you currently work with this person (which would live in avocation or vocation), would you still desire a separate and distinct key relationship with this person?

4. Is placing this person on your tree as a key relationship a strategic or advantageous attempt to better a situation in another area of your tree, such as avocation, vocation, or play?

5. If you stripped away everything else—all other branches of your tree—would you be fulfilled by having this person as one of your only relationships in life?

If you answered yes to question 4, this is not a key relationship. Draw a line through the name. (Remember, if you answered yes to question 2 in the By Choice section and no to question 1 in this section, then draw a line through this person's name.)

PULLING IT ALL TOGETHER

Next to the names that remain, define your role in relationship to this person (e.g., husband, wife, mom, dad, BFF, brotha-from-another-motha).

Name: _____

Relationship/Role: _____

Name: _____

Relationship/Role: _____

Name: _____

Relationship/Role: _____

Name: _____

Relationship/Role: _____

Name: _____

Relationship/Role: _____

Now you have identified your key relationships. We'll be using both the nature of these relationships, or roles, and the names of those you chose when we craft our tree. We'll track how much time you're spending in a particular role and how you're affecting those on the other end of that role. As with any healthy, beautiful, vibrant tree we want to not only have strong branches jutting out from our well-grounded foundation, but we also want to ensure we're producing and inspiring blankets of hearty fruit and succulent leaves. We will dive deep into that specific area of our tree in part 4, "Impact." For now, let's craft our tree by bringing all the pieces of play, avocation, vocation, and key relationships together.

CRAFTING YOUR LIVING TREE

"To live is to express, and to express you have to create. Creation is never merely repetition. To live is to express oneself freely in creation."

—Bruce Lee, Striking Thoughts: Bruce Lee's Wisdom for Daily Living

Here we are in one of my favorite chapters of the book, where we get to express our creativity and craft our tree. Any opportunity I can get where I am able to focus on my life, do a little dreaming, and create a plan along the way is an opportunity I rarely miss. It's a bonus if it results in a piece of art or graphical representation. Being a visual person, I enjoy these kinds of cues. They sure beat the heck out of a Gantt chart or a long list of to-do items.

Our goal in this chapter is to craft our living tree, the visual representation of a fully connected life. We will use the model of a tree to display and represent all the facets of our inner life and the expressions of our desires. The model also serves as a visual reminder of our key relationships so while we're chasing down various dreams or playing outside, we never lose sight of what is equally important: the loves of our lives. In part 4, we'll explore strategies to maintain the health and wealth of our tree. But first, let's piece together the branches of our trees, our expressions.

EXERCISE: WHAT ARE YOUR EXPRESSIONS?

First, let's bring forward the work from the previous three chapters: "Play," "Avocation and Vocation," and "Key Relationships." Please refer to your answers from the exercises in chapters 5 through 7 to answer the following questions.

Step 1: State Your Expressions of Play

What are the expressions of play you identified?

_____

_____

_____

_____

_____

_____

_____

Next list the elements of play you discovered.

_____

_____

_____

Step 2: State Your Expressions of Avocation and Vocation

What are your current avocations and vocations? And what did you identify as your ideal avocations and vocations?

Current Avocation

_____

_____

_____

Current Vocation

_____

_____

_____

Ideal Avocation

_____

_____

_____

Ideal Vocation

_____

_____

_____

Step 3: State Your Key Relationships

Finally, what are the key relationships you identified and what is the nature of the relationship or role?

Name: _____

Relationship/Role: _____

Name: _____

Relationship/Role: _____

Name: _____

Relationship/Role: _____

Name: _____

Relationship/Role: _____

Name: _____

Relationship/Role: _____

Now that we have all of the potential elements of our expressions in one place, let's move on to the next exercise.

EXERCISE: YOUR CURRENT LIFE VERSUS YOUR IDEAL LIFE

Let's take a look at the components of a typical day for you, looking beyond your vocation and the work we did in that chapter. Having two young children, I know that there are times that I wonder what, exactly, a typical day is. Each day seems so terribly random that I've forgotten what normalcy feels like or what it's like to have things go as expected, so I understand if you're searching, wild-eyed, right now for "typical." Relax. I'm not going to come over and study you for a day to see if you nailed it just right. Rather, I want you to take all the components that most often come together to create a typical day and enter them in table 8.2. (Look at table 8.1 for an example.)

Then expand a bit to incorporate other fairly significant activities you do over the course of a week. For example, if you work out on Mondays or you meet with your writing club on Wednesdays, you will include those items in the shaded areas that indicate a rounded-out week.

> "Life isn't about finding yourself. Life is about creating yourself."
> —attributed to George Bernard Shaw

Step 1: Describe a Typical Day and Week

As you'll see with the example in table 8.1, choose the tasks, activities, and responsibilities that you feel are significant enough to note. Feel free to clump some items together into categories like "household errands" or "business meetings" that happen throughout the day in differing intervals. If you prefer to list things as they happen and not bundle anything together, that's okay too. As we did in avocation and vocation, we're looking to capture the overall essence of how you spend your days and weeks. Remember to include those activities that are just for you.

Here are some questions to prompt your thinking about each column in the exercise (again, the shaded rows at the bottom are provided for you to round out a typical week):

- Where are you? (environment, surroundings)

- What are you doing? (tasks, activities, responsibilities)

- Who are you doing this with? (those you are surrounded by or engaged with)

- For whom are you doing this? (who you are serving)

- What are you doing that is just for you? (exercise, art, journaling, etc.)

- Does the activity link with a value or statement from your personal manifesto or mission statement? Do you feel

What are you doing?	Where are you?	Who are you doing this with?	For whom are you doing this?	Does it connect?	What do you feel?	Which type of expression is this?
Early morning commute	In transit	Yourself	Work	No	Primarily agitated, anxious	Vocation
Work emails	Office	Yourself	Work: colleagues clients, business relations	No	Indifferent	Vocation
Meetings	Office	Various team members and partners	Work: business	Sometimes	Often frustrated but occasionally engaged	Vocation
Client calls	Office	Clients	Work: clients	Yes	Helpful, connected	Vocation
Managing team	Office	Employees	Work: employees	No	Disinterested, distracted	Vocation
Project work	Office	Clients and team members	Work: clients and team	Yes	Stimulated	Vocation
Evening commute	In transit	Yourself	Work	No	Agitated; anxious to get home	Vocation
Dinner	Home	Family	Yourself and family	Yes	Happy, peaceful	Key relationship
Chill time w/ family	Home	Family	Yourself and family	Yes	Joyful, loved	Key relationship
Workout (twice a week if I'm lucky)	Gym or outside	Yourself	Yourself	Yes	Invigorated, Alive	Yourself
Date Night	Varies	Wife	Yourself and wife	Yes	Connected	Key relationship
Soccer practice (once a week)	Outdoor practice field	Sam	Sam	Yes	Excited, proud	Key relationship
House errands (weekends)	Home	Yourself or family	Family	No	Obligated	Key relationship

Table 8.1. Example of a Typical Day and Week

What are you doing?	Where are you?	Who are you doing this with?	For whom are you doing this?	Does it connect?	What do you feel?	Which type of expression is this?

Table 8.2. Your Typical Day and Week

deep-rooted meaning or connection when engaged in this activity?

- What do you feel? (the primary feelings you experience when engaged in this *doing*)

(See tables 8.1 and 8.2.)

Now that you have sketched out your typical day and week, answer the following questions:

- When you consider your typical day and week, what do you feel?

- How are these typical days and weeks affecting you? How are they affecting others?

- What are the ramifications if nothing changes, both positive and negative? For yourself? For others?

If the net effect of doing this exercise is a realization that there are, indeed, some things you'd like to shift or some things missing altogether (like play or "me time"), don't fret. In fact, it's perfectly normal and okay to realize that the life you once carved out as fulfilling and rewarding is no longer attaining those same levels in the present day. We need to revisit. We need to adjust. We need to evolve incrementally over time. Life isn't just something we can "let ride." That would be easy, but it would get awfully boring at some point. Let's now move on to imagining what an ideal day and week would look like.

Step 2: Describe an Ideal Day and Week

Time to play and visit the other side of the spectrum, our *ideal* day and week. Table 8.3 shows an example of an ideal day and week. In table 8.4, put together the elements that would create an ideal day and week for you.

Don't hem yourself in; we'll get to the part of marrying reality with fantasy in our next step. The goal now is to create a new vision for yourself even if it is a bit (or a lot) fantastical. One that connects with your values, manifesto, and personal mission statement. One that makes you sit up a little taller, lean forward a little more, and smile from the depths of your soul. First, scan your expressions of play, avocation, vocation, and key relationships to remind yourself of the possibilities. If the issue is with where you work or whom you work with, rather than what you do, then note that in the "For whom are you doing this?" column. If you have a future employer in mind or would like to start your own business, then enter that. If you are unsure of where you might ideally land, then write in as much as you know, such as the industry or region or, perhaps, the new division of your current employer. And if all else fails, write "TBD" (to be determined) when you just aren't sure. Do this in any case where what you're *doing* is fine but whom you're doing it with or for needs to change. Again, fill in the shaded rows at the bottom to round out your ideal week, and use the following questions to prompt your thinking about the answers in each column. Have fun!

- Where are you? (environment, surroundings)

- What are you doing? (tasks, activities, responsibilities)

- Who are you doing this with? (those you are surrounded by or engaged with)

- For whom are you doing this? (who you are serving)

- What are you doing that is just for you? (exercise, art, journaling, etc.)

- Does the activity link with a value or statement from your personal manifesto or mission statement? Do you feel deep-rooted meaning or connection when engaged in this activity?

- What do you feel? (the primary feelings you experience or imagine experiencing when engaged in this *doing*)

What are you doing?	Where are you?	Who are you doing this with?	For whom are you doing this?	Does it connect?	What do you feel?	Which type of expression is this?
Morning meditation	Home	Yourself	Yourself	Yes	Calm	Yourself
Seeing kids off to school	Home	Kids	Yourself and kids	Yes	Happy, content	Key relationship
Short commute	In transit	Yourself	TBD	No	Relaxed	Vocation
Work emails	Office	Yourself	TBD: colleagues clients, business relations	Yes	Indifferent	Vocation
Meetings	Office	Various team members and partners	TBD: business	Yes	Engaged, vibrant, useful	Vocation
Client calls	Office	Clients	TBD: clients	Yes	Helpful, connected	Vocation
Sr. project management work	Office	Clients and team members	TBD: clients and team	Yes	Stimulated, improving	Vocation
Evening commute	In transit	Yourself	TBD	No	Contented	Vocation
Dinner	Home	Family	Yourself and family	Yes	Happy, peaceful	Key relationship
Chill time w/ family	Home	Family	Yourself and family	Yes	Joyful, loved	Key relationship
Hike in nature	Varies	Yourself and family	Family	Yes	Free	Play
Train for 10K races	Outdoors	Yourself	Yourself	Yes	Challenged, alive	Avocation
Work travel (once a month)	Varies	Clients, work	TBD: business and clients	Yes	Excited, happy	Vocation
Workout (3x a week)	Gym	Yourself	Yourself	Yes	Invigorated, alive	Yourself
Date Night	Varies	Wife	Yourself and wife	Yes	Connected, loving	Key relationship
Soccer practice (once a week)	Outdoor practice field	Sam	Sam	Yes	Excited, proud	Key relationship
House errands (weekends)	Home	Yourself or family	Family	No	Obligated	Key relationship

Table 8.3. Example of an Ideal Day and Week

What are you doing?	Where are you?	Who are you doing this with?	For whom are you doing this?	Does it connect?	What do you feel?	Which type of expression is this?

Table 8.4. Your Ideal Day and Week

Step 3: Reflect on Your Ideal Week

Now sit back and, once again, reflect on the vision you've created while answering the following questions:

- When you consider this ideal day and week, what do you feel?

- If you were to manifest your ideal day and week, turning them into reality, how would it affect you? How might it affect others?

- When you look at your ideal day and week, which activities would you consider luxuries (highly desired but not necessary)? Which activities are discretionary desires (nice to have but not required)? And, finally, which are requisite (what you couldn't do without)? Note this next to each activity you entered in your chart. Make sure you include at *least* one expression of play in your requisite list!

Once you sort out the entries in your worksheet, take a moment to review the luxuries, discretionary desires, and requisites. Did everything fall into one bucket, or predominantly so? Is everything a requisite? If so, why is that? Are you being realistic with your needs versus desires? Or maybe everything was a luxury? If so, why are you shortchanging yourself and not allowing for your own needs? Finally, was everything a discretionary desire? If so, why the noncommittal line of thinking? Why are you afraid to stake a claim one way or another? Do you need to recategorize your activities, being more honest and courageous with yourself this time around? Do you have at least one expression of play in your requisite list? The most essential piece of this exercise is nailing your requisites. We will come back to these shortly.

> "Don't let the noise of others' opinions drown out your own inner voice. And most important, have the courage to follow your heart and intuition."
>
> —Steve Jobs

Now that we have snapshots of your current and ideal situations, let's feather the two together to create your life, adjusted.

EXERCISE: YOUR LIFE, ADJUSTED

The third exercise within this set presents an opportunity to design your life, intentionally. Whether it requires only a few tweaks or a major overhaul, the work is just as essential. Small shifts, sometimes after making a few gigantic leaps, are necessary to stay current with yourself, your needs, and your desires. A fine piece of equipment requires periodic, routine adjustments to extend its lifetime and maintain peak performance. We are no different. Just because we don't have a decal sitting on our windshield reminding us when *our* next service date is doesn't mean we should ignore the need. To do so is to turn our back on ourselves.

Let's begin with hitting the "reset" button and building the life we desire. We will do this by designing a life that is attainable within the near future (six months to one year) so that we don't become overwhelmed by our own aspirations; making incremental shifts rather than completely exchanging one life for another is often a more realistic approach. However, if you have the courage, circumstances, and means to make that kind of major overhaul, then please go for it! I would never want to hold people back from revolutionizing their lives! For many of us, though, such drastic change isn't within reach, because we may have a spouse or children to support, commitments we need to see through, or any number of extenuating circumstances that make life a little stickier. In those cases, we'll need to take things a bit more slowly as we incorporate some new elements while maintaining much-needed stability. Here are the steps.

Step 1: State Your Requisites

Unlike the previous exercises we did in part 3, "Expression," include components that you'd like to see over the course of a day, week, month, and year. First, review the list of requisites from table 8.4,

Your Ideal Day and Week, and write them down in table 8.6, Your Life, Adjusted. The unshaded lines are for activities or expressions that you already do or could easily begin to do, meaning there's no great leap needed in order for you to begin or continue doing them. The shaded lines are for your "blue-sky" activities—expressions that aren't possible to begin today or tomorrow but you feel you could shift to in six months to a year.

Step 2: State Your Necessities

Next, identify which aspects of your life are necessities that haven't already been represented in your ideal day and week. By necessities, I mean anything that, for practical reasons, you need to hang on to. This might be your current vocation, for example. Let's use this step to capture anything that is downright essential to your life, even if it didn't make the cut in your ideal day and week. You'll place most necessities in the unshaded rows, as they are likely already happening. But if you have a current vocation that isn't making ends meet and you need to repair that ASAP, then write your new vocation in the shaded area as something you need to get to. Simply list "Current job" in the unshaded area instead of repeating all the activities, tasks, and responsibilities that go along with it.

Step 3: State Your Discretionary Desires and Luxuries

Now revisit your discretionary desires and luxuries and determine which ones can be included in this current vision. In other words, which can happen, or are happening, now? And which ones could become a reality in six months to a year? You can revisit those items that are more long-term desires next year during your personal retreat, when you complete this exercise again.

Review the example in table 8.5, and then fill out your own vision in table 8.6.

What are you doing?	For whom are you doing this?	Does it connect?	What is the need?	Which type of expression is this?
Morning meditation	Self	Yes	Requisite	Self
Morning commute	Work	No	Necessity	Vocation
Workout (3x week)	Self	Yes	Requisite	Self
Current job	Work	Mostly not	Necessity	Vocation
Dinner	Family	Yes	Requisite	Key relationship
Chill time w/family	Family	Yes	Requisite	Key relationship
Date night	Wife	Yes	Requisite	Key relationship
Soccer practice (once a week)	Sam	Yes	Requisite	Key relationship
Household errands (weekends)	Family	No	Necessity	Key relationship
Hike in nature (once a month)	Self and Family	Yes	Requisite	Play
Annual 2-week family vacation	Family	Yes	Requisite	Key relationship
				Key relationships
				KR
				KR
				KR
See kids off to school	Family	Yes	Requisite	Key relationship
Short commute	TBD	No	Requisite	Self
Senior role in project work at top firm (no employees reporting to me)	TBD	Yes	Requisite	Vocation
Train for 10K Races	Self	Yes	Discretionary desire	Avocation
Work travel (once a month)	TBD	Yes	Luxury	Vocation
Participate in one 10k race	Self	Yes	Discretionary desire	Avocation

Table 8.5. Example of a Life, Adjusted

What are you doing?	For whom are you doing this?	Does it connect?	What is the need?	Which type of expression is this?

Table 8.6. Your Life, Adjusted

Step 4: Do a Sanity Check/Reality Scan

Now that we have a complete picture, take a good, long, thorough look at your life, adjusted. Here are some questions to consider:

- What is your threshold for risk? Are you taking enough risk by including some substantial blue-sky desires in your adjusted life? Or are you playing it too safe? On the other end of the spectrum, are you being unrealistic and living only in the future, wanting to make too many shifts at once? Only you know the answer. Listen to your instincts, your inner coach. What is it telling you?

- Do you have balance? I don't mean in how your hours are parsed out; rather, does this exercise depict a life with at least one branch of each expression? Or are you heavily laden down in vocation with nothing to show for play or avocation?

- When you look at this picture of your life, are *you* happy? Are *you* inspired? Are you connected with *your* inspiration? Or are you dressing yourself up for someone else? Is there anything in here that's for show or to please another? Or is it all one hundred percent authentically *you*? This is your one life. Make it your own.

Step 5: Identify Roles and State Intentions

In the final step of this exercise, we want to take our adjusted life and assign the associated activities, tasks, and responsibilities to the appropriate role. For example, all work activity would be assigned to my role of "project manager," if that were my title. Once we have those distinctions, we'll write an intention for each of those roles. Our roles are how we will identify each branch of the living tree we will craft shortly that represents our life. The intended targets (who bears the impact of our roles) are the leaves on the end of that branch. Setting a clear intention for each role is one way in which we will keep an eye on our impact as we explore the fourth and final section of the tree.

When I speak of roles and multiple activities under one role, it might look something like this. If one of your activities is "reading to my daughter" and another is "coaching my son in Little League," these two activities could be combined into the role of parent, mom, or dad. Whom you are doing it for would be both your children. And the type of expression would be key relationship. It's also quite possible that your role of a Little League coach also serves as another type of expression: avocation. If that's the case (i.e., you have genuine interest and gusto about being a Little League coach, and you're not just doing it to spend time with your kiddo), then choose the expression that is most dominant. Identify the *primary* reason you are engaging in that activity and tag it as such. Again, refrain from judging yourself. If you put down Little League coach as an avocation over key relationship, there is absolutely *nothing* wrong with that. Let all of what you are passionate about have the permission and space to exist. There is room for everything. And everyone.

To identify intentions, get quiet and commune with yourself about why it is you're engaged with a particular role and what you wish the impact of this role to be on your intended audience or target. You can think of it as creating mini mission statements or a statement of intention. For example, as a mom, part of my intention is "to give my kids love and affection and to instill in them the belief that anything is possible." Given my own experience of how vitally important it is to receive *unconditional love and affection* as a child, it's essential for me to point that out in my intention for my role as a mom. Such love wasn't modeled well by one of my parents, so I need a strong reminder to do it myself. We tend to mimic or follow the patterns set down before us; this specificity is one of my strategies to break that cycle.

As an athlete, one of my avocations, my intention is "to challenge myself in ways known and unknown in pursuit of pushing my own limits, and to maintain health in all aspects of my life—relational, spiritual, physical, and mental." My intention states why I'm drawn to being an athlete while also reminding me to keep my feet on the ground. When I state, "to maintain health in all aspects of my life," it's a distinct reminder to not go overboard, to not sell out the health of my marriage for a faster bike split.

When you craft your intentions, slip yourself the reminders you need in order for you to embody that role as best you can while also reminding yourself why you chose it in the first place. Why did you become a mom or dad? Why did you marry your spouse or commit to your partner? What is it that calls to you as an artist, creator, inventor, or dreamer? Why have you said yes to the life you have created and what keeps you saying yes day after day? Find that core, the driving force or desire behind all of the yeses in your life.

To complete this step of the exercise, first bucket your activities into roles and then craft your intention for each role. For the expression of play, if you have several forms of play, like I do, simply use one line to encapsulate your intention for all forms of play. Refer to 8.6, Your Life, Adjusted, to ensure you've covered all the activities, tasks, and responsibilities listed. See table 8.7 for an example of this step of the exercise. Then state your own roles and intentions in table 8.8. Off you go!

(See tables 8.8 and 8.9.)

EXERCISE: A CALL TO ACTION

Now that you have all of the essential elements of your tree—both viable today and desired in the near future—let's tackle those expressions that are in your blue sky, your future pursuits. Every dream, every goal, every idea yearning to be manifested requires a plan. And, personally, I hate that, because I hate plans. Well, not *all* plans. I love a good operating plan, budget, and detailed project plan. But I don't care for plans that dictate how to achieve my own difficult dreams, like writing this book. I'd much rather fly by the seat of my pants and magically appear at the fairyland of "dreams come true" or "that shit got done somehow," but sadly for me, and others like me, that isn't the way things work. Or at least I haven't figured out how to hack it yet. And I have tried. Boy, have I tried.

Some of the strategies I have employed that *don't* work are

What is your role?	For whom are you doing this?	What is your intention?	What is the need?	Which type of expression is this?
Author, educator, and provocateur	Public	To restore deep, meaningful connection and well-being in people's lives. And to effect the same change in the American workplace.	Requisite	Vocation
Executive coach, mentor, and advisor	Business community	To support my peers by instilling in them the confidence and insights needed to grow themselves and their organizations.	Discretionary desire	Avocation
Mother	Niko and Uma	To give my kids unconditional love and affection. And to engender the belief that they can be and do whatever they dream.	Requisite	Key relationship
Wife	Deli	To give and experience deep, passionate love. And to bring joy and support to all facets of her life.	Requisite	Key relationship
Athlete	Yourself	To challenge myself in ways known and unknown in pursuit of pushing my own limits. And to maintain health in all aspects of my life—relational, spiritual, physical, and mental.	Requisite	Avocation
Play	Yourself	To remind myself that life isn't all about the *doing* and that some things are meant to be enjoyed free of judgment, outcome, and results.	Requisite	Play
Connector	Public	To bring like-minded experts together to raise awareness and solve the issues that have created an epidemic of stress and dissatisfaction.	Discretionary desire	Vocation

Table 8.7. Example of Roles and Intentions

What is your role?	For whom are you doing this?	What is your intention?	What is the need?	Which type of expression is this?

Table 8.8. Your Roles and Intentions

procrastinating, pretending to forget, crossing fingers, drinking shit-loads of wine, pushing pixels around in my writing app, and engaging in staring contests. This is only a partial list of strategies I employed to write (or not write) this book. The *hardest* thing in the world for me to do was sit down, alone, and write the thoughts that come into my head, most of which were surprising in their sheer absurdity and utter lack of helpfulness in anything that had to do with this book and its topic! One second it was kittens, another it was how to be a better parent. It was very confusing. But then I realized that I needed a Plan and, yes, one with a capital *P.*

If I were to ever finish this book, I was going to have to hire a coach. Which I did. And without my coach, this book might have taken me ten years to write. No joke. Why am I shar-ing this? Well, because for you to manifest what *you* desire then you, too, need a plan. Sheer passion, enthusiasm, and desire isn't enough to mate-rialize your dreams. If that were so, look out, world! I'm positive that by now we'd have those hover boards promised to us in *Back to the Future* (the real deal, not the wheeled, fire-prone ones!). But no, things aren't that simple, especially when we're working on behalf of our-selves. Give us a mandate to benefit someone else and we're usually all over it. But when it comes to us, we often slip into old patterns of placing ourselves last on the list.

> "If you do not change direction, you may end up where you are heading."
> —Lao Tzu

To navigate from here—wherever "here" is for you—to your goal of "there," you'll need to do just as I did and figure out what kind of support you need. Whether it's getting a coach—someone you're accountable to and who can help you create that plan—attending classes, gaining specific experiences, or getting your questions answered. Whatever it might be, do it! And start with a game plan to get the ball rolling.

Table 8.9 will help you consider obstacles to your progress. Will you get distracted? Will you sabotage yourself because, deep down, you don't feel you're worthy of achieving your desire? Will you get stuck in overwhelm, not knowing what to do and freeze? Will it be some combination of all of these? Hopefully you get the idea.

For me, it was distraction, and if I'm totally honest with myself, a good dose of self-sabotage. I had built success for other people for so long that I forgot how to do it for myself. And somewhere inside, I wasn't sure if I deserved success. Working diligently on my inner life is what finally snapped those tethers around my spirit. Between those practices and hiring a coach, I was able to manifest this book. Now it's your turn.

Step 1: Know Your Needs and Potential Obstacles

First, identify the needs and potential obstacles for each blue-sky item. What is going to try and stop you from manifesting your vision?

Potential Obstacles/What I Need

Example
Blue-Sky Item: Author
Book coach for accountability

Blue-Sky Item: _____

_____

Blue-Sky Item: _____

_____

Blue-Sky Item: _____

_____

Blue-Sky Item: _____

_____

Blue-Sky Item: _____

_____

Blue-Sky Item: _____

_____

Blue-Sky Item: _____

_____

Blue-Sky Item: _____

_____

Blue-Sky Item: _____

_____

Step 2: Make a Plan

Once you've identified your obstacles and needs, let's craft a call to action for each one. For each potential snafu, hurdle, gremlin, underminer, or hindrance, identify at least two, if not three, actions you will take to help smooth out the bump. I'd also like to see you identify one partner in crime or confidante, especially if hiring a coach isn't in your plan. There have been a lot of studies on whether or not it's helpful to share your goals with others and, quite frankly, the data is split right down the middle. Turns out, putting your goals on blast and telling everyone is often detrimental, as it can trick our brains into thinking we've already achieved our goal. It can also put extra negative pressure on us to succeed.

That said, I don't recommend running out of your home and telling everyone about your new vision. Instead, find one person to share your entire vision with, or at least one element of it. This should be someone you can trust not to blab it all over the neighborhood, someone who can support you in the way you ask them to—whether it's to lend an ear, hold your hand, or kick your booty. The best option, if possible, is to find someone you can do an element of your plan *with*. For example, if there's a course you need to take, is there someone who can join you? If not, network with at least one of the other students and become support buddies so you can cross the finish line together.

Bottom line: Telling too many people is usually counterproductive to achieving our goals. On the flip side, doing it alone is also often counterproductive. My advice is to find one person whom you feel safe sharing your vision with or bringing along on a piece of the journey.

In table 8.9, I share an example of an action plan. Create your own action plan in table 8.10.

Blue-Sky Item	Obstacles or Needs	Actions Needed	Resources Needed	Conversations Needed	Time frame	Confidante/ Supporter
Find senior project work at XYZ, Inc.	Need resume.	Freshen up resume.	Find out from recruiter how I should format resume.	Call Joe.	Joe: End of next week.	Annie
	Need to find out if it is as good as I think.	Contact Joe who works there.	Ask Joe what recruiter he used.	Call recruiter, once I have a referral.	Recruiter: By end of this month.	
	Need recruiter.	Hire recruiter.	Search LinkedIn and other websites for job postings and salaries.			

Table 8.9. Example of an Action Plan

Blue-Sky Item	Obstacles or Needs	Actions Needed	Resources Needed	Conversations Needed	Time frame	Confidante/ Supporter

Table 8.10. Your Action Plan

This is the part where you proverbially shake my hand, look me in the eye, and agree to commit to your action plan. Or, better yet, this is where you call the name in the last column and share what you are doing and what kind of support you need. If this is the case, I recommend sharing everything in the table row that this person's name is associated with, especially the "time frame" data. That's something your confidante can stick on a calendar, along with a prompt to check in with you two to three weeks before that deadline arrives.

Here in Seattle, our football team, the Seahawks, has a tradition that I quite like. Before players run out to the field for practice or for a game, they reach up and tap a sign above the threshold that says, "I'm ALL IN." It reminds the players that they have just committed wholeheartedly to what lies ahead. It's time for you to do the same. Be "in!" today, tomorrow, and next week. Hit that sign in whatever way you want to, but make it a ritual. We all need reminders; no exceptions here. Now on to bringing all this work together.

EXERCISE: CRAFT YOUR LIVING TREE

I've saved the best for last, which is nice considering the colossal amount of work you've just undertaken. The culmination of all of this effort is that you'll now craft your living tree, representing your connected life—one that brings all facets of your life together—as we've now worked through every component of the model. Your soil is your foundation, the nutrients that feed and sustain your inner life, physical well-being, and environment. Your inspiration represents the roots. Your expressions, specifically the roles within each expression, are your branches and are the physical manifestation of your inspiration. And, finally, the leaves sitting at the end of each expression, or branch, are your intended targets—*whom* you are doing this expression for or whom you are intending to reach. Figure 8.1 is an illustration of my tree at the time of publishing this book. While I suggest you craft your living tree to represent your current or adjusted life, you can certainly craft a second version to represent your ideal life. I have found it incredibly powerful, especially when working on large goals, to have a visual in front of me. The choice is yours.

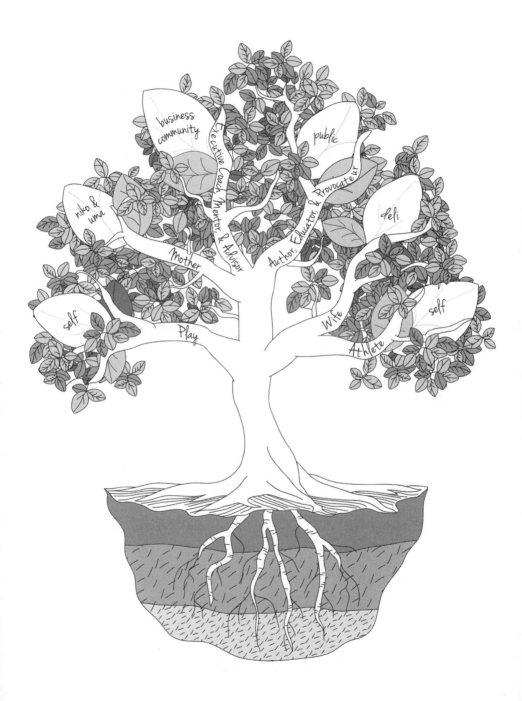

Figure 8.1. My Tree

Figure 8.2. Blank Tree

To create your own tree, either freehand it if you have that type of talent (I do not), or use the template provided here. (You can also download the template from www.lifeincorporated.co.) Once you've designed your living tree, I recommend printing it out and placing it somewhere you will see it each day. This is your visual of your *life*! This is your reminder of why you're here, what your intentions are, and what needs your time and attention. If and when things change for you, reshape your tree to reflect what's current. Keeping yourself aligned with your inspiration is essential, and when your inspiration changes, your expressions may change, too. As with all living and growing things, we must constantly nurture what we have and make adjustments when needed.

> "You don't need anyone to tell you who you are or what you are. You are what you are."
> —John Lennon

It is my hope that when you look at your tree, you have a profound sense of pride and joy. You can see what makes you unique, and I hope that from now on, you *never* lose sight of it. See figure 8.2 to create your own tree.

CONCLUSION

You did it! You have crafted your living tree and laid out a vision of how you'd like to see your life shift in the future. Through your hard work, you've identified your inspiration—what makes you tick—and you've explored ways to express your inspiration so it continues to fuel you and, in many cases, fuel others. Too often, we know deep down in our hearts the life we wish to lead and the passion we want to follow, but we don't give ourselves permission to do it. Or we don't have the tools to navigate the waters. Now you have permission to create the life you want and the tools to make it happen.

In this section, we learned the four types of expressions—play, avocation, vocation, and key relationships. Play is time spent without purpose and at one's own free will; it's time we wish we could extend and time we lose track of; it's adventurous, and it's something that makes us feel good—so good we couldn't care less about how we're perceived. The intent of play is to benefit us, first. It's the most personal expression and, indeed, the most important. Yet probably the most forgotten. Avocation is the next ripple out and, while it isn't play, it's an expression that ought to bring us great joy. In it is our opportunity to participate in something out of enjoyment, without the added pressure of expectation. This is where many people build a slash career, ensuring they're engaged with an endeavor that brings joy even though it doesn't pay the rent. It's also a great avenue in which we can build a bridge from a current vocation to a new one. Speaking of which, vocation is often where we sell out or accept less than we desire. Yet, one way to define "vocation" is work that we feel we should be doing—not just out of obligation but because we feel called to do it. And, finally, key relationships are the deep relationships we have made with others out of profound love and connection. These are the people who we've signed up for in a big way and who we envision in our life for the long run.

Once we identified what represents each of these expressions for ourselves, we then crafted our living tree. We will use this visual to remind us of all that we desire to be and do, along with who will reap the benefits of our efforts. It is here that we arrive at the leaves, the last major element of our tree.

Part 4

LEAVES:

IMPACT

If you think you're too small to have an impact, try going to bed with a mosquito.

—Anita Roddick

I love this quote. In an effortless, whimsical, yet potent way, it describes the extraordinary impact *any* creature can have on *any* thing. Being the unfortunate one in my family who is regularly feasted on by mosquitoes (why is that, by the way?), I can especially appreciate the havoc one teeny tiny insect can have on a grown-ass adult. Which brings me to the topic of this next section: impact.

I wonder how many of us flit around doing our thing while knowingly or unknowingly creating a stream of deserters behind us. I think of the giant in "Jack and the Beanstalk" traipsing through the forest, the seismic quakes from each of his heavy footfalls causing everyone to scream and run for cover. We're probably not being quite as destructive, but is there something in the way we are going about our life that is creating less than desirable results for others? Are we so focused on our own outcomes that we are unaware of or numb to the aftermath we leave behind? Or are we keenly aware of our impact on others? So much so that we forsake ourselves in the name of helping or pleasing others, causing the leaves on our branches pertaining to ourselves to dry up and crumble? In this section, we'll learn how to keep the leaves on our trees vibrant and green, our relationships healthy and flourishing.

The thing is, I *know* that deep down we want what's best for everyone, including ourselves, but sometimes something derails us from presenting our best selves and acting from that place of loving-kindness. So what is it? Why do we so often short-circuit from the life we aspire to lead to the one that's locked up in dissatisfaction and strife? That's the question I was pondering when I hopped on my trusty bike and dialed up a podcast from one of my aforementioned favorite Buddhist teachers, Tara Brach.

In this particular podcast, called *Compass of Our Heart*, she shared a story about a time when she was on a panel with several other teachers and thought leaders, and the moderator posed this not-so-trivial question: "What is the secret to finding happiness and inner freedom?" The moderator then told each panelist they had ten minutes to answer the question. Tara was second in line; Richard Baker, the American Soto Zen Master, was first. Baker stood up, walked to the microphone, and said, "The key to freedom is intention and attention." He then turned around, walked back to his chair, and sat down. I'm not sure what the Buddhist equivalent lingo of "mic drop" is, but that's exactly what happened when Baker delivered his short but very powerful insight.

> "A life is not important except in the impact it has on other lives."
> —Jackie Robinson

Baker's words helped me to clarify what it is that I am trying to articulate in this part of the book. Impact has two components, intention and attention. If we sleepwalk through the day, are unclear about our intentions, or act from a shallow place in ourselves, then our impact on others and ourselves is adverse. We get caught up in the trance of solving problems, acquiring stuff for the sake of acquiring, or simply trying to keep up with the day. However, when we take the time to set our intention and do it from a place of heart and depth, our impact is positive in nature. While my spin on intention and attention will vary from Baker's intended meaning, we would both agree that intention and attention are where the real work is in regard to impact. Impact is a result. Intention and attention are the drivers. With these two in hand, we can thoughtfully guide our impact instead of our impact landing on us.

In the following two chapters, we will explore each prong of impact—intention and attention. We will come into deeper understanding of how and why our intention can create positive results and how it can also seemingly turn against us. We'll raise our consciousness of the impact intention has on our lives, our relationships, and our results. We'll then dip into attention, focusing on being attentive to how we're actually affecting others versus what we hope to be true. Finally, you'll be introduced to the Life, Incorporated Journal, where we will measure our impact on all facets of our lives. We will explore the impact we have on ourselves, from our root system all the way out to the leaves on our tree, those in relationship with us. Holistically, we'll gauge the health of not only ourselves but also of all those engaged in our ecosystem. We'll start with intention.

INTENTION

"Our entire life arises out of the tip of intention."

—Buddhist teaching

You know that saying, the road to hell is paved with good intentions? Yeah, me too, and it's frustrating as hell. When I think about this saying, a couple of scenarios come to mind. First, there's the foot-in-mouth situation, like when you see someone you know after having not seen her in a while, and she's sporting a baby bump. So wanting to acknowledge and participate in the joy over this momentous event, you say, "Congratulations! When are you due?" But she looks you squarely in the eyes, lips pressed thin, and says, "I'm not pregnant." Ugh! That's a mistake you make only once. Trust me.

And there's the more hapless, oafish scenario where your idea is *awesome*, but your foresight and execution not so much. The term "unintended consequences" comes to mind. Here I'm reminded of one of my favorite movies, *National Lampoon's Christmas Vacation* and the ill-fated Clark Griswold character played by Chevy Chase. Two of the unintended consequences in the movie are Clark finding *the* perfect

Christmas tree only to discover it's about five feet too tall for the house and methodically stringing lights on every inch of the home only to blow the circuit breaker and electrocute the cat. Time and time again, Clark's best efforts to create a magical holiday experience for his family are thwarted by his inability to execute his vision or just plain rotten luck.

Of course it's hilarious when it happens to him, but it's usually not so amusing when we're the ones in the midst of a plan backfiring on us. Obviously, these two examples are on the lighter side of good intentions gone awry, because they represent what can go wrong when our intentions really are aligned with creating or doing good. But I have come to understand that the intentions predominantly paving our road to hell are far more insidious than the examples I shared. This is not because they are rooted in any kind of evil. It is because we are completely unaware of them. Let me share a story.

One evening, Deli and I were chatting in bed before shutting off the lights. Nothing unusual here except that I had had something on my mind the entire day, and I was desperate to share it. With two young kids, any kind of activity requiring privacy, including conversations and sex, usually takes place in our bed right before lights out. It's our sanctuary. Typically we end the evening on an up note. But as I said earlier, something had been gnawing at me. I was in the process of writing this book and was in full freak-out mode over the fact that I was not yet earning a regular income and neither was Deli at the time. She's a world-class facilitator and trainer and was still in the process of ramping up and getting certified in the new programs she wanted to deliver. Along with my anxiety over finances, I was having one of many moments authors regularly have, wondering how the *heck* I was going to make a living out of my writing! I was pretty convinced I'd sell exactly one copy of the book—I assumed my wife would be in for one, at least. So there I was. Churned up, anxious, and ready to chew through the mattress if I didn't get my concerns off my chest.

Deli, on the other hand, was in her usual relaxed la-la bedtime mode. She was writing in her gratitude journal, making a note about what the kids needed tomorrow, and meditating on the day. She was calm and serene, and I was about to "express" my concerns. You can see where this is going. It started out innocently enough with me blurting out that I was stressing over our financial situation. Deli responded calmly and said, "Okay, what's going on?" I started to describe our situation, how neither of us was making any money yet and how we were spending our small nest egg, which would eventually run out, and, by the way, what was her plan to start making money, anyhow? Did she have a timeline? What was her focus? Because, ya know, if my efforts were going to create an income, it was going to be a little while ,because I still had a lot of work after I was done authoring the book to get the word out. On and on it went like that. After each question, Deli would begin to reply in her Zen way, but I would quickly cut her off, my intensity ratcheting up another level. By the end of my five-minute, what-I-thought-would-be-a-conversation oration, Deli was as panicked as I was. It was 10 p.m., and any hope of a good night's sleep had flown out the window along with our sanity.

I'll pause the story there and ask the same question I asked myself when I finally managed to shut my jaw and sit in the awkward, tense silence that ensued. What had just happened? How had I gone from wanting to process a concern with my wife to saddling her with the weight of the world? And why had I steamrolled over Deli, flattening her with the same emotions that had cemented me in panic? It didn't make sense. I had honest, *good* intentions going into this. How could something so well meaning end up so wrong? I'll answer that question in a moment. First, I want to finish the story.

After a long silence, Deli bravely made one more attempt to respond. In an exhausted but sweet voice she said, "I don't know what to do, Halley. What do you want me to do?"

The sincerity and compassion in her voice slammed into my heart like a hammer; I was overcome with emotion. "I don't know," I said. "I'm just scared, and I don't want to be alone with it. I just wanted you to know."

From that moment on, we had a relaxed, productive conversation exploring our options and processing the efforts we were currently making. By the end of it, we realized that while our lives were, indeed, a bit chaotic at the moment, we did in fact have a plan, had had one all along, and we were actually doing quite well in meeting our goals, thank you very much! Our night ended on a bright note, and we felt as connected as ever. End of story. Now, we'll explore that sloppy middle part.

THE TWO INTENTIONS: PRIMORDIAL AND TRANSCENDENT

What I've come to understand is that there are always two intentions at play in any given moment. Our primordial intention sits on top of the water, is shallow in nature, and is reactive. It serves our ego and looks to fulfill our immediate, most basic, and obvious needs such as approval, superiority, and comfort.

The second, our transcendent intention, sits way below in the depths and is nestled in our heart, our best self, and serves a more noble and aspirational purpose—to fulfill our more subconscious, persistent desire for human connection, love, and belonging.

While we may step into every situation initially connected to our transcendent intention, our primordial intention often takes over at the slightest challenge or perceived threat to us obtaining what our heart desires. Or we are only conscious of our primordial intention and don't understand that what we are really after is far beyond the chip shots we're making on the surface. Our heart desires the deeper, transcendent intention, but our mind isn't in on the script. We bluster and grope along until we finally land on what soothes our heart. We don't know why it took so much to get there or, perhaps, why we were never able to reach a point of satiation, but in our gut we know it shouldn't have been as hard as all this. Both of these scenarios occur in us for differing reasons. One reason is that threat taps into our most basic human survival instincts. The other reason is that we lose touch with our most intimate needs.

My "conversation" with Deli perfectly demonstrated how two

> "Our intention creates our reality."
> —Wayne Dyer

intentions can be at war with one another and revealed a pattern in my behavior that explained a lot about why my interactions under stress usually created more stress before eventually finding a peaceful end. I can trace it back to my childhood and the learned behavior that was unconsciously instilled in me from watching a parent do the same thing. The pattern was that in order to gain the more deep-seated desire, or transcendent intention, of understanding and connection, I first needed to make others feel what I was feeling. In short, the only way I knew how to create connection was through the transfer of emotions. Instead of navigating directly to understanding and connection, my avenue was either fraught with potholes on a bad day or lined with wildflowers on a good day. If I was joyful then I needed everyone to feel joy, which is the upside of this particular pattern! Except, of course, on the odd occasion when others couldn't be roused into a good mood. Not only would I be confused but also disappointed in those situations. And guess what? If I was feeling disappointment then others would too, and that was the dangerous underbelly of the pattern. If I was feeling any discomfort, in order to feel connection, then those I was interacting with needed to feel the same discomfort, sort of meet me where I was before we could travel forward and obtain connection.

When I got eyes on that pattern, when it was lifted out of my subconscious into consciousness, it knocked the wind out of me. Yes, I was incredibly thankful for the discovery, because I could now shift this pattern within myself, but I also had to face the fact that I had inadvertently created a lot of unneeded discomfort in others. Feeling myself getting pulled down the muck-mired road of self-shame, I did the best thing I could at that moment: I began talking with others about my discovery, about these two intentions riding on top of one another and how I had allowed one to override the other, time and time again, for the sake of obtaining the other. It was in those conversations that I realized that I was far from alone. When brought to a level of awareness, it turns out that many of us are either unconscious of our own pattern of behavior or we simply lack the framework in which to consider how our intentions manifest results. I knew at that moment that this discovery was key in the stewardship of our relationships, the leaves resting atop our branches.

Using my example with Deli, I will illustrate how my particular pattern played out. You might catch a glimpse of yourself or gain a better understanding of how primordial and transcendent intentions work to create results—both good and bad. At the onset of my exchange with Deli, before I opened my mouth, I had my sights on the transcendent intention of wanting connection. I knew in my gut that I wanted to feel as though she were *with* me. That I wasn't alone in shouldering what felt like an unwieldy burden, that we were together and connected. As with most interactions at their onset, I was clear on the deeper desire, but my strategy to attain my desire was flawed. To arrive at connection, my strategy was to first satisfy the primordial intention of gaining comfort and safety by way of Deli matching my internal state. Here's how it played out.

The fear I was carrying around about our financial situation was big. It was intimidating, almost suffocating, and being the kind of person that I am, I do *not* like to feel out of control. It's like putting gasoline on a flame; it intensifies an already highly combustible situation. As soon as I put voice to my fears and felt the full impact of them, I engaged my limbic system, and my primordial intentions took over. When we engage our limbic system, shit gets real—or at least we *think* shit's real.

The limbic system is that area in our brain that helps us survive perceived threats. It's a complex system of nerves and networks that influences our instincts and moods. It controls basic emotions, such as fear, pleasure, and anger, and our drives, such as hunger, sex, dominance, survival, and care of offspring. The limbic system also goes by the name of "paleomammalian brain," which should give you an idea of just how long we humans have operated from this particular wheelhouse. The decisions made based on input from the limbic system are what have kept us alive throughout the decades of our evolution. When the alarm bells of the limbic system sound, our brain hijacks everything. Reasoning? Out the window. Thoughtfulness? Not a chance. Desire quickly turns into angst-fueled, electrified *need.* We start beating our chests and shift into fight, flight, or freeze mode where our focus becomes *very* self-centered. We're looking to get what we need—whether it's status, safety, advantage, or comfort of any kind—and, typically, attaining these needs comes at the cost of our own spiritual ease and well-being, as well as that of others.

As I talked to Deli that night, I engaged my limbic system, which, for me, meant a default swap from focusing on my transcendent intention of connection to my primordial intention of "feel what I feel" where, unfortunately, I had learned to find comfort and safety. I think we've all heard the saying, misery loves company. I now understand it on a whole new level. I might have once believed that this saying referred to callous people who drag others down into the mud with them. I now realize that it's simply the human condition: striving for comfort while being consumed by fear.

Every time Deli responded to me in a calm, soothing manner, it made me more agitated, because she wasn't matching my emotional state. My internal dialogue went something like this: "Why isn't she freaking out? Why am I the only one worried about this? Does she think this anxiety is all for nothing?" Because she was in a different emotional state than I was—calm instead of freaking out—I was unable to satisfy my primordial intention, and I had to keep ratcheting up the emotional static. Up, up, up, until finally, she flipped her lid. Then both of us were lit up like Christmas trees, wired for flight and buzzing like bees in a jar. That's when my nervous system calmed down. Why? Because my primordial intention of needing her to feel what I felt had been met. Without that need standing in the way, my transcendent intention of connection became obtainable. When she asked me what it was that I needed from her, I was not only able to hear her but I was able to calmly respond. I needed her to lock arms with me and understand what was troubling me. Which she did, and we connected.

As totally shitty as it was, my strategy got me what I wanted that evening, and that same strategy had delivered me a positive end result time and time again in the past. It was an insidious pattern that hijacked my interactions without me even being aware of it. In hindsight, my pattern should have been fairly easy to spot since it's a bit on the dramatic side. I see similar patterns in others unfold much more subtly, yet they are equally capable of preventing us from obtaining what it is we truly, *truly* want.

Here's another example. Linda, a marketing professional in a large software company, had the pleasure of meeting her new colleague, Beth, who had been hired to oversee sales in a particular vertical, or segment, of the business. The CEO had made it clear that the two sides, marketing and sales, were to collaborate together and put their best thinking toward kick-starting some seriously pathetic revenue numbers. Linda, being the social marketing butterfly that she was, was eager to lock arms. Beth, on the other hand, was much more reserved in personality and not quite as eager to pull the trigger on new messaging and strategies. This "lack of enthusiasm" in Beth bothered Linda, and the two of them had one awkward interaction after another. Beth would walk away wondering why Linda was constantly trying to cram her ideas down her throat. Linda would walk away wondering what flaws Beth was finding in her proposals. The more Linda tried to come back to the table, the more it seemed Beth would pull away. The situation was becoming an impasse, and the CEO wanted numbers soon.

A former colleague of mine, Linda is one of those rare gems who comes up with plenty of amazing insights. Perhaps that's why she's so good at marketing—she's made a living out of studying other people's behaviors. The gift that Linda has is that she can often turn her own instruments on herself. After the last big "hurrah" where Linda trotted out all her best ideas to, at best, a lukewarm reception, she realized that what she was after in that moment—and the ones preceding—was Beth's respect. Having worked with many other sales leaders throughout her career, Linda was all too familiar with the commonly held belief that marketing is a soft skill, only there to make things look pretty while sales wields all the power and has all the answers. Sales leaders are the ones who bring in the dollars, after all, and dealing with the egos that perpetuate that line of thinking had become nauseating for Linda. She was exhausted from sales leaders constantly devaluing her contributions and riding roughshod over her. She had brought that baggage with her into this new relationship with Beth, and instead of focusing on her transcendent intention of creating a partnership, she had been focused on her primordial intention of achieving the admiration and *respect* of the newly appointed sales director. In short, Linda had been getting in her own way. If there was to be a partnership between them, Linda needed to focus on the long-term trajectory and goal instead of her more immediate, basic needs of validation.

With this new realization in hand, her next meeting with Beth went very differently. Before Linda walked into the room, she paused to remind herself of the longer-term, deeper intention of partnership. Instead of throwing glossies on the table and flipping through slide decks full of concepts, she sat down quietly with nothing in hand but pen and paper. Taken aback by Linda's quiet demeanor, Beth was curious and pulled a chair up to the table. What happened from that meeting on would result in Beth's vertical outperforming the annual goal by over two hundred percent, thanks to savvy leadership from both marketing and sales. And the trajectory didn't stop there. The CEO wisely put the pair on another languishing product in which they engineered a similar turnaround. To this day, Linda is one of Beth's most trusted friends, and I always get a kick out of seeing them together at social engagements, clearly feeling such ease around one another.

> "From intention springs the deed, from the deed springs the habits, from the habits grow the character, from character develops destiny."
>
> —attributed to an ancient Chinese text

I have no doubt, as the quote states at the beginning of this chapter, that "our entire life rises out of the tip of intention." Life is not a passive exercise, and to choose passivity is, in actuality, an extremely active and definitive choice. Life can happen to you or you can happen to life, right? Wrong. No matter your philosophy, an intention precedes you. You have, indeed, actively contributed to your outcome by choosing to simply accept what comes your way or pull up to the wheel and grab hold. *You* are happening to your life, most definitely. And if you're reading this book, then you're certainly not the kind of person who has a laissez-faire attitude about your experience in this lifetime. You've already demonstrated that you're leaning in, wanting to understand more. That, in and of itself, suggests a transcendent intention to evolve and connect more deeply with yourself and others.

So what happens, then, during the other 364 days of the year when you aren't reading this book? How is it that we derail and end up engaged in difficult dynamics and encounters really not worthy of our time and effort? It certainly isn't that we have a *lack* of intention or that we're void of great intention. In fact, I'd argue the opposite. Our hearts are indeed in the right place; it's just that our brains cloud the path. We mistake our primordial intention for our most valuable need, and in doing so, we follow the wrong star home.

Primordial intentions are *full* of emotions that fill us with certainty that *a* particular battle or need is the most important thing in the universe. Winning an argument with a spouse, one-upping a colleague in accolades, or bolstering our self-worth with the affirmations of others seems paramount to our existence, to our happiness. When we step back from those escapades (usually after we're "sober" again), we see that those battles produced no winners, that the transcendent intention running underneath has gone unfulfilled. We played in the shallows, shadowboxing our demons and never embracing what it is our souls actually desired: love, connection, and belonging. Playing to primordial intentions rarely delivers us to this bedrock of fulfilling relational gold. Or if it does, it's because you've done what I did with Deli, navigated your way there via the shallow waters. While this may work temporarily, in the end, it is a damaging course to traverse. What we must do, instead, is become conscious of our primordial and transcendent intentions while finding ways to remind ourselves that our transcendent intention is what matters most. This is what Linda did as she looked to evolve her relationship with Beth.

When I asked Linda about her new strategy for approaching Beth, I was prepared for her to reply that she had revealed her "misguided ways" to Beth, divulging her noble desire of wanting to forge a solid, successful partnership. Wrong. Linda, it turns out, never said a thing about partnership, about wanting to be a good collaborator, about wanting to be a better fit. She simply showed up differently, her energy firmly grounded in her transcendent intention of forging a meaningful partnership. As a result, Linda immediately felt a shift in both of them, simply because of the different way she was showing up. And whenever she felt the *need* to put on some sort of display, which would happen from time to time, she would quickly and quietly lift herself off the primordial need of wanting respect or recognition and reset her sights on the larger goal. Three weeks after that transformational meeting, their relationship was unrecognizable. Within three months, they had forged a deep and trusting partnership.

The linear, process-oriented part of me kind of hates this story. I sort of wanted a detailed account of what Linda had said to Beth so that I could replicate it and then hand it over to you. You know, like some sort of transcendent Mad Libs; by magically inserting a couple new verbs and nouns, we'd have in our hot little hands the perfect passport to the land of best intentions. Sounds about as hokey as it is in real life. Without a transcript, what do we do? How do we navigate toward and manifest our transcendent intentions? And how do we know when we are locked on a primordial intention versus a transcendent intention?

PRIMORDIAL VERSUS TRANSCENDENT

When it comes to impact, we need to be ever mindful of the nature of our intentions, because they not only lead to our results, directly or indirectly, but they shape the kind of journey we experience and the legacy we leave. When I think of the initial path Linda and I took to fulfill our primordial needs, the road was difficult to traverse; it felt jarring to us and those on the receiving end of our intentions. Plenty of times, that path enabled me to achieve the end result I desired but at a significant cost to myself and the people in my life. Linda corrected her path midjourney, which allowed her to arrive at a result she wouldn't otherwise have been able to achieve. Thankfully for myself and for most others, the primordial intention isn't always the intention we lead with, but when it is, it's inevitably damaging to everyone involved. It is mostly dangerous to ourselves as we experience the emotional "spinning" that can wreak havoc on our inner life. In more extreme cases, the damage can be greater to those we are in contact with; we suck them into our cyclone of need.

For our well-being and the well-being of others, it's essential that we not only become aware of our intentions but also gain the ability to identify which kind of intention is in the lead so we can course correct when necessary. For this, there are two main indicators of primordial versus transcendent intentions.

INDICATOR 1: STRUGGLE VERSUS EASE

"Slow is smooth; smooth is fast." This is what Mike, the coach of masters swimming at the club I attend, said to me several years ago after watching me perform sprint drills with disappointing results. As I climbed out of the pool, exhausted and out of breath and definitely a bit bummed, he casually delivered the message with a compassionate grin and a singsong voice. I looked up at him and got it immediately. "Right," I exhaled, letting the word draw out as long and as heavy as my arms felt after beating the water for sixty minutes. Those words immediately became my mantra in the water, and they remain the best swimming advice I've ever received. That mantra has now extended beyond the deck of the pool and into my day-to-day interactions. Let me explain.

> "All doubt, despair, and fear become insignificant once the intention of life becomes love, rather than dependence on love."
> —Sri Da Avabhasa

In water—a medium roughly eight hundred times denser than air—streamlining is key, and with streamlining comes more relaxed, purposeful, elongated movements, not to mention increased speed. Whenever I jump into a pool and get caught up in trying to swim fast at all costs, I end up displacing a lot more water than I'm moving through. My strokes get jerky, short, and wasteful. My body position twists and my movements become choppy, because I over-tense each muscle set. Any aerodynamics and efficiencies I could be creating are lost due to the thrashing around I'm doing. But when you watch a professional swimmer at the 1500-meter distance or above, it's almost deceiving how relaxed they look in the water compared to the unbelievable speed at which they're moving. If you want to see this in action, google "Sun Yang 1500m Freestyle 2012" and watch him smash the world record at the 2012 Olympic Games. You won't see a bunch of white water and froth behind a robotic machine. Instead, you'll see a relaxed swimmer who almost appears to be taking a nap as he glides through the water. There is rock solid strength within a fluid, yet purposeful, approach. No tensing. No overreaching or pan-icking even though he was performing on the world's largest sports stage with everything at stake.

This same analogy holds true for every activity I can think of. Whether it's horseback riding, running, knitting, or drawing, the more relaxed we are, the greater the opportunity for better results. The tenser we are, the likelier it is our efforts will result in failure or disap-pointment. Ever tried to come up with a catchy headline with someone standing over you? Yeah, not the best circumstances in which to create. Ever tried to ride a trotting horse with stiff legs shoved in the stirrups? Yeah, um, ouch. Yet when we let go, when we soften our eyes, soften our knees, soften our hearts, we glide. Often, we soar.

> "You can still achieve certain things through effort, struggle, determination, and sheer hard work or cunning. But there is no joy in such endeavor, and it invariably ends in some sort of suffering."
>
> —Eckhart Tolle, *A New Earth: Awakening to Your Life's Purpose*

It's fascinating to me how as soon as we disengage from the "struggle," which is always entailed in a primordial intention, our abil-ity to navigate and obtain our transcendent intention becomes almost effortless. Whether the intention is self-focused in nature (such as idea generation, creative work, physical performance) or focused on another (such as reaching an understanding, communicating, experiencing intimacy), this dynamic between struggle and ease and the results we can expect remains. The physical sensation of being in a relaxed state versus a grasping or tense state is the first indication of which path of intention you're following. Because our primordial intentions so often occur when our limbic system's been engaged, the tensing sensation is almost a given. It's the body's fight, flight, or freeze mode—none of which occur in a relaxed state. On the flip side, when we experience serenity and easefulness, we are likely follow- ing our transcendent intention; our limbic system stays switched off, allowing clarity and reason to guide the way.

Exercise: Know the Sensations of Struggle versus Ease

Step 1: Identify Ease

To identify the opposing sensations in yourself, close your eyes and think of a time when you were engaged in an activity that had pur- pose and meaning—alone or with others—where you felt a com- plete sense of ease. Perhaps you were sharing stories over a glass of wine with a friend, engaging in a meaningful exchange with your partner, painting in the studio by yourself, or taking a long swim in a lake. Close your eyes, recall a time like this, and then ask yourself the following questions:

- What physical sensation(s) do I notice?

- What are the characteristics of my breath? Where is it originating from? Chest or belly?

- Where in my body do I feel relaxed? My jaw? My chest? Legs? What do I feel in my hands and toes?

- Where in my body do I feel a sense of aliveness? Are any muscles tingling or twitching? Am I smiling? What are my eyes doing?

Now list the physical sensations you experience while at ease. Describe the sensations in whatever way conjures the experience most vividly for you.

For me it would look something like this:

> Tingling on top of head. Breath is deep, eyes and mouth smiling. Body is leaning in and my attention is focused. There's a relaxed feeling throughout my body with electricity traveling through my spine. I've lost track of time and feel energetic connection with others.

_____

_____

_____

_____

_____

Step 2: Identify Struggle

Now settle back down into your body, close your eyes, and recall a time when you were engaged in an activity—alone or with others—where there was a great sense of struggle. Perhaps you were having an uncomfortable exchange with a friend, arguing with your partner, writing a creative essay, or running a race where achieving a new personal record or winning was critical to you—any time when you experienced negative friction and tensing within yourself while engaged in something that had meaning to you. Then ask yourself the following questions:

- What physical sensation(s) do I notice?

- What are the characteristics of my breath? Where is it originating from? Chest or belly?

- Where in my body do I feel tension? My jaw? My chest? Legs? What do I feel in my hands and toes?

- Where in my body do I feel a sense of angst? Are any muscles contracted or tense? What are my eyes doing?

Now write down the physical sensations you experience while engaged in a struggle. Describe the sensations in whatever way conjures the experience most vividly for you.

An example of this could be:

> Breath is shallow and eyes squinting, focus in eyes is hard. Slight headache in temples and chest feels tight. Staying present is very difficult as my thoughts lean toward how I can escape. Entire body is tense. Toes curled.

_____

_____

_____

_____

_____

Step 3: Do Your Homework

Next read the descriptions you wrote about the physical sensations associated with ease and struggle every day for fourteen days. Doing so will help raise your awareness about what is physically going on with you at all times, especially when you are engaged in a struggle. Similar to our discussion in inner life, your ability to recognize moments of derailment—when your limbic system has taken over—is *essential* to navigating your way off such a crazy, often damaging ride. Being able to quickly recognize when you are struggling, as it pertains to an intention, is an invaluable asset in giving yourself pause so you can then make a different choice.

INDICATOR 2: EXTERNAL VERSUS INTERNAL FULFILLMENT

Indicator 2 is more spiritual or psychic in nature. Often when we're operating from a primordial intention versus a transcendent one, we experience the physical sensations of struggle automatically. But for those of us who are more attuned to our thought patterns versus our physical patterns, this second indicator is another great opportunity to spot when a primordial intention is in the driver's seat. Another reason for this second indicator is that the activity we are engaged in may require us to traverse a path that is uncomfortable, thereby creating physical sensations of struggle in our body. That alone doesn't automatically indicate a primordial intention, but when paired with this second indicator, it does.

> "At the constitutional level where we work, ninety percent of any decision is emotional. The rational part of us supplies the reasons for supporting our predilections."
>
> —William O. Douglas, former justice of the US Supreme Court

I love William O. Douglas's quote. If a former US Supreme Court justice stating that ninety percent of the court's decisions are made on an emotional level doesn't convince you that we operate primarily from a heart-based wheelhouse, I don't know what will! Perhaps reading Daniel Kahneman's book *Thinking, Fast and Slow* will tip you over.[17] Here he describes two modes of thought: System 1 and System 2. System 1 is "fast, instinctive, and emotional," and System 2 is "slower, more deliberative, and more logical." Guess which system Kahneman found people overwhelmingly use when making decisions? Yep, System 1. Our emotions lead us into a decision; we then rationalize our decision with reason.

I think back to when Apple first announced the iPhone. I wasn't currently using a PDA and really had no need for one, but watching all the hype and that cool, sexy, sleek design . . . well, let's just say I was one of the hundreds of people lined up in front of my local wireless

---

17   Daniel Kahneman, *Thinking, Fast and Slow* (New York: Farrar, Straus and Giroux, 2013).

store on the morning of June 29, 2007. When I was confronted with the steep price, I quickly performed some mental acrobatics and came up with reasons to justify my purchase: "Well, I really do need a PDA, but I just haven't liked the design of the others. I use a Mac as my laptop, so buying this one makes more sense with the system I use. It comes with an unlimited data plan, so I'll be saving money on my monthly wireless bill." At that point, I had enough reasons to calm my nervous system and feel good about my decision to get an iPhone. It was an exercise many others would go through during that summer.

Did I *need* the phone? No. Did I *desire* the phone? Yes. We all have desires, and we all have needs. This is generally not a problem, depending, of course, on the nature of those desires and needs. But when a desire calls for something external to fulfill it or when a need can only be met by something outside of ourselves, we are likely operating under a primordial intention, just as I was when I purchased the iPhone, which has the potential to run us into trouble.

Did my purchase of an iPhone run me into trouble? Eh, not really. Aside from the temporary damage to my bank balance, the consequences were fairly insignificant. Wanting the phone was a primordial intention that I was able to fulfill with little impact on myself or others. But what if I had been at a casino and had gotten caught up in the rush of things and had lost over $1,000 at the blackjack table? Then that would have been another story, an example of a primordial intention that resulted in a lot of damage to myself and my family.

If we look back to my previous examples of Linda and me, you may be able to spot the need for external fulfillment already. For Linda, her primordial intention was her need to be externally validated by Beth; her transcendent intention was a desire to forge a partnership. My primordial intention was the need for someone to experience my emotions, what I *thought* was connection; my transcendent intention was the desire for support and understanding. Table 9.1 provides more examples of transcendent versus primordial intentions under the lens of desires that may be internally fulfilled versus needs that can only be met through external means.

Transcendent (internal fulfillment)	Primordial (external fulfillment)
I desire a sense of belonging.	I need you to validate me.
I desire an understanding of my feelings.	I need you to feel what I feel.
I desire peace from my past.	I need you to fix me.
I desire to forgive.	I need you to atone.
I desire joy.	I need you to make me happy.
I desire the courage to follow my heart.	I need you to make it safe for me.

Table 9.1. Transcendent Desires versus Primordial Needs

I could go on, but paper is expensive, so I'll stop here. You may identify with one or all of these transcendent versus primordial intentions. I know I certainly can; they've all shown up in my life in different periods and under varying circumstances. Now that I'm conscious of these intentions, I can pause before I enter an interaction or when an interaction has gone sideways and ask myself, "What is the intention? What is the desire or need? Am I looking for something or someone outside of myself to fulfill it? Does fulfilling this intention come at the cost of another person's well-being?" A great way to tell if a primordial intention is at play is if you find yourself rehearsing a scene with someone, especially when the final act paints you as the hero. Making someone else wrong, manipulating the situation so we can be right, or creating dependency of any kind are all clear signs of primordial intention. We are in reactive mode seeking the external validation of an ego-driven need, plain and simple.

Often, when I do spot the primordial intention I can express it to those close to me who are familiar with this work. I can simply say, "You know, I have a need right now to be validated (or built up, or soothed, or whatever it is) that feels really important right now, and I just want you to know what's going on with me." Then they'll usually say something like, "Okay. So what's the internal desire? What's beneath the primordial need, and how can you cultivate that for yourself?" Whether it's conducting my own version of a pep talk, recalling a memory that gives me confidence, or speaking about my need in an even manner that calms the nerves, I can often deliver myself what it is that my heart desires. And, of course, having the people close to you understand you and connect with you in those moments doesn't hurt. That said, when I'm alone or without my kula, I ask myself the same questions, which helps me navigate back to my transcendent intention most of the time.

Exercise: Know Your Intentions

Step 1: Identify Your Primordial Intentions

Now I'd like you to spot some of your primordial intentions, especially the ones that frequently override your transcendent intentions, such as my decades-long pattern of needing others to feel my feelings as a means to achieving connection instead of just creating connection by sharing my feelings. These are two roads to the same destination, but one is clearly more perilous than the other. Spotting that pattern within myself has absolutely revolutionized my relationships, including the one I have with myself! Let's see if we can scare a few of these up for you. Answer the following five questions:

1. What needs in you often feel like *needs*? The kind that create physical and emotional stress. Name as many as you can.

_____

_____

_____

_____

2. What do you find yourself grasping for, fighting for, from other people? (For example, I seek attention from others. I constantly try to prove I am worthy of love. I am desperate to be needed.)

_____

_____

_____

_____

3. What patterns do you notice within yourself when it comes to achieving transcendent intentions (such as connection, love, courage, peace, self-worth) through primordial needs? Are you seeking from others before settling into yourself?

_____

_____

_____

_____

4. What beliefs about yourself or others contribute to the creation of primordial intentions? (For example, I believe that I am owed something before I can give something. Real love involves pain and suffering. If so-and-so loved me, then that person would know what to say. If I don't please this group, then there's something wrong with me.) Name as many beliefs as you can.

_____

_____

_____

_____

_____

5. Finally, complete this sentence at least three times: If I had
_____, then I would be or have _____. (For
example, if I had approval from my boss, then I would have confidence in myself.)

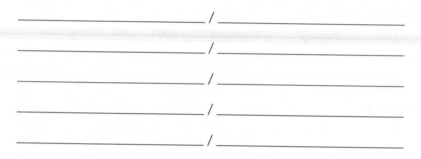

Step 2: Identify Your Transcendent Intentions

Those five questions should have produced at least one primordial
intention, if not a handful! Now the question becomes, what is the
transcendent intention underneath? Once we know that, we can
begin lifting that intention up to avoid unconsciously defaulting to
our primordial intention whenever we're under stress. Using table 9.2,
create your own list of primordial intentions and their transcendent
counterparts. First, name the primordial intentions you identified
from the preceding exercise and then seek out the transcendent intentions underneath.

Primordial (can only be fulfilled externally)	Transcendent (may be internally fulfilled)
I need	I desire
I need	I desire
I need	I desire
I need	I desire
I need	I desire
I need	I desire

Table 9.2. Your Primordial Needs versus Your Transcendent Desires

PULLING IT ALL TOGETHER

Ever since sitting down and doing this exercise, I've been able to shift more than a few patterns that were hijacking my ability to keep my transcendent intentions in sight and on top. Just having the awareness was more than half the battle. Having the discipline to hold myself to a higher bar and actively shift my intentions was the other half. It isn't easy work; we become addicted in some way to these patterns.

Being aware of our intentions also allows us to question what we really stand to gain by continuing a pattern that constantly creates negative outcomes. Looking down the road to what prices we may pay for our behavior can be a great reality check; we can no longer pretend that these prices are harmless or no big deal. I think of the relationship I lost with a best friend as one of the biggest call-to-action moments around rewiring my intentions. If I hadn't learned to connect with others through a transcendent intention, then I would have eventually become an island unto myself.

Because I'm highly attuned to my physical self, my method of spotting a primordial intention relies about eighty percent on indicator 1, sensing struggle over ease. When my chest tightens and my breath becomes shallow, I know to stop what I'm doing. Even if I have to say that I'll be back in twenty minutes (the time it takes our limbic system and the effects of adrenaline to subside), I'll take my time out. During that time, I ask myself the questions about intention I posed earlier on page 257. This helps me to not only get back into my reasoning brain but also identify the transcendent intention.

Other times, I don't feel the physical sensations of struggle. This is perhaps because I've slipped back into a primordial pattern that I'm used to, which doesn't spawn the same physical rush as another pattern would. My cues at these times are to listen to myself and notice if I'm asking for something repeatedly. Or if I'm unwilling to disengage until *x* happens, such as getting an apology, being told I'm loved, or receiving a message I want to hear. When those things occur, I've typically switched into primordial mode and, here again, I will either shift midstream or take a few moments to explore within myself before continuing.

Once you've identified your transcendent intention—whether you knew it all along or pulled it out from under a primordial intention—I find the *best* way forward and the most likely path to attain what you desire is this: Give whatever it is that you seek. We're all at least somewhat familiar with notions around the law of attraction. The concept that like attracts like dates all the way back to Plato in 391 BC; then Sir Isaac Newton popularized the term in 1687. The phrase "You get what you give" comes to mind, and I couldn't agree more with this universal law. Just as we discussed in the section on nurturing, we need to impart whatever it is that we desire to reap. The same holds true for our intentions and relationships. If I desire understanding, I must seek to understand. If I desire courage, then I must demonstrate courage. If I desire affection, than I must show affection. And if I desire peace, then I must be in a place of peace.

The truth is, it's impossible for someone to give us something we cannot give ourselves. Yet sometimes we persist in trying to attain it from others anyway. This framework of intentions provides the tools for us to learn how to physically and spiritually embody our desires. In this way, we will learn how to give to ourselves and fulfill our transcendent desires. It's an elegant and realistic path from dependence on others to reliance on the strengths within. I highly encourage each of you to take on this work, because it will transform your relationship with yourself, first. Then with others. Now for your homework.

Just like you'll do for the exercise about indicator 1 (feeling the physical sensations of struggle versus ease), review your Primordial versus Transcendent Intentions Chart (page 261) once a day for fourteen days. This will help you become aware of the predominant patterns that are getting in your way of having a positive impact on yourself and those around you. Commit to heightening your awareness of these intentions and bring them to the forefront of your mind before entering into any conversation or interaction that feels as if there's something at stake. Before you hit "go" on the conversation or the activity, pause and scan your intentions. Then identify and connect to the transcendent intention, naming it so that you can come back to it and remind yourself of it anytime you feel a primordial intention want to take over. Finally, embody the transcendent intention, remembering that like attracts like and that we truly are the only ones who can give ourselves what we desire.

Having this self-awareness is key. As with everything in this book, we must first work with ourselves, from within, before stepping out and focusing on others. Now that you are conscious of the impact of your intentions on others, we can focus on attention. There we'll learn to be mindful of not only our needs but also the needs of others, especially those connected to the branches on our tree.

ATTENTION

*"You cannot get through a single day without having
an impact on the world around you. What you do
makes a difference, and you have to decide what kind
of difference you want to make."*

—Jane Goodall

And now we put our focus on the leaves perched atop our branches. I know for myself that this area, along with inner life, is one I tend to overlook. My attention is typically focused on building strong branches and a strong physical foundation, but I forget to look up to what it's really all about—the people I'm building it for, including myself. Nothing like having a tree that resembles winter in the middle of spring.

It was actually the struggles around this area of the tree that inspired me to begin writing this book. During all my years working in the relationship field, it struck me how many of us don't understand why so many of our relationships suffer. This, to me, is the basis of all the talk around work-life balance, a term we already know makes me cringe. But while the term may be flawed, the desperation and desire to resolve it isn't. We work so damn hard; of course we want to know why it is, then, that there's so much unfulfilled want in ourselves and those around us.

My ensuing studies around this übertopic of relationships and lack of "balance" is what compelled me to search deeper and deeper, culminating in the examination of my tree, from soil, to roots, to branches, to finally, the leaves. So much of what we do in those areas affects our ability and capacity to manage our relationships. Without laying those levels of foundation and clarity, we'd be waving in the wind, grasping at shadows, and, once again, doomed to fail. This is why I've left our impact, our relationships, for the end. It's the culmination of our work, not the beginning of the journey by any means. We cannot have a positive impact on ourselves, much less others, unless we are deeply grounded in the fabric of who we are, how we are, and what makes us tick. Only then can we begin pumping lifeblood outside of that core.

EXERCISE: THE REALITY OF TIME

Alexander Bell wasn't exaggerating when he said that time flies. Ever been caught telling a story about something that happened three years ago only to be corrected by your partner and reminded that it was more than eight years ago? Ever blinked and realized your children aren't small enough to fit in your lap anymore? Ever gone back to visit the town you grew up in only to find it transformed by urban decay? Time is fleeting. And so much—so much—happens while our eyes wander.

> "Time goes by so fast, people go in and out of your life. You must never miss the opportunity to tell these people how much they mean to you."
> —Alexander Graham Bell

For those of you who like to see things laid out, let's calculate just how much time we have available to us. Calculate how many hours you spend on each type of expression per week; then total up the hours.

> VOCATION(S): ___
> AVOCATION(S): ___
> KEY RELATIONSHIP(S): ___
> PLAY: ___
> TOTAL HOURS: ___

Now let's look at everything else. There are 168 hours in a week. We spend (or should spend!) at least 56 hours sleeping each week. That leaves us with 112 waking hours a week, or 16 hours a day. According to the Bureau of Labor Statistics,[18] we spend roughly 4 hours a day eating and drinking, doing household chores, and "other" activities. This brings our available hours each week down to 84, or 12 hours a day. Subtract the total hours above from 84 and see how your numbers add up.

The first time I did this exercise, I found myself with a 9-hour deficit! I couldn't figure out how I was doing everything while being 9 hours in the hole! Then I realized that I was "borrowing" from sleep, getting only 6 to 7 hours of sleep each night so I could cram everything else in. When I realized that I needed to replenish my sleep hours and shave hours off something else in order to do so, it was really sobering. I mean *really* sobering for me. How could I do it all? No wonder I never had any downtime! I was as overscheduled as most kids are these days. The reality was, something had to shift. Instead of spending 50 hours a week on my vocation, 15 hours a week on my avocations, with the remaining hours focused on family, I needed to pour some hours from one area into another; I also needed to reallocate some hours to make time for an element of play and much-needed downtime. In short, I needed to make a shift in my priorities while also ensuring I was making the *most* out of the little time I had.

---

18 Bureau of Labor Statistics (BLS), "Charts from the American time use survey" (BLS, 2015), http://www.bls.gov/tus/charts.

Regardless of whether or not your situation looks like mine did, just realizing that we have only about 12 hours a day available to us ought to make you sit up a little straighter. For those of you with a typical vocation that requires 8 hours a day, you've already lost two-thirds of your time to that expression alone. It becomes clearer than ever that we have to be *intentional* with where and how we place our *attention*.

ATTENTION + INTENTION = IMPACT

"Pay attention to one another." These were the words my dad wrote in our wedding card the day Deli and I tied the knot nearly two decades ago. These words were his most important piece of advice for two loving partners hoping to beat the odds and make their marriage last. Needless to say, I've never forgotten them. But I'm not sure I always understood them. At one point, I mistook his advice to mean quantity of time instead of quality of time. At another, I misinterpreted attention to mean how much money I spent on her versus how much time I spent *with* her. It wasn't until a few years ago that I understood that for true attention to take place, an intention has to be in place. And the depth of the intention affects what kind of impact my attention has on her. There's a mindfulness that a lot of us forget, especially when we're scrambling in the reality of our twelve-hour days. And with a paycheck screaming to get earned, we usually default to sloppiness or last-minute Hail Marys to keep our relationships afloat.

Going back to the analogy of currents sweeping us down shore, we must have our oars in the water on a regular basis to keep our key relationships where we desire them to be. It isn't enough to just pay attention, and it isn't enough to simply have a good intention. The two must be brought together if we want to have a positive impact on those important to us. How many of us have experienced losing someone special when we had such high hopes for this person?

For example, a key employee everyone is hot about slowly drifts into the "Maintenance" bucket where all great employees go to die. You may be familiar with this one: The once inspired one-on-ones become a series of tactical checking-things-off-lists interactions. No one understands why this person walks in one day and gives notice. The reason? The employee became a task someone was trying to complete; they forgot the person. Everyone saw this employee as integral to the company's success, but the intention was unspoken and the attention was frantic or split or just plain missing.

On the other hand, have you ever lavished attention on someone only to find it got you nowhere? In fact, it seemed to have the opposite effect and caused the chasm to span ever greater? The person walks away and you think to yourself, "How could so-and-so do that? I gave everything I had!" Want to know my guess? Either you were thoroughly without intention, merely slapping the water with the oars of attention—making a lot of noise and going nowhere—or you were misaligned with a primordial intention, desperate to receive something you *needed* that the person was unable to provide or was no longer in the mood to be harassed into providing.

> "Attention is the rarest and purest form of generosity."
> —Simone Weil

In both examples, the relationships ended, resulting in the loss of someone important to us. I might also ask here how many times you've treated *yourself* in one of these two manners, either not giving yourself any quality time or frantically running from thing to thing, doing, doing, doing to try and fill your cup only to end up exhausted and befuddled. Yeah, me too.

How we spend our time must be intentional. It's do or die when it comes to our relationships with ourselves and with others. In that vein, I'd like for us to set an intention for each key relationship. We will then take it a step further and set an intention for each expression on the day it occurs. Instead of making to-do lists or having a thirty-day plan, we will set intentions as a means to positively affect our lives and the lives of those we love.

PULLING IT ALL TOGETHER

We've spent a good deal of time talking about intentions, how they arise, and how they serve us. We've learned about the two types of intentions, along with tools to recognize when we're leading with a primordial intention versus the preferred transcendent intention. I can't imagine focusing on the impact we have on others until we have become fully aware of how we're entering into any interaction. Because we've done that work, we can now move forward in setting our intentions for others.

Homework

I want you to consider all of your key relationships and set an intention for each one on a weekly basis. We already have your overarching intention for those key relationships from the work we did in part 3, "Expression." This exercise isn't meant to override that intention; rather, the goal is to provide an opportunity to fulfill that overarching intention, be fully present in each key relationship, and ensure the expressions of our intentions are positive ones. For instance, I could have a lofty and inspiring intention for my role as a mom, so I know in my heart what it is I want to provide for my children. But if it only lives in me and has no regular opportunity to be expressed, it becomes an unfortunate secret I've kept to myself. We need to move from our heads into our bodies and demonstrate our intentions for these incredibly important key relationships. Here is how we'll do that.

"I'm convinced of this: Good done anywhere is good done everywhere. As long as you're breathing, it's never too late to do some good."

—Maya Angelou

First, before the start of a new week, write in your Life, Incorporated journal how many hours you plan to spend on each expression. After each day, record how much time you actually spent. At the end of the week, total up the hours and see what you notice. Did something take more time than anticipated? If so, what expressions were sacrificed? Take this into consideration as you plan out the next week. As you write in the numbers, take into consideration the amount of downtime you need. As you'll see in my example, my hours don't add up to 84, because I'd be going, going, going nonstop. This is not realistic, especially for an introvert like me who needs alone time and white space to recharge. Instead, my approach was to pencil in realistic projections that I felt would not only ensure I was taking care of business but also ensure I was showing up in a meaningful way for all my expressions. See table 10.1 for an example.

Week 1 (Planned)	Week 1 (Actual)
Vocation: 40 hours	Vocation: 49 hours
Key Relationships: 28 hours	Key Relationships: 23 hours
Avocation: 6 hours	Avocation: 6 hours
Play: 4 hours	Play: 1 hour

Table 10.1. Planned versus Actual Hours for Expressions

As you can see from my example, work took over and I sacrificed time allotted for key relationships as well as play, a scenario that I'm sure occurs quite often in our lives. But the point of this exercise isn't to beat ourselves up or finagle a way to force our lives into evenly dispersed buckets so that we might achieve "balance." No, this is an exercise in awareness. So much of our ability to have an impact on something important to us is directly tied to the amount of meaningful time we can spend on it. If we're unaware that work has completely taken over our lives and is gobbling up hours like Pac-Man gobbling dots, then we aren't aware of the handicap we're placing on ourselves when it comes to accomplishing our other intentions for the expressions important to us. Worse yet, our lack of availability to ourselves or to others may be having a damaging impact that we are unaware of.

It's here that I want to pause and talk a bit further about the importance of downtime or white space. In 1973, prominent social psychologists John Darley and Daniel Batson performed a study called "From Jerusalem to Jericho"[19] that examined the influence of situational variables on behavior. In their study, they recruited 67 students from the Princeton Theological Seminary. Some were asked to give a short talk about the parable of the Good Samaritan while others were asked to speak about jobs seminary students would be well suited for.

Before their talks, the students were each given a campus map so they could find where their speech was to take place. On of the following three instructions was also given:

1. "Oh, you're late. They were expecting you a few minutes ago. We'd better get moving."

2. "The assistant is ready for you, so please go right over."

3. "It'll be a few minutes before they're ready for you, but you might as well head over."

These instructions created three different levels of hurry: high, medium, and low. Little did the students know that on the way to giving their speech, they would encounter an actor depicting a person very much in need. The test was whether or not the students would actually practice what they preached—would they be Good Samaritans and stop to help someone clearly in need? Or would they pass right by?

As you might have figured out by now, most of the students who felt a high level of hurry chose to ignore the person in need of help. Only ten percent of the students in high hurry stopped. Forty-five percent in medium hurry stopped, and sixty-three percent in low hurry stopped. So clearly feeling pressed for time makes us act against our own best judgment. We become untethered from our core and

---

19 J.M. Darley, D.C. Batson, "'From Jerusalem to Jericho': A study of situational and dispositional variables in helping behavior," *Journal of Personality & Social Psychology*, 27 (1973): 100-108.

easily set aside our values when we slip into hurry-up mode and make the clock our commander in chief.

The reason I share this study is so you will be ever mindful of placing white space between activities and events throughout your day. Taking the time to ground yourself in your deepest transcendent intentions each day is essential but not enough. Create space between your meetings, between activities, between shifts in roles so you can remain true to your authentic self.

In order to put everything into practice, I'd like you to track your time for twelve weeks. You may find that no matter how much you want your time to fall a certain way, it doesn't. So there are expectations or other decisions to reconsider. Or you may find that you are able to come fairly close to your plan but run into a week or two where things go sideways. Perhaps in those cases, you'll want to carve out more time on a following week for the expressions that were sacrificed. It's up to you. The core purpose of this exercise is to become aware of how you spend your time so you can manage it instead of *it* managing you!

The next step in your journal is to set your weekly intentions for each expression and describe a meaningful act or way in which you will take action and demonstrate that intention. Please note: These intentions are intended to benefit others; this isn't a place to find a way to get what you need or desire. Yes, we all want to bring positivity and progress to those important to us, but ask yourself how it is that *they* would like to receive that positivity and progress. For example, setting an intention of "have him tell me he loves me" for your spouse isn't an appropriate intention when serving others. In fact, even if it were your own intention, it lies in the primordial realm, because you're seeking something external from yourself.

For both reasons, I would scratch that one off of the list. Instead, write down what you'd like to demonstrate (your intention) and then how you'll demonstrate that (your meaningful act or action). Make it something you know or sense would be important or meaningful to your key relationships. You won't be sharing your intentions, just expressing them, so there's no need to go over the top or stress in any way. All your key relationships will be aware of is your action. That said, your weekly intentions for them might look something like this:

Intentions for Key Relationships	Meaningful Act
Wife: She is the priority.	Plan date night; keep everything a surprise!
Kids: I can be silly, too!	Make Sunday "can't say no day"; for eight hours, they call the shots

Table 10.2. Intentions and Actions for Key Relationships

Now that you have your intentions set for your key relationships, move through the rest of your expressions and set intentions for these as well. These intentions will look more like typical goals. I'd recommend five goals each week for more involved expressions, such as vocation, and three for less involved expressions, such as avocation. For play, we'll insert one intention so that we've been thoughtful about how we'll get our playtime in this week! Oftentimes, if we don't schedule it in, it doesn't happen. It's equally important to consider ourselves when setting intentions for the week. In addition, I'd also like you to add one relational intention for each of your other expressions. Choose someone associated with that expression and perform a meaningful act. Again, we want to maintain the health of the leaves on our tree, so many of whom are relationships. Finally, consider any other relationships where you sense an opportunity has cropped up to perform a meaningful act. Consider your kula here. See table 10.3 for an example of what a week might look like for me.

Each week, you have an opportunity to set your intentions, record the impact of those intentions, and review the results. Again, the goal isn't to ace the test and have life always go as planned. I know of no such world. Rather, the goal is to develop *awareness* of how you spend your days and the impact you have. Because life shifts week to week (sometimes hour to hour!), it's important to stay current with what is

Expression	Important Relationship	Meaningful Act	Intentions
Vocation: Author, Educator, Provocateur	Book Coach	Write her a card thanking her for encouragement!	• Begin book proposal. • Finish conclusion. • Review and edit beginning chapters. • Secure website domain name. • Identify agency for branding work.
Avocation: Advisor/Mentor	Dave	Send him a bottle of wine as appreciation.	• Schedule coaching call with Noah. • Review budget for arts organization. • Email Heather regarding finance committee.
Avocation: Athlete	John	Schedule coffee to catch up on how his work's going.	• Swim three times this week. • Keep heart under 160 for all runs. • Do five pull-ups.
Play			• Work on my jigsaw puzzle at home. • Send Dad photos of kids. • Invite Paul over for dinner.

Table 10.3. Intentions and Meaningful Acts for Expressions

actually occurring in our lives and our relationships instead of allowing things to drift into an already uncertain future. My hope for you is that you gain clarity on what is important to you by noticing where you tend to add more hours to the day while also noticing from where you often borrow. This information provides a great opportunity for you to notice any incongruence in what you *say* and what you *do*. Don't judge. Just notice. And if you feel a shift needs to be made, you now have the data to support your decisions. Turn to your journal and begin!

CONCLUSION

We've now done the important work of taking responsibility for our impact by bringing attention to intention. So often we spend hours and hours keying up our passion and drumming up all the ways in which we can achieve something only to slip into mindless maintenance mode. We leave it to milestones and awards to determine our success when the real success of life resides in our relationship with ourselves and others. A quote attributed to Maya Angelou articulately expresses this sentiment: "I've learned that people will forget what you said, people will forget what you did, but people will never forget how you made them feel." In the end, the same phrase goes for ourselves as well and deserves a reminder. We need to ensure we're living a life that makes us feel as fulfilled as we leave others feeling.

In this section, we learned the two forms of intentions—primordial and transcendent—that are at play at any given moment. We learned that primordial intentions are distinguished by the engagement of our limbic system, resulting in the physical sensation of struggle, and the need for fulfillment through external means. Whereas a transcendent intention, originating from within and fulfilled internally, often brings a sense of calm. How we fulfill that transcendent intention is by first identifying it and then embodying whatever it is that we desire. When we desire courage, we engage from a courageous mind-set. When we desire comfort, we bring comfort to others. In this way, we are able to fulfill our transcendent intention while demonstrating that we are truly the only source of what it is we seek. Nothing external to us can provide what we desire with any long-term, lasting results. The only path to experiencing a fulfilling life is to learn how to become our own providers. We create wholeheartedness in ourselves as we travel through our day having a positive impact on the ecosystem we belong to.

"Never believe that a few caring people can't change the world. For, indeed, that's all who ever have."

—Margaret Mead

Once we brought our intentions into our awareness—especially those intentions that are meant to serve us—we then turned outward to those we wish to serve, creating intentions for our key relationships, those associated with our avocations and vocations, and those who are part of our ecosystem but, perhaps, not wrapped up in an expression. We also reviewed how many hours we have available in the week so we can be ever mindful of just how it is and where it is we are spending our time! Again, we can have all the good intentions in the world but when we don't match that against reality, we fall short—at least one aspect of our lives often paying the price. Keeping a journal to record your weekly intentions will not only provide you with a reality check but will also allow you to shift each day or week so that no component of your tree becomes malnourished.

Being present and aware of our impact is essential if we want our tree to be healthy, fruitful, and thriving all year round. Set your intentions, track your progress, and notice the results. Shift when necessary so that you can stay current in an ever-changing, complex world! You now have all the tools you need to sustain your living tree.

CONCLUSION

*"It was when I stopped searching for home within others
and lifted the foundations of home within myself
I found there were no roots more intimate
than those between a mind and body
that have decided to be whole."*

—Rupi Kaur

As I write the last pages of this book, it's late December here in Seattle—full-on winter. Driving across the floating bridge that spans the water between my home and my writing nook, I notice waves splashing over the guardrails; further on, I see tree limbs littering the roads and leaves swirling in the air in what seemed equal parts desire to alight and remain afloat. Winter in the Northwest can be meek or wild. Just like our lives. This stark contrast of unpredictable, harsh, and trying weather with the warm and easy summer months when I was in the thick of writing this manuscript gave me pause. How quickly our world can shift and how necessary it is that we become adaptable to these contrasts.

Each life goes through its fair share of autumns when a death of some kind is experienced, but how it is that we transform those moments into new possibility and sustain growth is what I chose to explore in this book. My story, and the stories of others I've shared in this book, are a few examples of the epidemic I first witnessed many moons ago when I realized just how disconnected we've become from ourselves and our own experience of life. What I know from my experience in the field, my subsequent study and research, and the development and impact of the tools found within these pages is that we all struggle with remaining deeply rooted and connected in some way. Whether our entire tree has been knocked to the ground, laying us bare, or a fragility or unrest lives within, threatening to undermine our stability, we each struggle because we have been lulled into believing that focusing on one particular area or achieving one particular "thing" will give us peace, deliver us happiness, give our lives meaning, or achieve this elusive thing called "balance."

Nothing external can deliver any of that to us. If our life is to have meaning that stands the test of time, our life—both the content and the form of it—has to be created internally before we push it out onto the stage in the external world. No amount of money, fame, Facebook likes, Instagram followers, or pats on the back can act as a long-term surrogate for nourishing our soul. If we wish to experience long-term well-being, then we must work on every aspect of our life, and the work must be done from the inside out. Take it from someone who had to say good-bye to her own fantasy because it was based on a primordial need—that of gaining acceptance from someone outside of myself. It shattered like glass in my delicate hands. It was as fragile and hollow as my own capacity to accept myself. Truth is, we can't build a solid vision if it's anchored in air. Also, life doesn't deposit itself into neat and tidy containers for us to pull out and manage on a day that suits us, yet we treat it as if we could. We "dust off" our health every New Years or "polish" our marriage when the boards begin to shake loose. We grope around from corner to corner, spinning one plate after another, never truly wrapping our arms around the totality of life.

This book, this work, asks you to erase the black, erase the white, and embrace the vast gray nature of life. To approach our gardens as we so often do with our lives, applying a "one-size-fits-all" approach, we would find ourselves in a year-round patch of dirt. You would never overwater a cactus to produce more fruit. You would never prune a tree without considering its form. You would never fertilize a rose in the middle of a freeze and expect blooms. And yet this is what we do day in and day out.

We have unrealistic expectations of ourselves; we try to contort ourselves into a mold that does not fit, or we bounce around from fad to fad, focusing on the part of our life that is either crying out the most or gives us the quickest high. I know—I've done it. I toned up my body to make up for the devastation I felt inside. I puffed up my chest and dressed up in the title of a high position while feeling more and more dissatisfied. I poured money into a problem, hoping it would somehow fix itself. I strived for forty-four years to heal the past by seeking solutions outside myself. Of course, none of these tactics worked. They created short-term, false senses of accomplishment and contentment that were quick to fall apart.

To opt out of a disconnected life and embrace a fully connected life is to live from the inside out, fully integrating *all* aspects—from your inner life all the way to the impact you have on the world. Making this shift requires you to take full responsibility for your life and cultivate what you need, rather than seek it from others. If you take on this work wholeheartedly and practice the tools regularly, you will notice both your internal and external barriers begin to erode. They will be replaced with fluidity and strength as you come into the wholeness of your being—of your life. I don't care where you begin, but I, and this planet, do care that you do begin. Today.

Journal

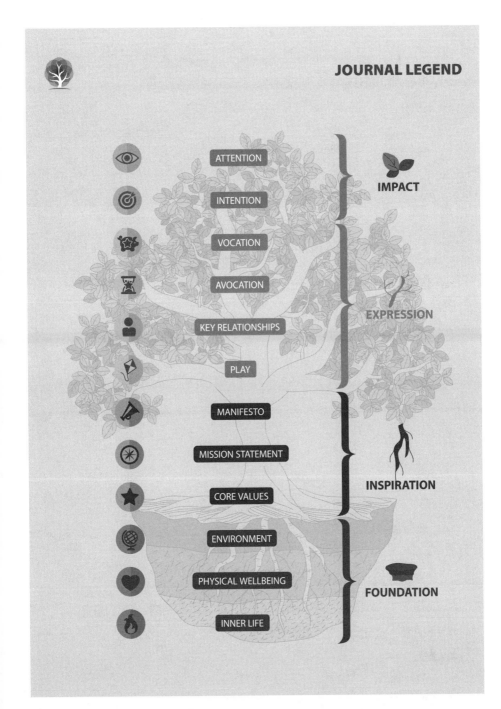

JOURNAL LEGEND

ATTENTION

INTENTION

IMPACT

VOCATION

AVOCATION

KEY RELATIONSHIPS

EXPRESSION

PLAY

MANIFESTO

MISSION STATEMENT

CORE VALUES

INSPIRATION

ENVIRONMENT

PHYSICAL WELLBEING

INNER LIFE

FOUNDATION

FIRST MONTH | on your first day, use this form to set up your first month

EXPRESSION

my life, **ADJUSTED** | record specific goals you want to reach this month and circle the expression that goal is associated with

MONTHLY GOALS

1 _____

2 _____

3 _____

4 _____

5 _____

my life, **ADJUSTED** | record weekly milestones needed to meet your monthly goals listed above

WEEKLY MILESTONES

WEEK 1

_____
_____
_____

WEEK 2

_____
_____
_____

WEEK 3

_____
_____
_____

WEEK 4

_____
_____
_____

FOUNDATION

my **KULA** | record an action you intend to complete for a member of your kula as well as an action you intend to complete for your greater kula

ENVIRONMENT

This month I intend to _____ for _____ MY KULA

This month I intend to _____ for _____ GREATER KULA

FIRST WEEK | on your first day, use this form to set up your first week

IMPACT

set **ATTENTION** goals | record the number of hours you would like to spend on your expressions this week

82 HOURS AVAILABLE IN A TYPICAL WEEK

👁 ATTENTION

I will spend _____ hour(s) on **PLAY**

I will spend _____ hour(s) on **VOCATION**

I will spend _____ hour(s) on **AVOCATION**

I will spend _____ hour(s) on **KEY RELATIONSHIPS**

set **INTENTIONS** | record your weekly intentions and the meaningful act or action you will take to demonstrate the intention

👤 KEY RELATIONSHIPS	INTENTION	MEANINGFUL ACT OR ACTION	BY WHEN
1			
2			

🛒 VOCATION	INTENTION	MEANINGFUL ACT OR ACTION	BY WHEN
1			
2			

⏳ AVOCATION	INTENTION	MEANINGFUL ACT OR ACTION	BY WHEN
1			
2			

🌿 PLAY & OTHER RELATIONSHIPS	MEANINGFUL ACT OR ACTION	BY WHEN
1		
2		

DAILY | complete this form each day

FOUNDATION

my **INNER LIFE** | record your inner life practices below and the time you you dedicated to each practice

INNER LIFE

AWARENESS _____ practice(s) for _____ minutes

CONNECTION _____ practice(s) for _____ minutes

NURTURING _____ practice(s) for _____ minutes

my **WELLBEING** | record your nutrition, sleep, movement and exercise below

PHYSICAL WELLBEING

NUTRITION

BREAKFAST	SNACKS	LUNCH	DINNER
_____	_____	_____	_____
_____	_____	_____	_____
_____	_____	_____	_____
_____	_____	_____	_____

Dd you use your 80/20 today? ☐ YES / NO ☐   What was it? _____

SLEEP

I slept for _____ hours *(7–9 hours is your goal)*   The quality of my sleep was   POOR / GOOD / GREAT

I woke up feeling _____

MOVEMENT & EXERCISE

I exercised or moved for _____ minutes *(a minimum of 20 minutes is your goal)*

The activity I did was _____

today, I felt 😃 🙂 😐 🙁 ☹️

I attribute this feeling to _____

DAILY | complete this form each day

IMPACT

my **INTENTIONS** | check in with your intentions for today and record your intentions for tomorrow

⊙ INTENTION

BUT FIRST Did I act on my intentions from yesterday? ☐ YES / NO ☐
If not, what got in your way? _____

TOMORROW I WILL ...

1 _____

2 _____

3 _____

4 _____

5 _____

my **ATTENTION** | record the time you dedicated to each expression, gauge how your day went, and record any adjustments you'd like to make for tomorrow

👁 ATTENTION

I spent _____ hour(s) on **PLAY**   I spent _____ hour(s) on **VOCATION**

I spent _____ hour(s) on **AVOCATION**   I spent _____ hour(s) on **KEY RELATIONSHIPS**

Did today go as I had hoped?

COMPLETELY
OFF COURSE   AS PLANNED

What I noticed and what I would like to adjust

_____

_____

_____

_____

_____

_____

DAILY | complete this form each day

FOUNDATION

my **INNER LIFE** | record your inner life practices below and the time you you dedicated to each practice

INNER LIFE

AWARENESS _____ practice(s) for _____ minutes

CONNECTION _____ practice(s) for _____ minutes

NURTURING _____ practice(s) for _____ minutes

my **WELLBEING** | record your nutrition, sleep, movement and exercise below

PHYSICAL WELLBEING

NUTRITION

BREAKFAST	SNACKS	LUNCH	DINNER
_____	_____	_____	_____
_____	_____	_____	_____
_____	_____	_____	_____
_____	_____	_____	_____

Dd you use your 80/20 today?   ☐ YES / NO ☐   What was it? _____

SLEEP

I slept for _____ hours *(7–9 hours is your goal)*   The quality of my sleep was   POOR / GOOD / GREAT

I woke up feeling _____

MOVEMENT & EXERCISE

I exercised or moved for _____ minutes *(a minimum of 20 minutes is your goal)*

The activity I did was _____

today, I felt   😃 🙂 😐 🙁 😣

I attribute this feeling to _____

DAILY | complete this form each day

IMPACT

my INTENTIONS | check in with your intentions for today and record your intentions for tomorrow

INTENTION

BUT FIRST Did I act on my intentions from yesterday? ☐ YES / NO ☐
If not, what got in your way? _____

TOMORROW I WILL ...

1 _____

2 _____

3 _____

4 _____

5 _____

my ATTENTION | record the time you dedicated to each expression, gauge how your day went, and record any adjustments you'd like to make for tomorrow

ATTENTION

I spent _____ hour(s) on **PLAY**   I spent _____ hour(s) on **VOCATION**

I spent _____ hour(s) on **AVOCATION**   I spent _____ hour(s) on **KEY RELATIONSHIPS**

Did today go as I had hoped?

COMPLETELY
OFF COURSE   AS PLANNED

What I noticed and what I would like to adjust

_____

_____

_____

_____

_____

_____

DAILY | complete this form each day

FOUNDATION

my **INNER LIFE** | record your inner life practices below and the time you you dedicated to each practice

🔥 INNER LIFE

AWARENESS _____ practice(s) for _____ minutes

CONNECTION _____ practice(s) for _____ minutes

NURTURING _____ practice(s) for _____ minutes

my **WELLBEING** | record your nutrition, sleep, movement and exercise below

❤️ PHYSICAL WELLBEING

NUTRITION

BREAKFAST	SNACKS	LUNCH	DINNER
_____	_____	_____	_____
_____	_____	_____	_____
_____	_____	_____	_____
_____	_____	_____	_____

Dd you use your 80/20 today? ☐ YES / NO ☐ **What was it?** _____

SLEEP

I slept for _____ hours *(7–9 hours is your goal)*   The quality of my sleep was   POOR / GOOD / GREAT

I woke up feeling _____

MOVEMENT & EXERCISE

I exercised or moved for _____ minutes *(a minimum of 20 minutes is your goal)*

The activity I did was _____

today, I felt 😄 🙂 😐 🙁 ☹️

I attribute this feeling to _____

DAILY | complete this form each day

IMPACT

my **INTENTIONS** | check in with your intentions for today and record your intentions for tomorrow

INTENTION

BUT FIRST Did I act on my intentions from yesterday? ☐ YES / NO ☐
If not, what got in your way? _____

TOMORROW I WILL ...

1 _____

2 _____

3 _____

4 _____

5 _____

my **ATTENTION** | record the time you dedicated to each expression, gauge how your day went, and record any adjustments you'd like to make for tomorrow

ATTENTION

I spent _____ hour(s) on **PLAY**   I spent _____ hour(s) on **VOCATION**

I spent _____ hour(s) on **AVOCATION**   I spent _____ hour(s) on **KEY RELATIONSHIPS**

Did today go as I had hoped?

COMPLETELY
OFF COURSE   AS PLANNED

What I noticed and what I would like to adjust

_____

_____

_____

_____

_____

_____

DAILY | complete this form each day

FOUNDATION

my INNER LIFE | record your inner life practices below and the time you you dedicated to each practice

🔥 INNER LIFE

AWARENESS _____ practice(s) for _____ minutes

CONNECTION _____ practice(s) for _____ minutes

NURTURING _____ practice(s) for _____ minutes

my WELLBEING | record your nutrition, sleep, movement and exercise below

❤ PHYSICAL WELLBEING

NUTRITION

BREAKFAST	SNACKS	LUNCH	DINNER
_____	_____	_____	_____
_____	_____	_____	_____
_____	_____	_____	_____
_____	_____	_____	_____

Dd you use your 80/20 today? ☐ YES / NO ☐ What was it? _____

SLEEP

I slept for _____ hours *(7–9 hours is your goal)*   The quality of my sleep was   POOR / GOOD / GREAT

I woke up feeling _____

MOVEMENT & EXERCISE

I exercised or moved for _____ minutes *(a minimum of 20 minutes is your goal)*

The activity I did was _____

today, I felt 😁 😊 😐 🙁 😣

I attribute this feeling to _____

DAILY | complete this form each day

IMPACT

my **INTENTIONS** | check in with your intentions for today and record your intentions for tomorrow

◎ INTENTION

BUT FIRST Did I act on my intentions from yesterday? ☐ YES / NO ☐
If not, what got in your way? _____

TOMORROW I WILL ...

1 _____

2 _____

3 _____

4 _____

5 _____

my **ATTENTION** | record the time you dedicated to each expression, gauge how your day went, and record any adjustments you'd like to make for tomorrow

👁 ATTENTION

I spent _____ hour(s) on **PLAY**   I spent _____ hour(s) on **VOCATION**

I spent _____ hour(s) on **AVOCATION**   I spent _____ hour(s) on **KEY RELATIONSHIPS**

Did today go as I had hoped?

COMPLETELY
OFF COURSE   AS PLANNED

What I noticed and what I would like to adjust

_____
_____
_____
_____
_____
_____

DAILY | complete this form each day

FOUNDATION

my **INNER LIFE** | record your inner life practices below and the time you you dedicated to each practice

INNER LIFE

AWARENESS _____ practice(s) for _____ minutes

CONNECTION _____ practice(s) for _____ minutes

NURTURING _____ practice(s) for _____ minutes

my **WELLBEING** | record your nutrition, sleep, movement and exercise below

PHYSICAL WELLBEING

NUTRITION

BREAKFAST	SNACKS	LUNCH	DINNER
_____	_____	_____	_____
_____	_____	_____	_____
_____	_____	_____	_____
_____	_____	_____	_____

Dd you use your 80/20 today? ☐ YES / NO ☐ What was it? _____

SLEEP

I slept for _____ hours (7–9 hours is your goal)   The quality of my sleep was   POOR / GOOD / GREAT

I woke up feeling _____

MOVEMENT & EXERCISE

I exercised or moved for _____ minutes (a minimum of 20 minutes is your goal)

The activity I did was _____

today, I felt 😃 🙂 😐 🙁 😫

I attribute this feeling to _____

IMPACT

my **INTENTIONS** | check in with your intentions for today and record your intentions for tomorrow

○ INTENTION

BUT FIRST Did I act on my intentions from yesterday? ☐ YES / NO ☐
If not, what got in your way? _____

TOMORROW I WILL ...

1 _____

2 _____

3 _____

4 _____

5 _____

my **ATTENTION** | record the time you dedicated to each expression, gauge how your day went, and record any adjustments you'd like to make for tomorrow

○ ATTENTION

I spent _____ hour(s) on **PLAY**   I spent _____ hour(s) on **VOCATION**

I spent _____ hour(s) on **AVOCATION**   I spent _____ hour(s) on **KEY RELATIONSHIPS**

Did today go as I had hoped?

COMPLETELY
OFF COURSE   AS PLANNED

What I noticed and what I would like to adjust

_____

_____

_____

_____

_____

_____

DAILY | complete this form each day

my **INNER LIFE** | record your inner life practices below and the time you you dedicated to each practice

INNER LIFE

AWARENESS _____ practice(s) for _____ minutes

CONNECTION _____ practice(s) for _____ minutes

NURTURING _____ practice(s) for _____ minutes

my **WELLBEING** | record your nutrition, sleep, movement and exercise below

PHYSICAL WELLBEING

NUTRITION

BREAKFAST	SNACKS	LUNCH	DINNER
_____	_____	_____	_____
_____	_____	_____	_____
_____	_____	_____	_____
_____	_____	_____	_____

Dd you use your 80/20 today? ☐ YES / NO ☐ **What was it?** _____

SLEEP

I slept for _____ hours *(7–9 hours is your goal)*   The quality of my sleep was   POOR / GOOD / GREAT

I woke up feeling _____

MOVEMENT & EXERCISE

I exercised or moved for _____ minutes *(a minimum of 20 minutes is your goal)*

The activity I did was _____

today, I felt   😀 🙂 😐 🙁 ☹️

I attribute this feeling to _____

DAILY | complete this form each day

IMPACT

my **INTENTIONS** | check in with your intentions for today and record your intentions for tomorrow

INTENTION

BUT FIRST Did I act on my intentions from yesterday? ☐ YES / NO ☐

If not, what got in your way? _____

TOMORROW I WILL ...

1 _____

2 _____

3 _____

4 _____

5 _____

my **ATTENTION** | record the time you dedicated to each expression, gauge how your day went, and record any adjustments you'd like to make for tomorrow

ATTENTION

I spent _____ hour(s) on **PLAY**   I spent _____ hour(s) on **VOCATION**

I spent _____ hour(s) on **AVOCATION**   I spent _____ hour(s) on **KEY RELATIONSHIPS**

Did today go as I had hoped?

COMPLETELY OFF COURSE   **AS PLANNED**

What I noticed and what I would like to adjust

_____

_____

_____

_____

_____

_____

DAILY | complete this form each day

my **INNER LIFE** | record your inner life practices below and the time you you dedicated to each practice

INNER LIFE

AWARENESS	_____	practice(s) for	_____	minutes
CONNECTION	_____	practice(s) for	_____	minutes
NURTURING	_____	practice(s) for	_____	minutes

my **WELLBEING** | record your nutrition, sleep, movement and exercise below

PHYSICAL WELLBEING

NUTRITION

BREAKFAST	SNACKS	LUNCH	DINNER
_____	_____	_____	_____
_____	_____	_____	_____
_____	_____	_____	_____
_____	_____	_____	_____

Dd you use your 80/20 today? ☐ YES / NO ☐ **What was it?** _____

SLEEP

I slept for _____ hours *(7–9 hours is your goal)*   The quality of my sleep was   POOR / GOOD / GREAT

I woke up feeling _____

MOVEMENT & EXERCISE

I exercised or moved for _____ minutes *(a minimum of 20 minutes is your goal)*

The activity I did was _____

today, I felt 😄 🙂 😐 🙁 😣

I attribute this feeling to _____

DAILY | complete this form each day

IMPACT

my **INTENTIONS** | check in with your intentions for today and record your intentions for tomorrow

◉ INTENTION

BUT FIRST Did I act on my intentions from yesterday? ☐ YES / NO ☐
If not, what got in your way? _____

TOMORROW I WILL ...

1 _____

2 _____

3 _____

4 _____

5 _____

my **ATTENTION** | record the time you dedicated to each expression, gauge how your day went, and record any adjustments you'd like to make for tomorrow

👁 ATTENTION

I spent _____ hour(s) on **PLAY**   I spent _____ hour(s) on **VOCATION**

I spent _____ hour(s) on **AVOCATION**   I spent _____ hour(s) on **KEY RELATIONSHIPS**

Did today go as I had hoped?

COMPLETELY
OFF COURSE   AS PLANNED

What I noticed and what I would like to adjust

_____
_____
_____
_____
_____
_____

IMPACT

my **ATTENTION** | record the time you spent on your expressions and your intentions for next week

82 HOURS AVAILABLE IN A TYPICAL WEEK

ATTENTION

LAST WEEK

I spent _____ hour(s) on **PLAY**

I spent _____ hour(s) on **AVOCATION**

I spent _____ hour(s) on **VOCATION**

I spent _____ hour(s) on **KEY RELATIONSHIPS**

NEXT WEEK

I will spend _____ hour(s) on **PLAY**

I will spend _____ hour(s) on **AVOCATION**

I will spend _____ hour(s) on **VOCATION**

I will spend _____ hour(s) on **KEY RELATIONSHIPS**

my **INTENTIONS** | record your weekly intentions and the meaningful act or action you will take to demonstrate the intention

INTENTION

WEEK IN REVIEW

I was able to demonstrate all of my intentions ☐ YES / NO ☐

BUT FIRST   The expressions and / or relationships I neglected were _____

The expressions and / or relationships I attended to were _____

NEXT WEEK

KEY RELATIONSHIPS

	INTENTION	MEANINGFUL ACT OR ACTION	BY WHEN
1			
2			

VOCATION

	INTENTION	MEANINGFUL ACT OR ACTION	BY WHEN
1			
2			

AVOCATION

	INTENTION	MEANINGFUL ACT OR ACTION	BY WHEN
1			
2			

PLAY & OTHER RELATIONSHIPS

	MEANINGFUL ACT OR ACTION	BY WHEN
1		
2		

WEEKLY | complete this form at the end of each week

IMPACT

my ATTENTION | record the time you spent on your expressions and your intentions for next week

82 HOURS AVAILABLE IN A TYPICAL WEEK

ATTENTION

LAST WEEK	NEXT WEEK
I spent _____ hour(s) on **PLAY**	I will spend _____ hour(s) on **PLAY**
I spent _____ hour(s) on **AVOCATION**	I will spend _____ hour(s) on **AVOCATION**
I spent _____ hour(s) on **VOCATION**	I will spend _____ hour(s) on **VOCATION**
I spent _____ hour(s) on **KEY RELATIONSHIPS**	I will spend _____ hour(s) on **KEY RELATIONSHIPS**

my INTENTIONS | record your weekly intentions and the meaningful act or action you will take to demonstrate the intention

INTENTION

WEEK IN REVIEW

I was able to demonstrate all of my intentions ☐ YES / NO ☐

BUT FIRST

The expressions and / or relationships I neglected were _____

The expressions and / or relationships I attended to were _____

NEXT WEEK

👤 KEY RELATIONSHIPS	INTENTION	MEANINGFUL ACT OR ACTION	BY WHEN
1			
2			

🛒 VOCATION	INTENTION	MEANINGFUL ACT OR ACTION	BY WHEN
1			
2			

⌛ AVOCATION	INTENTION	MEANINGFUL ACT OR ACTION	BY WHEN
1			
2			

🌱 PLAY & OTHER RELATIONSHIPS	MEANINGFUL ACT OR ACTION	BY WHEN
1		
2		

INDEX

A

acceptance, 4, 28, 30, 280

achievement- and goal-oriented focus, 2–3, 28, 31, 46, 109–110, 117–118

Achilles' heels, 62–64

action plans, 226–228, 227t

Affirmation Meditations app, 55

affirmations, 55

Alboher, Marci, 166–167

Amiel, Henri-Frédéric, 101

Angelou, Maya, 59, 270, 276

anxiety, 114, 240

  lack of movement and exercise and, 73

  present-moment awareness, 36

  Relationship Gauge, 84

"Any Road" (Harrison), 107, 109

Arruda, William, 138

aspiration

  inspiration vs., 121, 122t

  problems with letting aspiration lead, 117–118, 124

"attend and befriend," 38–39

attention, 265–277

  allocating time for, 271t

  meaningful demonstrations of intention, 273, 274t–275t

  paying attention with intention, 268–269

  reality of time, 266–268

  setting intentions for key relationships, 270–275

Avabhasa, Da, 244–249

avocation, 165–190, 232–233

  allocating time for, 271t

  compared to play and vocation, 166–168

  comparing current and ideal situation, 188–189

  hours spent on weekly, 267

  identifying potential, 177–180

  listing expressions of, 205

  meaningful demonstrations of intention, 273, 275t

  as "slash career," 166–167

  special OPS, 170–177

B

Baker, Richard, 236

Batson, Daniel, 272

Bell, Alexander Graham, 266

Benn, Gottfried, 162

Bija, 52

Bock, Halley

  personal mission statement, 139

  self-love, 25

box breathing, 71

Brach, Tara, 38, 44, 236

breathing

  box breathing, 71

  filling process, 52

  as fuel of life, 115–117

Brown, Brené, 54, 150

Brown, H. Jackson, 165

Brown, Stuart, 150–154

Buddha, 81, 121

Bureau of Labor Statistics, 267

Byrne, Rhonda, 54

C

caffeine, 64, 68, 70

call to action, 221, 224–228

  action plans, 226–228, 227t

  knowing needs and potential

    obstacles, 225–226

cancer

  lack of movement and exercise

    and, 73

  lack of sleep and, 69

  sitting too long and, 76

cardiovascular disease, 76

caregiver relationship, 193–194

chakras, 52

Chase, Chevy, 239

"choice" criteria for key relationships,

  192–195, 199

coaches, 224

community, 82–100

  defining positivity and negativity,

    87

  focusing on influence of

    individuals, 85–86

  hoarding relationships, 86

  impermanent nature of

    relationships, 85–86

  kula, 88–100

  re-creating relationship dynamics

    from past, 83

  Relationship Gauge, 84–85

compartmentalizing life, 3–5, 15

Compass of Our Heart (Brach), 236

Comprehensive Physiology, 74–75

Connally, John, 150

connection, 37–39, 280–281

  "attend and befriend," 38–39

  defined, 7–8

  drift from, 5–6

  elevating positivity, 45–47

  examples of disconnection, 4–5

  healing negativity, 39–42

  living from the outside in vs. inside

    out, 9–10, 10t

  plan for reconnection, 14–15,

    16f, 17

  positive neuroplasticity, 38–39

  possibility of reconnection, 11–14

  technology and disconnection, 1–2

Visiting Hour, 42–45
core values, 131–137, 140–141
  choosing, 132–133
  drafting list of, 132–133
  finalizing list of, 133–134
  questions to reflect on, 132
  refining list of, 133
  struggles involving, 134–136
counterphobic response to negativity,
  40–41, 43
Csikszentmihalyi, Mihaly, 7

D
Dalai Lama, 191
Darley, John, 272
debt, ix
depression, 114
  lack of movement and exercise
    and, 73
  play vs., 151
  prevalence of, x
  Seasonal Affective Disorder
    (SAD), 5
detox diets, 67–68
dharma, 187
diabetes
  lack of sleep and, 69
  sitting too long and, 76
Dib, Deb, 138
dietary demons, 63–65
Dillard, Annie, 47–48
discretionary desires
  defined, 214
  stating, 216

*Ditch, Dare, Do: 3D Personal
  Branding for Executives* (Arruda
  and Dib), 138
Douglas, William O., 255
Dyer, Wayne, 242

E
80/20 rule, 62–63
  grocery shopping and, 65–67
Einstein, Albert, 124, 160
E-Motion (film), 34
emptying process, 50–51
environment, 22–23, 81–106
  community, 82–100
  surroundings, 82, 100–105
exercise. *See* movement and exercise
Expression component, 16f, 143–232
  avocation and vocation, 165–190
  crafting your living tree, 203–232,
    229t–230t
  key relationships, 191–201
  overview, 17
  play, 149–163

F
filling process, 52–55
*Flow: The Psychology of Optimal
  Performance* (Csikszentmihalyi), 7
Foundation component, 16f, 19–106
  environment, 22–23, 81–106
  inner life, 22, 25–56
  overview, 15, 17
  physical well-being, 22, 57–79

Fowler, Jen, 139
freewriting, 51
"From Jerusalem to Jericho" study, 272

G

gamification of life, ix, 114, 141
Gide, André, 131
gluten-free foods, 66
Godin, Seth, 125–126
gratitude, practice of, 54

H

Harrison, George, 107
Hay, Louise, 55
Headspace app, 35
Heal Your Body (Hay), 55
healthy fats, 66–67
heart disease
    lack of movement and exercise
      and, 73
    lack of sleep and, 69
Hebb, Donald, 39
"Here's a Horrifying Picture of
    What Sleep Loss Will Do to
    You" (Schocker), 68
high blood pressure, 73
"high engagement/high
    commitment" criteria for key
    relationships, 192, 195–196, 199
high-intensity interval training
    (HIIT), 75
The Huffington Post, 68

I

Impact component, 16f, 233–277
    attention, 236–237, 265–277
    intention, 236–237, 239–263
    overview, 17
incorporated life, 10–11, 10t
inner life, 22, 25–56
    connection, 37–47
    filling life with busyness, 27–29
    frequency and cadence of
      foundation-strengthening
      practices, 55–56
    life-changing events affecting,
      26–27
    mindfulness, 32–37
    nurturing, 47–55
    projection of feelings on others,
      29–30
    pursuing happiness through goals
      and acquisition, 31, 37–38, 46
Inspiration component, 16f, 105–106,
    113–141
    being vs. doing, 114–115
    breathing as fuel of life, 115–117
    chasing passions vs. goals, 109–111
    comparing inspiration with
      aspiration, 121, 122t
    core values, 131–137, 140–141
    evolving nature of inspiration, 123
    keeping inspiration front and
      center, 123–124
    lack of authentic life, 113–114
    loss of inspiration, 118
    overview, 17

personal manifesto, 125–130, 140–141

personal mission statement, 137, 140–141

problems with letting aspiration lead, 117–118, 124

reward for passion, 119–120

intention, 236–237, 239–263

giving what you seek, 262

indicators of, 250–260, 257t, 261t

primordial, 242, 244–249

transcendent, 242–249

unintended consequences of good, 239–242

J

Jobs, Steve, 214

Johns Hopkins University, 73

Jung, Carl, 154

K

Kahneman, Daniel, 255

Kaur, Rupi, 279

key relationships, 191–201, 232–233

allocating time for, 271t

codependency vs., 193–194

criteria for, 192–198

defining own role in, 200–201

hours spent on weekly, 267

listing, 198–200, 206

meaningful demonstrations of intention, 273, 274t

relationships by obligation vs., 193–194

setting intentions for, 270–271

kula, 88–100, 105–106

creating, 90–96

defined, 88

defining, 88–89

greater, 99–100

populating, 96–97

solar system of relationships, 90–96

your contribution to, 97–99

L

Lady Chatterley's Lover (Lawrence), 20

Lamott, Anne, 32

Lao Tzu, 116, 224

Lawrence, D. H., 20

Lee, Bruce, 203

Lennon, John, 228

Life, Incorporated Journal, 285–303

daily, 288–301

first month, 286

first week, 287

legend, 285

weekly, 302–303

light, healthy sleep habits and, 70

limbic system, 244–245

living tree, 14–15, 16f, 17, 203–232, 229t–230t. *See also* Expression component; Foundation component; Impact component; Inspiration component

call to action, 221, 224–228

current life vs. ideal life, 206–214
life, adjusted, 215–221
listing expressions of avocation
    and vocation, 205
listing expressions of play, 204–205
listing key relationships, 206
Long Walk to Freedom (Mandela), 73
Loving-Kindness Meditation (Metta
    Meditation), 53–54, 70
luxuries
    defined, 214
    stating, 216

M

Maclaren, Ian, 85
The Magic (Byrne), 54
Mandela, Nelson, 72–73, 76, 123
A Man's Life (blog), 125
mantras, 52
Masahide, Mizuta, 29
Mason, John, 140
MCTs (medium-chain triglycerides),
    66–67
Mead, Margaret, 276
medication, ix, 41
meditation, 32, 35–37, 51–54
    commitment to practice daily, 37
    emptying process, 51
    filling process, 52–53
    Metta Meditation, 53–54, 70
    object or sensory, 35–36
    present-moment-awareness, 35–37
    Yes Meditation practice, 44–45

medium-chain triglycerides (MCTs),
    66–67
melatonin, 70
memory loss, 69
Metta Meditation (Loving-Kindness
    Meditation), 53–54, 70
Michelangelo, 170–171
mindfulness, 32–37
    allowing thoughts/emotions to
        pass, 33–34
    defined, 32
    hanging on to thoughts/feelings,
        32–33
    ignoring thoughts/emotions to
        pass, 33–34
    practicing, 34–35
    present-moment-awareness
        meditation, 35–37
Mindfulness Daily app, 35
mobile devices, viii, 1–2, 7, 48, 70,
    255–256
money and profit, 12–13, 146, 282
    living from the outside in vs. inside
        out, 10t
    people vs., viii
movement and exercise, 72–78
    emptying process, 51
    homework, 77
    mix of activities, 75
    personal trainers, 75–76
    practice, 77–78
    risks from lack of, 73–74
    sitting, 76–77
music, healthy sleep habits and, 71

N

naps, 71
National Institute for Play, 151
National Institutes of Health, 69
National Lampoon's Christmas Vacation (film), 239–240
negativity
 being hard on oneself, 39–40
 defining, 87
 harmful loops, 41
 phobic/counterphobic response to negativity, 40–41, 43
 practicing love and compassion on self, 41–42
 Relationship Gauge, 84–85
A New Earth: Awakening to Your Life's Purpose (Tolle), 251
Newton, Isaac, 262
Ngo, Kevin, 188
Nhat Hanh, Thich, 42
Nietzsche, Friedrich, 113
Nisargadatta, Maharaj, 40
nurturing, 47–55
 choosing how to begin each day, 48
 emptying process, 50–51
 filling process, 52–55
 rebooting each day, 50
nutrition, 60–68
 80/20 rule, 62–63, 65–67
 Achilles' heels, 62–64
 dietary demons, 63–65
 grocery shopping, 65–67
 healthy fats, 66–67
 homework, 67–68
 sugar, 60–66

O

obesity
 lack of movement and exercise and, 73
 lack of sleep and, 68
 prevalence of, ix
One Person/Multiple Careers: The Original Guide to the Slash Career (Alboher), 166–167
organic food, 65
The Organization of Behavior (Hebb), 39
osteoporosis, 69

P

personal manifesto, 125–130, 140–141
 beliefs, 127–128
 organizing, 130
 revising, 129–130
 truths, 129
 wants, 128–129
 writing, 127–129
personal mission statement, 137–141
 examples of, 138–139
 writing, 138–140
personal trainers, 75–76
phobic response to negativity, 40–41, 43
physical well-being, 57–79
 adrenal fatigue, 58
 focus on outward appearance, 57–58

movement and exercise, 58–59,
    72–78
nutrition, 58–68
sleep, 68–72
Plato, 262
play, 149–163, 232–233
    allocating time for, 271t
    comparing past to present,
        158–159
    exploring past images of, 155–156
    exploring present images of,
        156–158
    hours spent on weekly, 267
    identifying expressions of,
        154–163
    listing expressions and elements of,
        161–162, 204–205
    meaningful demonstrations of
        intention, 273, 275t
    properties of, 152–154
*Play: How It Shapes the Brain, Opens
    the Imagination, and Invigorates
    the Soul* (Brown), 152
Play Is Just More Fun (Brown),
    154–155
positive neuroplasticity, 38–39, 54
positivity, 39–42, 45–47
    defining, 87
    heightening awareness of, 46–47
    rushing through joy, 46
    viewing joy as unsafe, 45–46
The Postal Service, 100
Power of Vulnerability course, 54
primordial intention, 242, 244–249,
    261–263

external vs. internal fulfillment,
    255–257, 257t
identifying, 258–260, 261t
struggle vs. ease, 251–252
profit. *See* money and profit
P.S. I Love You (Brown), 165
psychological neoteny, 151
pushing the scene, 33

Q
Quindlen, Anna, 167

R
Radical Acceptance (Brach), 38
Relationship Gauge, 84–85
requisites
    defined, 214
    stating, 215–216
reset diets, 67–68
risk threshold, 219
Robinson, Jackie, 236
Roddick, Anita, 233
Rohn, Jim, 57
Rumi, 102, 143

S
Sanfilippo, Diane, 67
Schocker, Laura, 68
Seasonal Affective Disorder
    (SAD), 5
Seattle Seahawks, 228
self-love, 9, 25

self-worth, viii–ix, 9, 28, 95
    drift from, 5–6
    living from the outside in vs. inside
        out, 10t
Shaw, George Bernard, 149, 207
sitting, 76–77
"slash careers," 166–167
sleep, 68–78, 267
    health risks from lack of, 68–69
    healthy sleep habits, 70–71
    homework, 72
    never-sleep mentality, 68
    practice, 72
sleep apnea, 71–72
Smith, Brian Sutton, 151
social media, ix, 88, 95, 114, 280
solar system of relationships, 90–99
    black holes, 90, 92–93, 97
    moons, 90–94, 98
    planets, 90–91, 95–96
    suns, 87, 90–91, 99
special OPS (opportunities, passions,
        and strengths), 170–177
    asking others to identify in you,
        174–176
    determining which are currently
        expressed, 173–174, 176–177
    identifying, 170–173
    "stands alone" criteria for key
        relationships, 192, 196–198, 200
Stevenson, Robert Louis, 47
Striking Thoughts: Bruce Lee's Wisdom
        for Daily Living (Lee and Little),
        203
stroke, 68

success, 110, 118–120, 276
    achievement-based societal norms,
        2–3
    living from the outside in vs. inside
        out, 10t
sugar, 60–66
Sumner, Zach, 125
Sun Yang, 251
surroundings, 100–106
    actual, 104
    ideal, 101–103
    modifying actual, 105
    temporary uncomfortability,
        100–101

T
technology
    addiction to Internet, ix
    Affirmation Meditations app, 55
    Headspace app, 35
    healthy sleep habits, 70
    Life, Incorporated website, 17, 63,
        67
    Mindfulness Daily app, 35
    mobile devices, viii, 1–2, 7, 48, 70,
        255–256
    social media, ix, 88, 95, 114, 280
    Tara Brach's website, 44
    Thinking, Fast and Slow
        (Kahneman), 255
    Thoreau, Henry David, 95, 123
    Tolle, Eckhart, 251
    transcendent intention, 242–249,
        261–263

external vs. internal fulfillment,
  256–258, 257t
identifying, 260, 261t
struggle vs. ease, 251–252
Twain, Mark, 137
*The 21-Day Sugar Detox: Bust Sugar
  & Carb Cravings Naturally*
  (Sanfilippo), 66–67

V

Vaughan, Stevie Ray, 7
Visiting Hour, 42–45
visualization, 52
vocation, 165–190, 232–233
  allocating time for, 271t
  compared to job, 169
  comparing current and ideal
    situation, 188–189
  defined, 168–169
  hours spent on weekly, 267
  identifying potential, 177–180
  key relationships vs., 198
  listing expressions of, 205
  meaningful demonstrations of
    intention, 273, 275t

special OPS, 170–177
vocation/job spectrum, 181–185,
  182t

W

Walden (Thoreau), 95
Weil, Simone, 269
"What to Remember When
  Waking" (Whyte), 49
Whitman, Charles, 150–151
Whyte, David, 49
Wigmore, Ann, 63
Wilde, Oscar, 126
Winfrey, Oprah, 138–139
work-life balance, 3–4, 266
The Writing Life (Dillard), 47

Y

Yes Meditation practice, 44–45

Z

Ziari, Amy, 139

ABOUT THE AUTHOR

HALLEY BOCK is the founder and CEO of Life, Incorporated—an organization that fosters mindful connection in all areas of life as the means to experience a wholehearted, fulfilling, and joyful life. Previously, Halley spent over a decade as a shareholder and CEO of a successful training and development company, where she both worked on and studied human dynamics and relationships and their impact on business and individual success. The focus of her company was on developing the art and skill of conversation as the vehicle for creating connection with teams, employees, leaders, and individuals, as well as transforming individual and collective results.

Based out of Seattle, Washington, Halley now spends her time spreading the message of life through writing, teaching, and speaking, as well as coaching executives. As a prominent thought leader, Halley has spoken to leaders and audiences across the globe on the topics of relationships, connection, culture, management, and fulfillment. She has also been relied on by substantial media outlets for her expertise. In addition, Halley serves on the boards of several nonprofits and can often be found exploring the trails with her family.